CONTENTS

Preface

1. Introduction: Place, the Media and Popular Culture
   Jacquelin Burgess and John R. Gold
2. Television in the Third World: A High Wind on Jamaica
   Peter Gould, Pennsylvania State University and Anne Lyew-Ayee, University of the West Indies
3. The Changing Concept of Place in the News
   Susan R. Brooker- Gross, Virginia Polytechnic Institute and State University
4. Natural Hazards in Novels and Films: Implications for Hazard Perception and Behaviour
   Diana M. Liverman, University of Wisconsin, Madison and Douglas R. Sherman, University of Southern California
5. 'The Truth is only known by Guttersnipes'
   Bob Jarvis, Tyne and Wear County Council
6. From 'Metropolis' to 'The City': Film visisions of the Future City 1919-1939
   John R. Gold
7. The English Television Landscape Documentary: A Look at Granada
   Martin J. Youngs, London School of Economics
8. Racism, Nationalism and the Creation of a Regional Myth: The Southern States after the American Civil War
   Catherine P. Silk, Reading College of Technology and John A. Silk, University of Reading
9. News from Nowhere: The Press, the Riots and the Myth of the Inner City
   Jacquelin Burgess
10. News and the Dissemination of Fear
    Susan J. Smith, University of California, Los Angeles

List of Contributors
Bibliography
Index

GEOGRAPHY, THE MEDIA AND POPULAR CULTURE

Geography The Media & Popular Culture

Edited by
JACQUELIN BURGESS and JOHN R. GOLD

ST. MARTIN'S PRESS
New York

 For information, write:
St. Martin's Press, Inc., 175 Fifth Avenue, New York, NY 10010
Printed in Great Britain
First published in the United States of America in 1985

Library of Congress Catalog Card Number: 84-40465
ISBN 84-40465

CONTENTS

PREFACE

Edited collections of essays are notorious for their pretensions. Usually derived from conference or seminar proceedings, they consist all too often of a diffuse set of contributions replete with optimistic editorial claims that the end-product is a comprehensive survey of the field in question.

This book has no such origins and, we sincerely hope, has no such affectations. It did not stem from any specific event but from long-standing personal interest in the media - an interest which we realised was shared by a number of other geographers on both sides of the Atlantic. The essays contained here were written, on invitation, by friends and colleagues whom we knew to be interested in the media and represent a first compilation of a fascinating source material. At the outset we would stress that there is no intention of establishing yet another sub-discipline of human geography. Rather, we seek to explore a series of avenues by which geographers could profitably study the media and to demonstrate the contemporary and historical insights that can be gained. Case-studies of different approaches and perspectives are provided, as well as some introductory grounding in the accompanying theoretical debates from the fields of media research and cultural studies. Above all, we aim to persuade colleagues and students that this neglected aspect of everyday life should be included in geographical research and teaching curricula; that Raymond Chandler is as valuable a source as Thomas Hardy and that the *Daily Mirror* has as much to say about the nature of places as the *Geographical Journal*.

As always, thanks are due to a large number of people for their assistance and support. Ann Mason and Chris Cromarty made a superb job of producing the diagrams and illustrations. Claudette John performed miracles with often indecipherable manuscripts. Joy Dalton produced the final typescript and supplied her invaluable knowledge of the Lasercomp process, without which the editors would have been totally lost. Alick Newman pasted up the final copy, another task which was totally beyond the editors. We would like to record our gratitude to the various owners of copyright material who have given their permission for reproduction here. Despite all reasonable endeavours, however, it proved impossible to trace copyright on Figure 6.2 and the photographs in Figure 9.2. We would be grateful therefore if the owners of copyright on these Figures would contact the editors, whereupon we would be pleased to settle matters.

Sincere thanks, as ever, to our families. Jacquie Burgess would like to thank Mike for his unfailing willingness to discuss the *real* meaning of *The Last of the Summer Wine* while trying to take his contact lenses out, and thanks Sharon Brown without whose help Gemma and Aidan would have delayed publication even longer. John Gold would like to express his gratitude to Maggie for continued forbearance and now promises to try and find out who Iain and Jennifer actually are.

JAB/JRG

ACKNOWLEDGEMENTS

We would like to thank the following copyright owners for permission to reprint material herein: cartoon, Chapter 1, *Punch* magazine; Fig. 5.1 McCormick Intermarco Farner, Molly Godet and Miles Gibson; Fig. 5.2 *New Musical Express*; Fig.6.1 Transit Film-Gesellschaft, Munich; Fig. 6.3 London Films; Fig. 6.4 British Gas Corporation; Fig. 9.1 Bill Caldwell and Express Newspapers; Fig. 9.2 *Daily Mirror*; Fig. 9.3 Les Gibbard; Figures 6.1, 6.2, 6.3 and 6.4 are reproduced from stills supplied by the Stills Department of the National Film Archive.

CHAPTER 1: PLACE, THE MEDIA AND POPULAR CULTURE

Jacquelin Burgess and John R. Gold

The media have been on the periphery of geographical inquiry for too long. The very ordinariness of television, radio, newspapers, fiction, film and pop music perhaps masks their importance as part of people's geography 'threaded into the fabric of daily life with deep taproots into the well-springs of popular consciousness' (Harvey, 1984, p7). The institutions and practices that comprise the media have a significance that demands our attention. They are an integral part of popular culture and, as such, are an essential element in moulding individual and social experiences of the world and in shaping the relationship between people and place.

In providing a context for the essays that follow, this introduction has five major sections. In the first part, we outline some of the key terms to be employed here. The second part discusses those branches of human geography where there has already been interest in the media, albeit in most cases somewhat tangential. The third part identifies the way in which interpretative approaches in geography have steered away from the study of the media and popular culture. It is suggested that the way forward here may well lie in closer attention to a range of studies drawn from sociology and related disciplines which are then discussed in section four. Some of the key works may well be familiar to geographers - such as the writings of E.P. Thompson, Raymond Williams and Richard Hoggart; others may be less so, for example the research done by Stuart Hall and his colleagues at the Centre for Contemporary Cultural Studies at the University of Birmingham. This section seeks to identify the various strands of theoretical debate in popular cultural studies, with attention being drawn to parallel themes in geography. It is also argued that there is an urgent need for theoretical debate about the ways in which environmental meanings and experience are shaped. In other words, we contend that a geography of the media must address the question of the ideology of places as well as focusing on their qualities and the emotional experiences that they generate. The final part of this chapter introduces the nine essays that follow in terms of two major perspectives: a behavioural approach derived principally from mainstream American media research, and critical approaches that draw upon a variety of Marxist formulations to explore the ideological role played by the media.

Defining Terms

At the outset, it must be stressed that the four major terms to be used - 'culture', 'popular culture', 'ideology' and 'media' - are the subjects of considerable debate. Each carries a variety of meanings and has changed in usage over time.

Culture, as Williams (1976) notes, is one of the most difficult words in the English language since it has two related, but distinct, associations - with Art and with Society. Although traditional criticism had assumed that expositions of culture were only to be found in literature and the Arts, the term 'culture' embodies a complex argument between general human development, in the sense of the 'cultural heritage', and particular ways of life. Proper use of the word needs to take into account the fact that each culture also involves the material and symbolic forms that characterise those ways of life. It includes the material practices and customs of a group, along with their expressions in places and landscape and the production of signifying or symbolic systems. A definition of culture, therefore, requires an understanding of these practices, customs and expressions, and, from the perspective of this book, it is important to emphasise that popular media, such as newspapers, music and film, be considered just as legitimate an expression of culture as literature, sculpture and the theatre.

This leads on to the term *popular culture*. Our definition is closely associated with the perspective on culture outlined above, since once again it is a concept that lacks any consensual meaning. 'Popular' can be taken to mean 'of the people' and conveys, in all senses, the notion of not being associated with an elite, whether in economic or social terms. Its usage is connected primarily with changing patterns of leisure and recreation, but can carry either positive or negative connotations. In literary-cultural formulations, for instance, 'high culture' represents those works of art and literature that are recognised by an elite to have aesthetic value and are revered for their insight into all aspects of human life. They are assumed to be of greater permanence than, say, pulp literature or popular music. The problem with such assumptions, however, is that evaluations of the worth of literature or music changes over time. A good example of this is supplied by Bennett (1982, p38) who summarised the reactions of the literary critic, Q.D. Leavis, to the intrusion of market forces into the cultural sphere during the 1930s:

> Pulp journalism has replaced respectable journalism, the novel has been sentimentalised, diversion has replaced edification as the motive for reading and, oh horrors! the presumption of the middle-brow public encouraged it to argue for a place for Arnold Bennett or even Ernest Hemingway on the university curriculum.

Popular culture is concerned with the everyday practices, experiences and beliefs of what have been called 'the common people' - that overwhelming proportion of society that does *not* occupy positions of wealth and power. Nevertheless, it should be stressed that involvement with and enjoyment of popular culture are not class-specific. Cunningham (1980), for example, explored the extent to which social classes intermingled in places of recreation and entertainment during the mid-Victorian period. He demonstrated that while the classes kept themselves apart, there could be equal enjoyment of the same entertainments. Cunningham also showed the ways in which leisure was seen as a dangerous force in the early nineteenth century and how it was gradually shorn of economic and radical political associations so that it no longer posed a threat to the dominant classes. This negotiation of consent through hegemony is an important theoretical concept in popular culture, as it asserts that there is a continuing interplay between the respective cultures and ideologies of dominant and subordinate groups in a society.

In turn, this leads us on to the term *ideology*. Ideology, in the sense used here, adds a political dimension to all forms of cultural expression. It may be taken to mean those systems of ideas and beliefs used by social groups to make the world more intelligible to themselves, and which, not infrequently, are justifications which serve to mask specific sets of interests (Bell, 1977; Bammer, 1981). While the concept of ideology itself tends to be associated with Marxist analyses (e.g. Althusser, 1970), in practice it has a much wider usage across a broad span of the social sciences and humanities (see Gouldner, 1976; Gregory, 1978).

From the point of view of the media, perhaps the most important question raised by the issue of ideology is that of the appropriation of meaning or, put another way, deciding what is to be the 'natural' meaning of events, activities and experiences. This issue is given particular emphasis in European schools of cultural studies. Semiologists, for example, have studied the ways in which ideology is presented and reinforced through language. In this context the media play an important part, especially through their role in mediating social knowledge and their function of bringing together and organising different conceptions in order to obtain consensus and consent (Hall, 1977).

Before pursuing this matter further, however, it is necessary to say something about our fourth and last term, *media* . We have not used the phrase 'mass media' in this text since, as already seen, it carries pejorative connotations connected with an undifferentiated, passive and unquestioning audience who are vulnerable to crude media manipulation. The media are taken to comprise all those channels by which specialised groups employ technological devices to disseminate symbolic content to their audiences (after Janowitz, 1968). Thus music, films, television, comics, radio programmes, journals, poster advertising and view-data systems can all be regarded as examples of media. The common theme that links them is that each is produced by an organisation with specific forms of production and working practices, and with its own background of commercial and institutional interests.

The history and development of the media cannot be discussed here, but a broad point may be made about the nature of media *research*. When examined as a whole, it is readily apparent that two distinct strands can be discerned which in turn relate to their origin, respectively, in American or European schools of thought. Mainstream media research in North America has been concerned primarily with the effects of media on individual attitudes and behaviour whereas, as has already been suggested, European studies have focused more on the production of meaning and the relations of the media to other cultural and political forms. Carey (1977), an American writer, has pointed to the dominance of the American paradigm over media studies since 1945 and lamented the fact that the USA remained 'blissfully unaware' of European work, which drew much more from phenomenology, structuralism and psychoanalysis. In his words:

European and American work derives from quite different kinds

> of intellectual puzzles and is grounded in two different metaphors for communication ... American studies are grounded in a transmission or transportation view of communication. They see communication ... as a process of transmitting messages at a distance for the purpose of control ... By contrast, the preponderant view of communication in European studies is a ritual one communication is viewed as a process through which a shared culture is created, modified and transformed ... A ritual view of communication is not directed towards the extension of messages in space, but the maintenance of society in time; ... If a transmission view of communication centres on the extension of messages across geography for purposes of control, a ritual view centres on the sacred ceremony which draws persons together in fellowship and communality. (Carey, 1977, p412)

The tensions between European and American media research are evident from this passage. Perhaps the key issue revolves around the theoretical viewpoint adopted which, in turn, influences the kind of questions being asked about the media. American work is characterised by a liberal-pluralist perspective, which presupposes a symmetry between media institutions and their audiences and presumes that the media reflect the full variety of views within society which *individuals* can then accept or reject. By contrast, European approaches argue in favour of a critical perspective that focuses not on the individual effects of media nor proceeds on assumptions of a liberal-pluralist society, but which sees the media as a conservative force encouraging consensus and consent with regard to existing conditions. The ideological role of the media, then, is to negotiate a continuing acceptance of the *status quo* and, from this perspective, the content of the media serves to reinforce specific ideological constructions of social realities.

The significance of this fundamental dichotomy is a matter to which we will allude on numerous occasions in this Chapter.

Geography and Communication Research

Over the last fifteen years, there have been various occasions on which geographers have acknowledged the importance of the media but, by and large, the quality of the ensuing analysis has been inadequate. One focus for analysis has been the phenomenal growth of modern telecommunications. The rapid diffusion of these media has attracted the attention of a wide range of social scientists concerned about the impact that *could* result in terms of the organisation and conduct of social, economic and cultural life (e.g. see Gold and Barke, 1978). The contribution of geographers to this debate, however, has been disappointingly small. The studies that are available have been preoccupied primarily with the impact of electronic media upon the spatial patterning of economic activity (see Kellerman, 1984). There is little adequate discussion of the content or significance of information flows and comments about social impact tend simply to reproduce hackneyed clichés about 'global villages' and 'wired societies' (for an honourable exception, see Gould and Lyew-Ayee, this volume). Those actually concerned with the analysis of the content and significance of messages did not necessarily fare much better.

This is particularly true for studies associated with behavioural geography , an area of research that developed in the late 1960s and early 1970s. The main problem lay in the inherent assumptions of this field of research. While behaviouralists have embraced many different approaches to the study of human perception and behaviour, most have proceeded on the premise that individual views of the world and environmental behaviour were dependent on the cognition of reality - the process by which mental representations of the environment are created. Individuals assimilate information from their physical and social environments and thereby construct their own unique psychological representations of reality (whether termed 'images', 'mental maps', or 'cognitive maps'). The construction of such imagery (the term that will be used here), is regarded as a *learning* process and one which develops with age.

The amount, type and quality of information therefore becomes the key to that process. Following the distinction made by Lowenthal (1961), geographers argued that individuals would be exposed to two forms of information and experience of qualitatively and quantitatively different kinds. On the one hand, direct experience provided the raw material of perception and cognition. Although such experience would be the minor source compared to all potential information, it supplied the main focus for work in geography . On the other hand, a vast array of indirect or secondary information sources are also available to individuals. These sources, it was argued, supply a quite different form of experience to the recipient.

The distinction between primary and secondary information is pleasingly simple and eminently suitable for experimental designs, but it served to polarise experience into two categories. Moreover, the polarisation carried with it connotations of 'good' (i.e. direct) and 'bad' (i.e. indirect) experience. This fails to acknowledge clearly the fact that individuals bring personal experience to bear on *all* information sources whether direct or otherwise. It also failed to recognise that mediated information is central rather than secondary in the information environment of the modern world.

Nevertheless, there was no denying the usefulness of this dichotomy for geographers. The way was opened up for studies of communication and the media as the most significant source of secondary information. The notion of 'far place' perception proposed by Goodey (1971, p6), in which images of people and place were those 'talked of ... (and) read about, heard about on the radio, or seen on the screen', was accepted without demur. For example, in the first paragraph of their state-of-the-art collection of essays, Moore and Golledge (1976, p3) identified the media as a significant source of secondary information:

> Environmental cognition is the study of the subjective information, images, impressions, and beliefs that people have of the environment ... We consider the ways in which these images arise, are influenced by direct environmental experience and by external sources like the mass media, and subsequently affect personal and group decisions and behaviour with respect to the environment.

None of their contributors, however, actually took up the question of the media. Indeed, we would argue that several factors, related principally to assumptions outlined above, have played an important part in suppressing media studies in geography. Of these, the primary reason concerns the emphasis on cognition and on mental representations of reality. This emphasis meant that geographers turned most readily to cognitive and social psychology for both theory and methodology. These are fields in which, as a noted social psychologist has argued: 'current research ... seems to be overwhelmingly individualistic, dominated by the information-processing paradigm' (Forgas, 1983, p129). By contrast, the sociological dimension of environmental cognition was much less fully developed. For example, Downs and Stea (1977) drew heavily on examples taken from media and popular culture to illustrate their arguments about cognitive mapping, but, by rooting their analysis firmly within the traditions of psychology, consistently failed to relate their material at a theoretical level to the social and cultural context.

In light of these comments, we can now consider the available studies of media by geographers. In many ways, they illustrate the first of the intellectual puzzles proposed by Carey (1977) in the quotation cited above, being concerned with messages in space and having strong behavioural overtones. There is no easy way to divide up this material but, for convenience, we may observe a distinction between research which emphasises media flows and that which focuses primarily upon media content.

Long Distance Information

A key area for geographical interest has been concerned with and the geographical coverage of news reporting. Pioneering papers by Cole and Whysall (1968) and Goodey (1968, 1969) explored public information available through media channels. Subsequent projects by Kariel and Rosenvall (1978). Walmsley (1980, 1982) and Brooker-Gross (1983) have investigated aspects of news flow and have extended the analysis into questions of news production. The broad conclusion from this work is that news reportage is spatially-biased. For example, Walmsley (1980) found evidence of parochialism in Australian newspapers, with each state giving prominence to its own affairs.

These studies also had a common basis in their use of content analysis, a methodology particularly well-developed in American mass communications research. Content analysis involves recording the number of times that an item is mentioned in the text. While often exhibiting considerable quantitative elegance, content analysis remains somewhat unsophisticated. As Walmsley (1980, p344) has noted:

> Despite its relative precision and unequivocal nature, place name counting pays no attention to whether the news about a given location is favourable or unfavourable. Nor does the technique take account of the fact that the format of the news and even the language used can be symbolic.

Moreover, it is too seldom realised that content analysis emerges from a particular view of the media. The analysis is clearly modelled around certain stages and functions, and is underpinned by the dominant American theoretical stance discussed earlier.

Is it true what they say about Dixie?

Another strand of research has been concerned more explicitly with the *content* of media reports and their impact upon individual and group images of places. Researchers have distinguished between direct and secondary experience, but have tried to assess the differences between detailed local knowledge of places and media descriptions of them. In consequence, one of the themes from this work implies a testing of reality, i.e. comparing the mediated image with local perceptions of reality. (The forebears of the insider/outsider dichotomy of humanist geography may be found in this research.) Studies have ranged from the apparently incidental stereotyping of places and regions to more deliberate attempts to manipulate media content for commercial or political reasons. They have covered both historic and contemporary periods. In historical geography, for example, papers by Thompson (1969), Jackson (1972) and Bowden (1976) have shown how migrants were attracted into the unknown by a combination of highly selective accounts of the frontier. For instance, the establishment of agricultural settlements in the highly marginal environment south of Salt Lake Valley by the Mormons was largely in consequence of Brigham Young reading, and believing, a propagandist emigrant guide-book.

The distinction between place images and place stereotypes is crucial for research of this genre, for it implies that 'images' are constructed essentially from firsthand experience and are information-rich. Stereotypes, on the other hand, are highly simplified generalisations about people and places which carry within them explicit or implicit assumptions about their characteristics and behaviours. As used in social psychology and as taken into geographical literature, stereotypes are part of a process of categorisation through which distinctive features of one group or one place are used to give identity. Stereotyped categories are extremely difficult to change. Additional or contradictory information is used to differentiate subtypes rather than confound the original misconception (Cauthen *et al*, 1971; Weber and Crocker, 1983). Within environmental cognition, stereotypes are a means of organising spatial knowledge and geographical identity. Yet as

Downs and Stea (1977, p90) have suggested 'they allow us to cope and simplify, but at a cost. We become ... victims of conventionality'. Although stereotypes are regarded as predominantly negative or derogatory in content, stereotypes of favoured places or regions can also exist (e.g. see Gold, 1980, pp128-42).

The media are centrally implicated in the production and maintenance of stereotypes for they 'create a vast cultural matrix in which images can develop and persist irrespective of the reality they are supposed to represent' (Karlins *et al*, 1969, p1). Recent analyses of the pervasive influences of news values have demonstrated that not only do journalists use stereotypes in writing their reports but also that the structural demands of the medium itself lead to stereotyped presentations.The concept of stereotype may be considered usefully in association with concepts of practical ideology and hegemony discussed later in the chapter, which raise a rather different reading of the phrase 'victims of conventionality'.

Empirical research on place imagery and stereotypes in media has concentrated on two issues. The first is place advertising which follows closely the model of mass communications research, since messages are clearly manipulated for particular purposes and the effects in terms of location decisions are apparently measurable. The second considers alternative views of local realities by contrasting the images of inhabitants/insiders with those of outsiders - visitors, tourists or media representatives.

Taking place advertising first, Goodey (1974) extemporised around the 'new' theme of sense of place which was emerging as a distinct focus in geographical enquiry. He wrote that while sense of place 'is an interesting theme and one which packages a range of traditional geographical interests in new wrappings, any real advances in knowledge in the area must be predicted on our understanding aspects of media sociology, advertising and psychology which are only poorly developed themselves' (Goodey, 1974, p133). At the time, he was unable to call upon much work done by geographers on place advertising, although a series of studies have appeared since which look more seriously at processes of place promotion in the context of economic regeneration (Gold, 1974; Holcombe and Beauregard, 1980; Burgess, 1982a; Burgess and Wood, 1984). Such work reveals the extent to which place promotion is part of the strategy of many new economic development schemes. While the officials involved often have no clear conviction about the effectiveness of such work and tend to resort to simplified and stereotyped advertising extolling the economic advantages and quality of life on offer, the evidence is that they remain committed to such advertising.

The second strand of this work explores the relationships between media content and the views of local inhabitants. The resulting tensions indicate great differences in perception of identity and meaning of place. Goodey (1974), for example, explored the media's approach to the British New Towns and noted the persistent negative stereotypes of both the physical environment and social life to be found there - a view that contrasted considerably with available studies of residents' views (e.g. Zweig, 1970). Burgess (1978) examined the role of the local, regional and national media in sustaining and reinforcing a variety of images of the city of Hull in northern England. The research traced the stereotyped images back through local and national media reports, finding that the inhabitants' image acted as the major framework for local press reports and promotional literature about the city. By contrast, the national newspapers used the external stereotype as the framework for news.

Interpretative Approaches

While getting to grips with the realities of media production and beginning to investigate the attitudes and contexts within which the the media operate, the style of research described above has limitations. In particular, certain questions about the meaning of places arose which could not be answered effectively by research that looked to psychology for its theoretical and methodological guidance. With the rise of so-called 'humanistic' geography, it might have been expected that the situation would improve. After all, the expressed intentions of humanist geographers included commitment to understanding everyday life from the viewpoint of the subject, celebration of the meaning and experience of place, and interest in the symbols which revealed individual and group attachments to their locality. Interpretative perspectives such as these required an empathetic understanding of the historical, social and cultural contexts in which individual experience took place.

Expectations that the media, as an important part of popular culture, would occupy a significant position in the new agenda for research proved to be ill-founded. Rather than embracing the wide range of popular cultural expressions about place and experience, research is focusing almost exclusively on the symbolism and meaning embodied in literature and art. The 'rediscovery' of literature has deflected attention from those more prosaic texts which tend to speak in the language of these 'inarticulate' people unable to response to complex psychometric techniques. More significantly, the 'geography and literature' movement embodies certain elitist assumptions about the value of various forms of culture.

From Image to Insight: Geography and Literature

In one respect, the emphasis on literature and elite culture is understandable. Geographers who accepted the force of the humanist argument would have found it hard to discover any alternative approaches to media studies other than those closely-aligned to the behavioural paradigm of American mass communications research. Other traditions, for example, from structuralism and cultural studies, were only just beginning to penetrate the discipline (see Jackson and Smith, 1984). Without a clear method by which to analyse items of popular culture, it is extremely difficult to break the assumption that it constitutes nothing more than 'entertainment'. Without a theoretical orientation, the study of popular cultural forms is highly susceptible to the criticisms of triviality and obviousness which have been levelled against humanistic geography in general (Gregory, 1981). Literary and artistic criticism, on the other hand, offers a body of theory and textual analysis that is familiar to geographers with links to the humanities. Furthermore, literature in particular has long been employed in geographical research: regional novels, for example, have been used to reconstruct topographies and historical landscapes (Darby, 1948; Watson, 1983).

It is not surprising therefore that a substantial body of material has developed on the subject of geography and literature. Within these writings, it is possible to discern three related purposes at work. The first is to gain insight and understanding of the qualities of environmental experience which appear to be beyond the powers of expression of ordinary people. Part of this process of insight relates to the experiences of the artist, part to the self-awareness of the researcher. Secondly, literature is held to be an exemplar for the geographer's own writings. Geographers are exhorted to *create* their own art (Jeans, 1979; Meinig, 1983) and it is hoped that the literary standards of the discipline may be raised in the process. The third purpose is to understand the ways in which literature moulds feelings and attitudes towards places and landscapes.

An illustration of the extent to which these purposes can overlap and interpenetrate is to be found in the work of Douglas Pocock, one of the figures most closely associated with the movement towards the study of geography and literature. In the final part of a textbook, Pocock and Hudson (1978) had considered the projection of images of the north of England and their likely significance for planning. Brief gobbets from Dickens, Gaskell, Hardy, Bennett, Orwell, Lawrence and others led into a discussion of promotional images. There was no expressed intention, however, to compare the different genres or varying insights offered by the texts. Subsequently Pocock (1979) again used literary quotations about the north of England as 'messages' from which, he argued, popular images of the region were constructed. Literature is thus regarded as another source of secondary information and he concluded that it offered a 'research field for geographers interested in relevance and the growing field of communications research' (Pocock, 1979, p73). Later publications (Pocock, 1981a, 1981b) reflected the impact of humanist perspectives. The introduction to *Humanistic Geography and Literature* (Pocock, 1981a, pp9-19) identified the different uses to which geographers might put literature, ranging from varieties of landscape description to personal enrichment and insight. Pocock (1981a, p13), however, retained an interest in the effects of literature: 'it provides an important secondary source of knowledge, including environmental knowledge, and thus contributes to the general learning process whereby values, attitudes and aspirations are acquired, the end-product of which is our cultural refraction of reality'. Cognition is thus placed in a literary frame.

Such varying, and at times conflicting, motives are understandable in the early development of any field of research, but it is hard to avoid the conclusion that much of what has appeared has taken the source material as a 'literary quarry in which to dig' (Pocock, 1979, p72). Most geographers continue to treat literature as a resource for other purposes and make insufficient effort to situate that literature in its proper historical, economic, social and cultural context. Lowenthal (1976, pp291-2) made this point forcefully:

> It is the quality of human life that matters most in environmental

> experience and a faith that the humanities afford the best insight into this realm of knowledge ... All insights about social, cultural and geographical environment - especially those exemplified in literature and painting - are embedded in the experiences of particular people in specific times and places. How people view and articulate their experience is a product both of their own place in history and that of their successive interpreters. The very words used to describe environmental conditions and responses alter in force, context and meaning over time.

It remains true that the most satisfactory expositions are those that have followed this advice as, for example, the work of John Barrell on John Clare (Barrell, 1972), landscape painters of the eighteenth and nineteenth centuries (Barrell, 1980) and Thomas Hardy demonstrates (Barrell, 1982). Barrell succeeded in informing a detailed textual analysis with a strong sense of the material conditions in which these works of art were created. He found, for example, that the sense of place celebrated in Clare's poetry emerged in response to his loss of identity and dislocation caused by the Enclosure Movement.

Another study which may be mentioned in this respect is by Lowenthal (1982) himself. Lowenthal took one aspect of culture that is very clearly not in the tradition of 'great' literature, namely, science-fiction. In using this material to ascertain contemporary attitudes towards the past, Lowenthal (1982, p80) commented that the 'immense popularity of this nostalgic genre, ranging from the romances of H.G. Wells to the adventures of *Doctor Who*, reflects a widespread and profound human concern'. Within science fiction, he isolated a feeling of repulsion towards all but those manifestations of previous lives which fit with high-minded cultural appreciations. He argued that in the act of preservation, only the best is retained while the bulk of the past is simply forgotten. What is retained then encompasses all that has gone before. Thus, the rare illustrated medieval manuscript, though seen by an infinitely smaller number of people than modern paperbacks, 'is admired today both as art and as an emblem of beleaguered culture, whereas the tawdry paperback is more apt to symbolise the debasement of culture and art alike' (Lowenthal, 1982, p92).

The Myth of Mass Culture

Lowenthal's last point is well-made. We have already argued that one motive encouraging an interest in literature rather than the wide spectrum of popular culture is a view of the relative 'worth' of elite versus popular culture. To judge from the published record, geographers emerge as being profoundly elitist in their interests, with a derogatory view of the 'mass' media and thus its 'mass' audience. The key to such attitudes may sometimes be just odd words, but they can carry a considerable meaning. Downs and Stea (1977, p25), for example, wrote about the imagery of America conveyed by popular media in the following words (our italics):

> For many people throughout the world, America is a land of pony tails, white socks, drive-ins, freeways, skyscrapers, and split-levels - a stereotype constructed from the residual debris of a diet of Hollywood movies and TV shows.
>
> *Fortunately*, there are more responsible sources that promote an understanding of the world.

The question of the acceptability of some forms of culture rather than others is even more apparent from the research agendas of geographers, singly or collectively.

Yi-Fu Tuan, for example, has made significant contributions to the geography and literature debate (e.g. Tuan, 1976a, 1976b, 1978). Literature, which he defined as folklore, stories, epics and lyrics (Tuan, 1976b), gives voice to the 'inchoate experiences' which ordinary people find hard to express and brings into consciousness that which was previously hidden. Great Literature is a major repository of the world views of particular epochs, and Tuan was exercised by the extent to which it could be said to shape and influence popular perceptions and attitudes towards the environment in different times and societies. He drew a clear distinction between 'high class' and 'pulp' literature. In the former he argued that the stories which portray people and society were 'realistic', for 'the characters appear real and do nasty things'. Serious literature disturbs, which is why 'pulp' literature, such as women's romances and men's adventure stories, is not to be considered realistic since it caters for the readers' fantasies. Tuan was even unsure of how far these fantasies are 'truly representative of their desires and aspirations'. He concluded that the serious literature of both science and fiction 'have the power to transform the image of the world; in both this power to influence the mass mind is proportional to the degree that literature is simplified and distorted' (Tuan, 1976b, p272).

"The rest of the family? In the parlour, glued to the bloody piano – as usual!"

The meaning here is clear: the 'mass mind', (i.e. the attitudes and world views of the non-elite), is susceptible to, and can be manipulated by, the commercial media.

The idea of a lumpen 'mass' set against a sensitive elite on the one hand or an idealised 'folk' community on the other, finds expression in a variety of guises in the work of other cultural and humanist geographers. Cultural geographers have long been engaged in the study of such cultural artefacts as vernacular buildings and concerned with rural and traditional landscapes, a focus which seems to reflect nostalgia for an idealised rural past. Carl Sauer, a key figure in the development of cultural geography, for example, was revealed through his correspondence as a man with a strong affection for rural life combined with a 'hopelessly romantic view of his country-bred origins' (Williams, 1982, p4). Although aspects of contemporary popular culture are discussed in the journal *Landscape*, and recent work by Rooney, Zelinsky and Louder (1982) challenged the conservation of US cultural geography, the desire to retain or recreate a nostalgic past is clearly indicated by a recent suggestion that there should be a new 'folk geography', which considers the non-material forms of traditional or 'folk' culture. However, since, in the words of the same advocates (Lornell and Mealor, 1983, p54), 'increased literacy, mass media, and improved transportation ... have contributed to the dissolution of most true folk societies in the US', one might have some doubts about the viability of such a field of study.

Similar themes can be traced in the work of humanist geographers. A work that demands attention in this respect is Relph's (1976) influential *Place and Placelessness*, an extensive commentary on place and landscape experiences which directly confronts the question of the (mass) media. Relph categorises place experiences as a spectrum ranging from the deepest authentic relationship to the most inauthentic, superficial experiences provided by the mass media. These mass images of place are passed on by 'opinion makers' and disseminated through the media, particularly through advertising. These forces can destroy other levels of authentic place experience 'because mass identities are based not on symbols and significances, and agreed on values, but on glib and contrived stereotypes created arbitrarily and even synthetically' (Relph, 1976, p58). The media, he argues, are directed at 'average people' and provide a levelling down of place experience which encourages the 'placelessness' of landscapes like Disneyland and the Mediterranean coast.

Outsiders to places become part of the mass for they only experience a place through its 'mass identity' and their 'observations are fitted into the ready-made identities that have been provided by mass media' (Relph, 1976, p60). He maintains that the power of the mass media over the mass mind is such that individuals exposed to these synthetic identities and stereotypes will almost inevitably be inclined to experience actual places in terms of them' (Relph, 1976, p58). Relph is also sure that people are vulnerable to the effects of the media constructions for these empty and trivial stereotypes increasingly influence and distort place experiences and can 'only be transcended by a considerable intellectual or social effort' (Relph, 1976, p59). Yet a little later in the argument he seems less convinced about the power of the media over the mass mind, for he writes that 'identities linked to the superficial qualities of place, that is mass identities, are rendered implausible more easily than those associated with existential and empathetic insideness ... Mass identity is indeed little more than a superficial cloak of arbitrarily fabricated and merely acceptable sets of signs ... (which) can be changed and manipulated like some trivial disguise so long as it maintains some minimum level of credibility' (Relph, 1976, pp60-1).

Thus in Relph's argument, on an issue close to the heart of interpretative approaches, the nature of place identity is seen to be destroyed by inauthentic experiences transmitted through the media which includes 'mass communications, mass culture, big business, powerful central authority and the economic system which embraces all these' (Relph, 1976, p90). Mass communications media have allowed the intrusion of national interests and values into local life, have destroyed those qualities of relatedness, of craft, of community and have replaced them with a standardised, consumer orientated, inauthentic mass society.

When used to describe people, the word 'mass' took on its modern usage from the late nineteenth century (Williams, 1976). As such, it carries two principal and contradictory meanings: a positive connotation of 'the people' - the subjects of social action; and a negative connotation of masses as objects upon which other forces are able to act. The geographical writings considered above carry something of this second meaning, in that 'average' people are willing victims of manipulation by advertisers, newspaper proprietors and theme park organisers. The 'mass' media are held to be party to the destruction of landscape quality and locality.

These criticisms of mass culture may be traced back to two highly significant strands of thought associated with the rise of the commercial media in the early twentieth century. The Marxist critique of the 'culture industry' blamed the media for the suppression of revolutionary activity through a process of cultural control which kept the working classes passive and acquiescent (Horkheimer and Adorno, 1972; see Silk, 1984). Members of the Frankfurt school, driven to the US by the rise of Nazism during the 1930s, were appalled by their perceptions of the impact of mass communications on American society. From its nineteenth-century role as an oppositional force, culture had, in their view, been deprived of all its critical force by the commercial media organisations (see Bennet, 1982). The second critique was not overtly political or sociological but drew instead on literary-cultural traditions going back through the writings of T.S.Eliot, and F.R. Leavis to Mathew Arnold (see Williams, 1958; Swingewood, 1977). It is this view which is most strongly represented in the interpretative work of geographers.

The so-called 'culture and society' movement held that moral standards and aesthetic values central to the continuation of civilised society were embodied in Great Literature. The elite, a narrow band of literate, cultured people - writers, artists and the minority able to appreciate their work - held the ground against the onslaught of mass culture. The critics were writing against the background of the rise of industrial capitalism, the extension of political representation to more of the population, and the advent of new types of cultural production associated with the cinema, broadcasting and cheap publishing. These forces conspired to destroy what was regarded idealistically as the harmonious, stable way of life in preindustrial, organic communities - 'the Old England' as Leavis and Thompson (1933, p87) called it. Asking how such a momentous change, 'a vast and terrifying disintegration', could take place so quickly, Leavis saw in mass production and standarisation an inevitable decline in emotional and spiritual life.

Williams (1958, p255) was critical of the concept of a cultivated elite, for set against 'a "decreated" mass, (it) tends towards a damaging arrogance and scepticism'. The elite in cultural terms are the best educated: 'literate Englishmen', and 'high class Americans' as Tuan described them. They are the people who read and appreciate stories in the *New Yorker* rather than *True Confessions*. The elite for Relph are those special individuals who are able to experience places at the deepest possible level. They are certainly not the people who actually enjoy going to Portmerion or Disneyland. There is no concept of class in any of Relph's writings but in every other respect, the tenor of *Place and Placelessness* accords with the profoundly conservative views of T.S. Eliot. Writing in 1948, Eliot stressed the need to preserve local loyalty and regional cultural diversity: 'the great majority of human beings should go on living in the place in which they were born. Family, class and local loyalty all support one another; and if one of these decays, the others will suffer also' (Eliot, 1948, p52).

Thus, conceptions of an elite able to appreciate 'high brow' culture combined with an idealisation of preindustrial 'folk' culture set the terms of analysis of contemporary cultural forms in 'mass' culture for a major part of the twentieth century. It was couched inevitably in terms of declining tastes and declining standards. The commentaries of those few who actually ventured down among the masses were those of outsiders, passing judgment on the culture of *other* people. It is difficult not to avoid the conclusion that certain geograhers are engaged in the same judgmental process.

Two movements in the 1930s more sympathetic to popular culture and experience may be seen as marking the beginnings of modern cultural studies. The documentary film movement under John Grierson celebrated the 'lost' lives of working people and retained a radical democratic rather than conservative stance during the period (Barnouw, 1974; Barsam, 1974). The second movement was that of Mass-Observation led by the anthropologist, Tom Harrisson, who worked in Bolton and Blackpool in the late 1930s. What emerges from these very detailed pieces of ethnography, and especially in the photographs by Humphrey Spender, are powerful evocations of the ordinary lives and landscapes of working and middle-class people both through the eyes of the Observers themselves, and the diaries of volunteers (see Harrisson, 1961;Spender, 1982; Calder and Sheridan, 1984).

The culture and society thesis was challenged by these documentaries, and later in the 1950s and early 1960s by three seminal books which triggered the recovery of popular cultural experience from 'the enormous condescension of history' (in E.P. Thompson's memorable phrase). These books were *The Making of the English Working Class* (Thompson, 1963); *The Uses of Literacy* (Hoggart, 1957) and *The Long Revolution* (Williams, 1961). The book by Hoggart is particularly interesting as a transitional study for, on the one hand, he explored sympathetically the 'whole way of life' of working class people in northern England, using the methods of literary criticism to read the living 'text' of working-class life, while on the other hand, he was deeply disturbed by the impact of the commercial media on working-class life. He defined this as a 'cultural struggle' between authentic working-class practices and the mass commercialised entertainment business:

> It is not a straight fight between ... what *The Times* and Picture dailies respectively represent ... the ability to read the decent weeklies is not a sine qua non of the good life ... There are other ways of being in the truth. The strongest objection to the more trivial popular entertainments is not that they prevent their readers becoming highbrow, but that they make it harder for people without an intellectual bent to become wise in their own way' (1957, p338)

Hoggart attacked the popular media for not concentrating on the truly personal and concrete, and for persuading people to become spectators rather than participants. In a lively review of changing British tastes, Hebdige (1982) draws a comparison between the conservative Leavis and Eliot and radical democrats like Hoggart and George Orwell. They shared concern about a 'levelling down process' associated with the mass media, and were equally worried about the 'Americanisation' of different levels of 'authentic' British culture. Across the spectrum of changing tastes for environmental settings, buildings, clothes and music, Hebdige in fact finds little evidence of the eradication of social and cultural differences feared by the critics.

Cultural Studies and the Media

Richard Hoggart was the first director of the Centre for Contemporary Cultural Studies (CCCS) whose members have played a significant role in the development of modern cultural and media studies (see Hall, 1980a). Hall (1981a) has classified European cultural studies in terms of two paradigms: the 'culturalist' strand introduced above and a second, later infusion of thought from a variety of 'structuralist' perspectives. Culturalism, the dominant force developing from the early theoretical work of Williams and Thompson, sees in popular culture expressions through which groups make sense of their common experiences. Culture is defined as particular ways of life whose socially constructed meanings are expressed in the widest possible range of institutions, behaviours, practices and artefacts. It entails not only historical criticism in the sense of studying works of art but also includes analysis of the material and symbolic elements in these ways of life. So, for example, in their study of youth subcultures, Clarke *et al* (1976, pp10-11) relate individual experience to the wider social structure:

> culture refers to that level at which social groups develop distinct patterns of life and give *expressive form* to their social and material life experience. Culture is the way ... in which groups 'handle' the raw material of their material and social existence ... (it) is the way social relations are structured and shaped: but it is also the way these shapes are experienced, understood and interpreted.

Cultural and media studies have been enriched during the last two decades by a variety of structuralist perspectives. The key figures have been Levi-Strauss (1963; 1966) whose application of the linguistic paradigm to the study of culture was a critical advance but one, Hall (1980a) argued, which was overshadowed by the work of Althusser (1970). Other figures of importance include Roland Barthes (1967, 1972, 1977) who has made most impact on literary and film criticism and whose concept of 'myth' is being used to consider the ideological interpretation of places (see Uzzell, 1984; Burgess, this volume). Another major contribution has come from the work of the French psychoanalyst, Jacques Lacan (1968), who has recovered a linguistic perspective in the work of Freud and whose work in psychoanalysis has had a considerable impact on the interpretation of media discourses (see Weedon *et al*, 1980)

Structuralists share a theoretical perspective which sees *language* as the fundamental structure of social life determining the signifying practices of different cultures (Hall, 1980a, p30). They also share a theoretical concern over the role of ideology in structuring social relationships and defining realities. Hall (1981a) argued that the major differences between the culturalist and structuralist perspectives hinge upon the concept of experience. Culturalist approaches stress the importance of human agency, arguing that experience provides the basis on which ordinary lives are lived. Meaning is embodied in individual experiences in different social milieux. Although Thompson emphasised the process of struggle between different cultures and classes, both he and Williams 'accord experience an authenticating position in any cultural analysis' (Hall, 1981a, p26). By contrast, structuralist approaches have not been concerned with the interpretation of meanings as expressed in different cultures *per se*, but with analysis of the mechanisms and processes whereby particular forms produce meaning. Structuralist approaches do not accept that experience is an independent component of social life. 'One could only "live" and experience one's conditions *in and through* the categories, classifications and frameworks of the culture. These categories, however, did not arise from or in experience; rather, experience was their "effect"' (Hall, 1981a, p29).

Material and symbolic conditions are experienced through language and thus through the rules or codes of the language system. Individuals can only think and speak by first accepting those codes. In the sense that language enables things to acquire meaning, people are engaged in the social practice of signification - meaning is a social rather than individual production. Language 'speaks us' rather than the reverse. Semiotics as one form of structuralism has done most to articulate the links between language and ideology by showing how relations between the signifier (words, visual images and so on) and the signified (the concept) can be arranged to meet the needs of particular ideologies (see Saussure, 1960; Barthes, 1972; Hall, 1977; Wollacott, 1982;).

Hall (1980a, 1981a) found the strengths of structuralism to be its insistence on determinate conditions, its decentralising of experience and its contribution in elaborating the neglected category of 'ideology' in cultural and media studies. The authenticating power and reference to individual experience in culturalism prevents the conception of ideology expressed as particular forms of unconsciousness. Ideology, as he argued elsewhere (1977), is not what is consciously concealed, rather it is embedded in commonsense wisdom in its most manifest and open form. The real foundations of ideology are 'hidden, repressed or inflected out of sight' through the signifying powers of language which hold together different aspects of social life in a web of preferred meanings. In a recent paper, Hall (1982) takes the notion of unconscious repression as the key to understanding the different approaches in American and European media research. The behavioural approaches have 'repressed' the ideological functions of media through their conceptions of a pluralist society held together by a central, core value system which, in the context of the American 'cultural melting pot', other cultures gradually accept as their own. It could be argued that the overwhelming emphasis in mainstream media studies on the role of media as agents of *change* bears on this theoretical position (see McQuail, 1983, p47).

Culturalist and structuralist perspectives have had a significant impact in three areas of media research, in each creating tensions between the theoretical perspectives of liberal-pluralist and critical-Marxist analyses. First, they have conceptualised the media as the major cultural and ideological force in contemporary life; one which occupies the central role in the production and consumption of 'social knowledge'. In the process of signification - 'making the world to mean' - greater attention is being paid to actual media practices. The conventional assumptions that the selection of news stories, for example, or the making of television documentaries is primarily a technical exercise - has been confounded by the realisation that media organisations comprise a set of social practices which fundamentally influence their 'symbolic' products. Contemporary research focuses on the autonomy of individuals within media organisations, the marketing of media products and the fundamental issue of whether the media reflects reality by 'holding a mirror up to society' or whether it actually shapes reality (see Gurevitch *et al*, 1982). Within geography, Jenkins (1984) has researched the making of the television series *Heart of the Dragon* to assess the impact of personal, organisational and production demands on the films' representations of China.

The second major area of research focuses directly on the texts of the media and here studies have been influenced profoundly by linguistic and semiotic perspectives. Meaning is not transparent and unambiguous. Whether dealing with linguistic texts like books and newspapers or visual texts like film and photographs, it is clear that we are confronted with complex symbolic structures which are mediations of social reality. Semiology has reasserted the need to study messages as a whole, rather than breaking them down into their component parts as in content analysis. Moreover in contrast to traditional content analyses, semiotics conceptualises texts as a discourse, as part of communication about aspects of social life. Thus, the products of popular media fictions and entertainments, through indirect and symbolic means, engage with social existence. The use of real locations in these fictions is a fascinating area for geographical research. For example, locations used in fictional crime series like the London dockland warehouses in *The Sweeney* or the backstreets of New York in *Kojak* are used to give surface realism to fictional dramas. It is highly probable that the places get caught up in the ideological web underpinning these law and order series and so real places are infused with the meanings of danger and threat to the existing social order.

Cultural studies have offered the means by which media texts can be taken 'at face value' as the evidence of lived practices and experiences among different subcultures as well as allowing for the apparent marginalisation of particular groups by the media (see for example, Hall and Jefferson, 1976; Hebdige, 1979; Cohen, 1980). Furthermore, by exploring the different levels of meaning within media texts, it is possible to tease out the ideological significance of messages. For example, Brunsden and Morley (1978) provided a 'reading' of *Nationwide*, a British networked, early evening television news and current affairs programme. Part of the discourse of the programme was an appeal to regional diversity within an overarching concept of 'national unity'. The 'regional' character of the programme is central to its identity but, the authors argued, *Nationwide* invents regional differences through the manufacture of cultural contrasts, such as using presenters with pronounced regional accents. Another study of interest to geographers is that by Taylor (1984) who explores the ideological forces operating beneath rural and landscape photographs.

The third area for research concerns media audiences. One crucial effect of cultural and structural perspectives has been recognition that groups and individuals will decode messages differently. Language is 'multiaccented' in that individuals can read and interpret messages and their channels in many different ways. Hobson (1980), for example, considered the uses to which women at home put radio and television programmes. Radio is integral to the working day whereas television is secondary to domestic labour in the evenings. In consequence, women decoded news broadcasts on television as being concerned with the masculine world of work and politics, and thus, as alien to their own values and concerns. The notion of encoding and decoding media texts is significant, for it links the complexity of institutional and technical demands within different media genres with a much more complex notion of the audiences who receive and interpret media products (Hall, 1980c). The encoding of reality within television, film and photographs is particularly interesting for their apparent literalness hide very careful constructions and manipulations of reality (Chanan, 1980; Hall, 1981b; see Burgess and Unwin, 1984).

Although irrevocably opposed in terms of their analysis of society, liberal-pluralist and critical approaches show signs of convergence over the role of the media in changing or maintaining social relations. The classical empirical studies of media effects 'revealed the central role of the media in consolidating and fortifying the values and attitudes of audience members. This tended to be presented in a negative way only because the preceding orthodoxy they were attacking had defined the influence of omnipotent media in terms of changing attitudes and beliefs' (Curran *et al*, 1982, p14). In other words, these studies were asking the wrong question: the media are not involved in the conversion of attitudes, rather they serve to reinforce the central, consensual values of society. Within liberal-pluralist research, this issue is currently defined in terms of an agenda-setting function. The media shape public awareness through their selection of news and events. Lomax-Cook *et al*, (1983), for example, found that public awareness of policy issues and official responses hinge on the actions of investigative journalists who seem, in consequence, to be playing a crucial role in policy making.

From a critical perspective, the most recent developments in cultural studies have been to move beyond orthodox culturalist and structuralist positions to detailed consideration of Gramsci's concept of hegemony (see Hall *et al*, 1977; Hall 1980a). Hegemony provides a means of conceptualising the process whereby the central, dominant meanings, values and practices of a society are maintained through the dilution and incorporation of oppositional ways of life. Hegemony demonstrates how, in the cultural sphere, the dominant classes are able to win consent for definitions of reality favourable to their own position. It includes all the processes whereby the fundamental social group achieves power over economic development and extends to social, political and cultural leadership. Hegemony is never permanent, never uncontested. It is, Hall argues, a most valuable concept for cultural and media studies because it allows for the relative autonomy of different cultural practices. The theory shows how cultural questions can be linked to other levels of political analysis and it 'enables us to think of societies as complex formations, necessarily contradictory, always historically specific' (Hall, 1980a).

Hall and the members of CCCS have produced some striking theoretical and empirical analyses of the role of the media in the maintenance of hegemony through its signifying practices (see for example Hall *et al*, 1978). Their work is however subject to critical comment from both Marxist and liberal-pluralist perspectives. Woollacott (1982) for example, while sympathetic, is critical of the secondary role given to the media which, she argues, appear to operate solely as agents of the people who define events for their own purposes. Blumer and Gurevitch (1982) are much less sympathetic, arguing that Marxist media analysts still need to show that audiences do in fact decode the preferred meanings in the ways suggested. Further, they demand empirical evidence to show that such acceptance supports the institutional *status quo*. In terms of audience effects, it is difficult to conceive of empirical studies which might *easily* demonstrate that 'the effectivity of the media lies not in an imposed false consciousness, nor in changing attitudes, but in the unconscious categories through which conditions are represented and experienced' (Curran *et al*, 1982, p24). Given the largely unconscious categories through which people experience their everyday environments, it represents a particularly challenging task for those geographers interested in the media.

What the Papers Say

We turn finally to the papers in *Geography and the Media* which reflect many facets of the preceding debates. We begin with three essays which adopt a mainstream social science/behavioural perspective. The opening essay by Peter Gould and Anne Lyew-Ayee is associated with the work of the International Television Flows Project, an innovative research programme in which geographers have been prominent. The authors note that until recently there was no way of monitoring, recording and coding television content in a manner that was consistent, (so that international data could be aggregated and compared), and useful to media policy makers and others. The paper demonstrates how the 'unconscious categories' of highly complex television programming structures can be made explicit through the use of a microcomputer data base which classifies content in terms of different levels of generality. The system allows broadcasters, researchers and others to ascertain, for example, the values being expressed in different kinds of programmes: this is a critical issue in Third World countries like Jamaica, who have few resources to produce indigenous programmes reflecting local values and interests, and who are very dependent upon imported material. The authors thus tackle many of the questions raised by the critical school discussed above from an entirely different perspective. The next paper considers a very different aspect of information flows. Susan Brooker-Gross analyses the impact of changing technology on the gathering, processing and dissemination of 'non-local news' during the nineteenth and early twentieth century in one US newspaper - *The Cincinnati Enquirer*. During the nineteenth century interest in 'elsewhere' was moulded by changing technology which meant that news from other places was obtained progressively more easily and more quickly. Ironically, the effect was to reduce considerably the variety and quality of information about specific places. She uses content analysis to show the extent to which news about places was usurped by an emphasis on events themselves. Until the 1870s the newspaper showed little discrimination in its selection of content. Indeed in the early part of the century, any news which managed to get through to Cincinnati was newsworthy! Using the theoretical formulations of Harold Innis, this essay demonstrates how, in the critical transition period between 1880 and 1920, news technology encouraged a transition from a time-biased, local society to a non-local, spatially-biased society. Susan contributes an empirical study to the debate about the role of the media in the apparent homogenisation of place experience and the loss of perceptions of place identity and uniqueness.

The following paper by Diana Liverman and Douglas Sherman explores another area of mainstream geographical research using an interesting form of popular culture. Both writers have considerable practical experience of natural hazards research, a field which straddles physical and human geography. Rather than asking what effect disaster movies and novels have on their audiences, Liverman and Sherman analyse the appeal such works of fiction have and consider how the need for dramatic effect influences the scenarios and characterisations of authors and film-makers. They find that most books and films provide a reasonably accurate portrayal of the specific physical events which make up the disaster - the floods and earthquakes are convincing. The need for dramatic effect, the creation of tension and the involvement of the audience with the film or book, however, encourages writers to misrepresent human responses to natural disasters. Mass panic, extreme shock and crime waves are not what normally happens after a real disaster, but then, as the authors acknowledge, staying calm is hardly the stuff of gripping fiction! It is interesting to note in passing how critical reactions to the fictional enactment of a nuclear holocaust *The Day After* which was shown world-wide in 1983, argued that the film did not in fact show the real and full horror of the aftermath. But then the film had to 'entertain' as well as 'inform' its audiences and part of that 'entertainment' demanded some hope for the future.

One of the major shifts in popular cultural research has been to acknowledge that academic work can also be fun and that researchers bring their own values and pleasures to the work. The culture and society critics without doubt hid their own enjoyment of literature behind an 'objective' definition of literary value. In the way that Dick Hebdige (1979) enjoys the changing styles of the 1960s and Angie McRobie (1980) enjoys the challenge issued by punk styles to middle class, middle-aged executives, so Bob Jarvis writes with great enjoyment about his own interests in music. 'The Truth is only known by Guttersnipes' considers the environmental imagery in the lyrics of rock music. He draws principally on American music to illustrate six interacting themes - on the road, cars and girls, promised lands, music as escape, the lure of the city, alienation and revolution. His paper charts the changing perceptions of male, youth subculture from the heady days of the 1960s to the much darker and more menacing perceptions of contemporary urban life in the 1980s. Rock music forms a major part of alternative culture while at the same time, it is produced, packaged and marketed with the full trappings of commercialised big-business. This raises interesting questions which Bob considers towards the end of the paper. So too does the relationship between the places in which music is produced and changing styles in environmental themes themselves: 'This year everyone's doing environmental songs - tower blocks an' that'.

Everyone was 'doing tower blocks' in the 1930s judging from the next paper by John Gold. He explores the urban visions of films of the inter-war period; those produced by the British and American documentary movements and those made by directors as science fiction 'entertainments'. John goes back to look forward by focusing on the visions of the future city that were being depicted during this period. In doing so, he explores a theme which has run through much of the preceding discussion about the relationship between 'high' and 'low' culture by studying the relationship between the then contemporary 'avant-garde' architectural designs for the future city and the imaginative creations of feature films and documentaries. The films examined reveal a future rooted firmly in the thinking of the times in which they were made. Yet, despite being made in different countries with different audiences, they reveal a consensus about the urban future in visualising cities of huge scale, dominated by tall buildings and restless highways. The selection of these images was related partly to the film-makers' judgement about box-office appeal but also pointed at a deeper level to a widespread belief about a future considered not only credible but also probable.

The following essay by Martyn Youngs brings us back to contemporary film making. He writes about the series of documentary films produced for Granada Television which examine the English landscape. Through interviews with the film-makers, notably Denis Mitchell and Ray Gosling, and through a close reading of the televisual texts, Martyn identifies the themes and intentions of the directors. He finds in films such as *Maryport, Never and Always,* and *A Writer's Notebook: The Pennines,* a perpetuation of an idealised arcadian myth: the nostalgic rural England of craftsmen and cottages and stone walls. The desire on the part of Denis Mitchell to produce visually pleasing films and the insistence of Ray Gosling to make an interpretation which reflects his own quirky, idiosyncratic and fundamentally optimistic views is revealed in Martyn's analysis. He shows how documentary films play an ideological role which strips the countryside of any political conflict by ignoring economic pressures and by masking the poverty to be found there. He argues that the landscape documentaries propagate a belief in an English landscape that has no spatial or historical context.

Martyn Youngs touches on the hegemonic role played by the television documentaries in the interpretations of the English countryside. Catherine and John Silk in the next essay provide the major exposition of the concept of hegemony in cultural studies in their paper on racism and nationalism in the Southern United States during the period 1865-1900. Through a detailed textual analysis of *The Choir Invisible* - a novel by James Lane Allen - they explore aspects of the crisis in hegemony engendered by the defeat of the South in the American civil war. The authors stress the complexity of material interests and ideologies in the US during that critical time of readjustment. They demonstrate how 'local colour' was used as a literary device to articulate themes of regionalism and localism. The theme of national unity in regional diversity was expressed through a racist discourse in which all whites, (whether from North or South), were to share a common destiny, unlike the blacks who had none. Catherine and John demonstrate that local colour - powerful images of plantation life, Southern belles and docile black servants - was being used to negotiate the crisis of hegemony. Northern industrial capitalists, (the people who dominated the emerging mass publications market), encouraged the racist discourse embodied in regional colour, thus reinforcing Southern whites in the mistaken belief that they had 'won' the civil war.

The last two papers in the book also deal with racist themes but those to be found in contemporary English newspapers. There are other links as well between Jacquelin Burgess's paper which considers the ways in which the national newspapers interpreted the disturbances which occurred in several English cities during the summer of 1981, and that by Susan Smith, which assesses the perceived relationships between crime and ethnicity as expressed in local newspapers in north-central Birmingham during 1979. These papers present expositions of the two major approaches to contemporary media studies. Susan adopts an agenda-setting theoretical framework drawn largely from the work of Robert Park who was himself a journalist: Jacquelin uses the semiotic theory of Roland Barthes to explore the ideological role of myth in the language of newspaper texts.

'News from Nowhere' begins with a detailed discussion of the processes of news production in the course of which dominant or preferred meanings of events are encoded into newspaper texts. The body of the paper is an empirical analysis of the texts of both 'quality' and 'popular' newspapers to demonstrate how a myth of the inner city was used by journalists and editors to locate and explain the riotous behaviour in Brixton, Toxteth and Moss Side during 1981. Jacquelin argues that the myth of the inner city is made up from four components which are woven together in the verbal and visual texts of the newspaper reports. These components are identified as being concerned with the physical environment, aspects of white working class culture, aspects of black culture, and finally, an interpretation of street culture. These significations create a commonsense understanding of 'the inner city' as an alien place, existing apart from 'normal' suburban, white, middle-class environments and culture. They serve to distance and marginalise the rioters and the places in which they took to the streets.

Susan Smith, in the final essay, takes up most directly the question of the effects of media messages and shows empirically how different ethnic groups in Handsworth and its adjoining areas in Birmingham actually use public information about the relationship between crime and ethnicity. She shows how the exaggerated reports about crime are clearly linked to ethnicity, thus, for example, West Indians are usually associated in news reports with fraud rather than other forms of criminal activity and that crimes by whites/ethnic minorities are given equal coverage in the local press despite the fact that ethnic groups are a minority of the population. Her theoretical orientation is one which treats news, especially local news as a particular form of gossip and rumour. The media focus and translate information into commonsense experience and everyday life. Susan relates the use of gossip and rumour to the means by which ethnic groups establish and contest territories in both social and physical space: different groups take up formal news agendas as expressed in the press and then elaborate, recast and selectively use that information through their own informal social networks. The public rather than the press, she argues, are the real agents of social change.

It has been our intention in this Introduction to suggest ways in which geographers might explore the wide variety of popular cultural forms and to justify our belief that the media should become a significant focus for geographical work. We hope that *Geography, the Media and Popular Culture* will stimulate research within the discipline and so we have offered an initial agenda of research which contains many challenges. In the essays which follow, readers will encounter mainstream geographical issues framed perhaps in novel ways. There are many differences in the theoretical and methodological orientations of our contributors - but we all share a commitment, interest and involvement in the material and symbolic expressions of the 'everyday' lives of 'ordinary' people and the places in which we live.

CHAPTER 2: TELEVISION IN THE THIRD WORLD: A HIGH WIND ON JAMAICA

Peter Gould and Anne Lyew-Ayee

International Television

If we confine our attention simply to television programmes and ignore the large quantities of television equipment and personnel moving from one country to another, we are still dealing with an international industry that generates about $1 billion a year. No-one knows for sure, because no-one monitors what is going on. In the past thirty years, we have generated what are undoubtedly the most potent flows of visual and verbal communication in human history, movements that carry an enormous baggage of values from one country and culture to another, yet we remain in virtual ignorance of what is happening.

There are essentially two reasons for this almost unbelievable state of affairs. First, we live in a world in which it is generally considered more important to spend tens of billions of dollars on smashing atoms, sending rockets to Saturn, and recombining DNA than finding out what is happening when powerful and value-loaded images from one human culture impact on another. Generating this sort of knowledge about our immediate human world is not given a very high priority in national research budgets. After all it is only about people, and these are obviously not as important as machines like cyclotrons, space craft and electron microscopes (Gould, 1984). Secondly, the truth of the matter is that no-one knew until recently how to monitor television programmes in a consistent and useful way: consistent in that international data could be aggregated and compared; useful in that a monitoring scheme could provide both policy-relevant information at a general level for broadcasters, as well as 'fine grain' data for social scientists. Numerous international committees of 'experts' have met every few years to announce the importance of the problem, and they invariably recommend that 'something should be done about it'. Their reports are filed away by UNESCO in Paris, or by other sponsoring agencies, and then four or five years later someone realises we know nothing about international television, that we really ought to have a committee of experts to study the problem and make recommendations ... and so it continues.

Quite apart from trying to understand an enormously powerful force of human communication, a basic reason for monitoring and recording what a television broadcasting system is doing is that it is impossible for anyone to make policy in any reasonable, rational and responsible way without knowing what the performance of the system is now. Policy making and planning always represent attempts to steer a complex system from a state we might label NOW, to another state labelled THE FUTURE, according to a set of goals that we try to make as clear and explicit as possible. In simple, straightforward terms, this means that we have got to have 'the facts', and that these facts have got to be as carefully defined and recorded as we can possibly make them. No subsequent analysis of television broadcasting for policy making is going to be better than the facts it is founded upon. This is so obvious that it hardly seems worth saying, and yet few national or private systems make any real attempt to monitor what they are doing, and those that try are generally dissatisfied with the inadequacy of the data base and analysis generated. At the national level it is impossible to make any meaningful comparisons between broadcasting channels or to compare the programming of a single channel from one year to the next. Nor can anyone know what several, often independent, television channels are creating in terms of an entire national structure.

As for the international scene, the problems are even more severe. If we assume roughly 100 countries around the world generating television broadcasting, then there is the potential for 100 x 100 = 10,000 flows of programmes. It is an alarming, but established fact that there is not one country in the world today that knows on a regular day-to-day basis what its own imports are, let alone records the content of these programmes, how they are treated, or what values they carry. Under these circumstances of totally inadequate information, policy making has no firm basis, no place from which it might start to steer towards a future it considers more appropriate. Fortunately, it is now possible to overcome all these problems by creating an inexpensive microcomputer data base of a radically new kind (Gould *et al*, 1983). Today, a broadcasting system can upgrade its data base on a daily basis, gain instantaneous access to any sort of programming information it requires, and use such a data system in an interrogative, question-and-answer fashion to plan for the future.

Breaking out of Partitional Thinking

Previous attempts to create reliable sets of data about television programming all ran into the same fundamental difficulties. The difficulties were both conceptual and definitional, and since they were not solved in any satisfactory way the sets of data produced were, at best, not very useful and, at worst, essentially meaningless. The basic conceptual difficulty was that the people who were trying to record the daily output of a television broadcasting system thought in highly traditional terms about the problem of 'classification'. In essence, this meant that they thought a television programme ought to be able to be placed in a little box, labelled in a certain way - such as 'Drama', 'Children's Programme', 'Cops and Robbers', 'Western', 'Situation Comedy', and so on. Then when the time came to make policy decisions, or compile annual reports, or answer questions from the public, government commissions or international agencies, all the labels on the boxes could be listed, together with the amount of broadcasting time they contained. It all seemed perfectly simple, obvious and straightforward.

The only problem was that television programmes were very rich and complicated things, and they obviously did not want to fit neatly into the non-overlapping boxes of the sort traditionally created by botanists and zoologists - and all the other people who admire (and sometimes force) intellectual tidiness on the natural world. If you take something as rich and, literally, *multi-dimensional* as a television programme, it is unlikely that it is going to be stuffed easily into a box with a single, over-simplified label. Unless, of course, you want to crush it down, lop off or ignore the bits that 'don't fit', and generally distort or destroy much of the information that the particular programme is trying to tell you. People who struggled with the problem of 'programme classification' often gave these inanimate electronic objects a will of their own, and labelled them 'intractable', when it was actually the frame of thinking that they were bringing to bear on the problem that needed a great deal of adjustment.

To get over this difficult problem, we have to make three careful conceptual distinctions and pay particular attention to questions of definition. First of all, we have to distinguish very carefully between the actual subject matter, the *contents* of a television programme, and the way a particular set of closely linked subjects forming a programme may be *treated.* We call the actual bits of subject matter that are connected together to form television programming the *backcloth*, and we think of each programme (or perhaps news item or advertisement) as a small geometric figure, called a simplex, whose points or vertices are the words we choose to describe the programme. It seems a bit strange at first, but we shall see that this is actually a very useful and practical way of thinking about the *structure* of television programming. For example, we might have a news item about floods in Southern California, broadcast on the evening of 21 February, 1980 by the Jamaica Broadcasting Corporation. We might represent it like this:

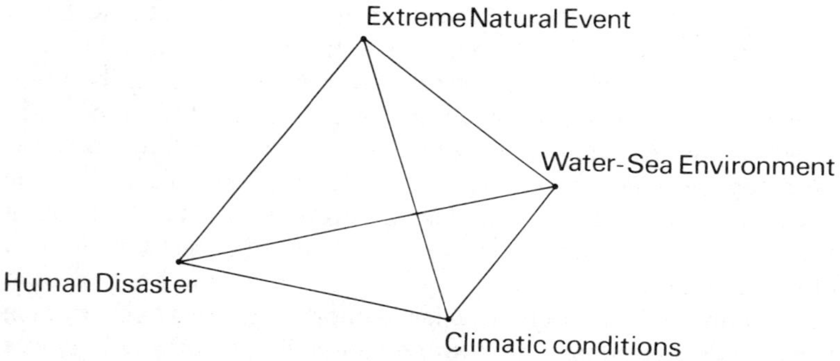

with each subject matter or content vertex coming from a list of several hundred words generated from the coding of thousands of television programmes around the world.

This brings us to the second conceptual distinction, because these descriptive terms exist at different levels in a hierarchy of generality. The words that make up the vertices in our example are at what we call the N + 1 level, and they aggregate in very carefully defined ways to more general terms at the N + 2 level. This means we can describe programmes in quite general ways (which is what broadcasters seem to like), or in more specific ways (more suitable for social scientists and people in communication research). Of course, you might want to code programmes at an extremely detailed level (say N-2?), and this would be perfectly possible if you were prepared to define your N-2 level terms with great care, and show how they aggregated up the backcloth hierarchy (Atkin, 1974).

Even so, something is obviously missing from the description of our news item as it stands: this particular set of well-connected subjects could conceivably form the content of an entertaining adventure story, or even as background material in an advanced educational programme for engineering students in a university learning to build dams. Also, we have no idea from our simplex description where these things are taking place. Outer Mongolia? Chile? Yugoslavia? So we have to specify the particular *treatment* we are going to give to these subjects, in this case, NEWS and USA - or, if it was considered to be useful to be more specific, INTERNATIONAL NEWS AND SOUTHERN CALIFORNIA, or an even finer geographic subdivision or location. The treatment NEWS, and the general country specification USA, are things we call the *traffic*. In a sense, they are carried by the backcloth, since we could have NEWS about all sorts of sets of subject words, and these could take place in the USA. The traffic terms are also hierarchically structured at three levels N, N+1, and N+2, to give us the same freedom to describe the treatment of programmes at different levels of generality. These traffic terms, the backcloth words, and all the problems of coding television programmes are described in coding manuals (Chapman and Johnson, 1979), and in books dealing with the methodology in detail (Gould, *et al*, 1983). Thus, a television programme is both traffic *and* backcloth 'glued together', and we shall see later that this is a very useful and highly informative way of thinking about the structure of television programming.

Just as one further example, consider the following:

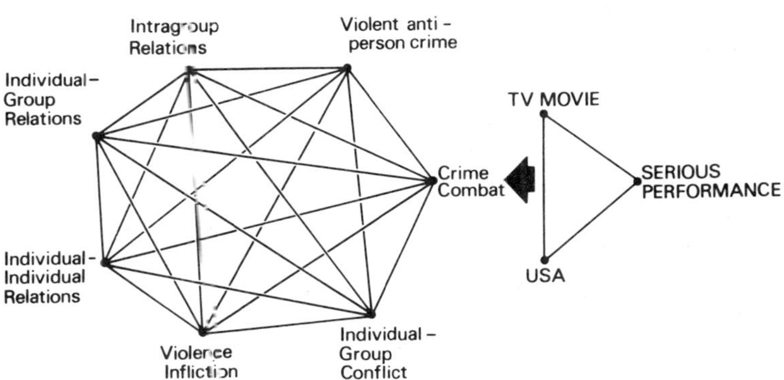

This happens to be *Police Woman*, a programme which sometimes seems almost perennial on Jamaican television. Notice that it is quite high-dimensional, because lots of things are connected together and are going on here. It seems to be a popular programme in Jamaica, which means that many people watch it, and this fact might mean that advertisers would like to get their products 'on screen' when it is being broadcast. Thus, we can think of other sorts of traffic that might 'live' on this part of the backcloth - for example, numbers of viewers, amounts of advertising revenues, and so on. In more advanced works, we could distinguish between treatment traffic (so-called 'super-traffic'), and such things as counts of viewers, revenues, Nielsen ratings, and so on ('ordinary' traffic), but for our purposes here it is sufficient to use the same term for both (Gould *et al*, 1983). Of course, when *Police Woman* is interrupted, and an advertisement comes on the screen, people watching may well feel a distinct change. Advertisements are usually very low-dimensional programmes (the advertising man's rule is 'keep it simple', and hammer it home to the viewer) and the sudden change in dimensionality may mean that people felt 'squeezed down', so that they temporarily switch off, or move away from the television set to get another beer. Thus,this sort of traffic in numbers of people watching, or dollars of advertising generated, may not be unrelated to the dimensionality of a particular programme.

The third concept we must understand is one that makes the intuitive, but often rather fuzzy idea of the 'structure of television programming' well-defined and operational. If we have a set of television programmes (perhaps those broadcast over a day, a week, a month, or whatever time period we are interested in), and a set of descriptive words (either backcloth or traffic words), we can define a *relation* between them. This can be done in a quite formal, mathematical way to create a multi-dimensional figure called a simplicial complex, which is our geometrical representation of the structure of television programming. Imagine a table or matrix whose rows are television programmes, and whose columns are the sets of words we might employ to describe the content (or the treatment) of a programme. As we have seen, programmes are represented as simplices, and if two programmes have two words in common, they would obviously be connected together by a one-dimensional face (a line whose end points were the two words they had in common). Thus, all the programmes, perhaps many hundreds of them, are linked together to form a highly connected structure - the simplicial complex.

Now notice what usually happens when someone approaches such a well-connected structure of television programming and starts applying conventional thinking about what classifications 'ought to be' - in other words, partitional box stuffing in all its eighteenth-century zoological and botanical glory. In order to take each programme, of varying dimensionality and varying degrees of connection to other programmes, and stuff it into a non-overlapping box, we have got to rip apart a highly-connected, multi-dimensional, and very complex *structure*. In the process of ripping things apart to satisfy an archaic 'tidiness complex' we are going to end up destroying much of the information about television programming itself. What we propose to do instead is to keep all the high connective 'tissue' intact, and teach people how to explore and interrogate these structures of television programming for informative and policy making purposes, rather than tearing them apart with outworn concepts. With the help of a computer, we can literally move around this complex structure asking questions that are relevant to us. With a bit of practice this is not too difficult, and all the evidence we have suggests that this approach can answer more questions than we would normally even think of posing.

Values, Coding and Communication Research

However, before we look explicitly at Jamaican television in these structural terms, there is one more very important question we must raise. This is the critical issue of *values* and how they shape the coding of television programmes, the raw data upon which all our subsequent analyses are based. Suppose we had a set of programmes broadcast in some Latin American country, and sets of well-defined backcloth and traffic words, and we asked a young and involved Marxist from that country, and a young American TV executive, to code the programmes. Would they describe the same structures? Even if they had been carefully trained, and knew the definitions of the terms thoroughly, it is unlikely that the same descriptions of the programmes would emerge. Indeed, the coder of Marxist orientation would probably feel there were a number of terms needed to describe the programmes that were not in the sets, and since these are always open we would have to add them. Does this mean that we can only have communications research modulo the ideology of the coders?

In dealing with television programmes, we are dealing with very delicate human materials that are often loaded with meanings that are, and indeed *have* to be, shaped by the values that human beings (viewers as well as professional coders) bring to bear upon a particular set of subjects. Can we ever have *totally* objective, value-free coding? In a very deep sense, we think the answer must be NO-there will always be the possibility of particular values shaping the choice of words we use to describe a television programme. It cannot be otherwise in the human sciences. But does this mean that the data sets are totally subjective, biased to a very large extent by the values of those who code them? Does this mean therefore that we must walk away from the task of trying to understand what is going on? Is cross-cultural, or even *human*, research impossible?

The answer to these two questions is also a qualified NO. In order to make proper policy decisions (themselves deeply shaped by local values), we must try to do the very best we can. This means having as clear and as hard definitions of the words as possible, having careful and well-trained coders, and having as our goal the capturing of the intent of those who chose to broadcast and add a particular programme to their television structure. One of the best ways of ensuring that local views and values will sensitively inform the coding process is to have nationals of the country or the broadcasting system involved as trained and practised coders. There is nothing less conducive to confidence than having people from a different culture 'descend' on another, and then shape the coding process totally oblivious and insensitive to local conditions and realities. On the other hand, it would be equally unfortunate if every country in the world were to develop its own, unique, coding scheme. Then international comparisons, in a highly dynamic international area of communication, would become quite impossible. In general, coding at the higher levels of generality in the backcloth and traffic hierarchies produces less stress and fewer differences, and this may mean that statements about international television can only be made in fairly general (i.e. $N+2$ level) terms. As we go down to the more specific $N+1$ and N levels, we must be increasingly sensitive to that effect that we called 'modulo the ideology of the coder'.

We can see this quite concretely in an advertisement shown frequently on Jamaican television for Panther condoms and Perle contraceptive pills. This government-sponsored viewing was coded as the simplex <Individual Health Maintenance, Birth Control, Sexual Relations>, but a coder whose deep religious beliefs forbade him or her from using mechanical and chemical contraceptive measures might have employed the <Morals-Ethics> vertex, while another might have incorporated <Personal Amusement>. Yet it seems to us (modulo the ideology Gould-Lyew Ayee!), that these were not the issues of the advertisement 'programmes' as they are shown on Jamaican television. The Perle advertisement, for example, shows a young woman getting ready for a party, sprucing up, making last-minute adjustments to her hair, and so on, and then suddenly remembering, just as she is about to leave for the party, to swallow her Perle. The scene implies the possibility of sexual relations, and there was a clear underlying concern for individual health and birth control. It was this set of three terms we finally decided upon, but this discussion itself makes a further important point - namely, that we cannot get away with fuzziness, a lot of hand-waving and a 'well, you know what I mean'. We have to code in clear, well-defined terms, and our choices are public and open to challenge. Such challenges can only improve the coding process. We feel that such open conditions and well-defined terms, together with as much sensitivity to local intent and culture as we can possibly generate, allow us to 'capture' the content and meaning of a programme *at a particular level* as far as human beings can record any sensitive human materials.

Television in Jamaica

Jamaica is an island nation of roughly 4,400 square miles lying in the centre of the Caribbean with about 2.25 million people, of whom approximately one million live in the capital, Kingston, and its immediate surrounding area. At the eastern end of the island the Blue Mountains rise up from the sea to over 7,000 feet, and the terrain over the rest of the island creates rather severe difficulties for radio and television transmissions. For television broadcasting there is a main station with studios at Half Way Tree (Kingston), and its signal is picked up and re-transmitted by eight other repeaters scattered strategically around the island. Television broadcasts outside of the main studios have proved difficult, and are confined to a radius of about 25 miles from the Half Way Tree station.

The Jamaica Broadcasting Corporation (JBC) was established in 1958, with a licence to broadcast awarded, and renewed to the present day, by the Jamaican Government. Funded by an initial grant of J$600,000, *radio* broadcasting started on 15 June 1959, with a service of 19 hours per day. All revenues for radio broadcasting are still derived from the sale of air time for advertising, and no other source. In 1962, the year of Independence, the Corporation was granted an exclusive franchise for *television*, and broadcasting was placed under the responsibility of the Ministry of Development and Welfare. Later, in 1969, it was transferred to the portfolio of the Prime Minister. Prior to this development, a Broadcasting Authority was set up in 1959 by the Government to ensure that JBC complied with the terms of its licence, and to offer the Corporation advice about broadcasting development.

Unlike radio, initial funding for television broadcasting came not from the Government, but from a consortium of foreign interests providing management and agency services and technical expertise. As in the case of radio, revenues for television were to be derived exclusively from spot advertising, and commercial transmissions started on 5 August 1963. Under the terms of its licence, the Jamaican Broadcasting Corporation is required to reserve broadcasting time for programmes provided by the Agency for Public Information (API) - since renamed the Jamaican Information Service (JIS) - and for educational programmes of the Ministry of Education. The former are usually half-hour daily programmes of local interest broadcast close to the start of commercial transmissions in the early evening (called the 'API programme'), while the latter are programmes for school children covering a wide variety of subjects for many different age levels.

Television broadcasting in Jamaica has been conducted over the past 21 years under conditions of considerable difficulty, and breakdowns and dead air times are common. Many stem from equipment incompatibilities - in the early years between American and European transmitters, relays, cameras, and other bits of paraphernalia, and by 1977 the annual reports were referring to 'dying equipment', and noted the difficulties of local production with the comment '[it is] not possible to maintain a regular schedule of weekly local programmes for several reasons: the breakdown of cameras, VTR machines and air conditioning units for long periods, and the inadequate supply of film stock' (Jamaican Broadcasting Corporation, 1977, p6). Further references to 'obsolete and worn-out equipment, the lack of spare parts, transportation, [and a] high turnover in personnel' emphasised the growing difficulties. The unavailability of equipment, particularly the breakdown of cameras, produced severe problems: even to cover the funeral ceremony of Sir Alexander Bustamante, one of Jamaica's national heroes, the Corporation had to borrow a camera in working order from the Educational Broadcasting Services down the street.

Producing programmes from local Jamaican materials also proved increasingly difficult. Part of the problem was the 'difficulty of getting commercial advertising support for local productions', and the report continued '[there is] a fundamental conflict to produce a majority of Jamaican programmes ... and to attract enough commercial revenue to do this' (Jamaica Broadcasting Corporation, 1973, p5). As early as 1972, John Hearne, a news analyst, was broadcasting pleas for Government funds so that more local programming could be made available:

> All we ask is that our Government invest money so that we see more plays by people like our own Barry Reckord or Trevor Rhone; that we get more documentaries in depth of where we as a people are going; that we see and hear our music and dance presented at some length in styles that are authentically Jamaican instead of bastard Anglo-American.
>
> All this will take money. And the people who buy the advertising times that pay for the alien canned stuff which is almost all JBC can now afford are not going to underwrite the sorts of programmes JBC should be offering. Only a government, in a country of this size, can afford that level of necessary money. ... A government of Jamaica that does not recognize this as a necessity, and a board that does not demand recognition of this necessity from the government that appoints it, might as well end the fiction of this so-called public corporation right now and offer it for sale to the highest private bidder.

As we shall see more than a decade later, the same problems are still around.

The Dynamic Structures of Jamaican Television

For the purposes of a small pilot study, we chose two identical three-week periods in 1980 and 1981 to allow us to make comparative statements particular to those times of the year. Although these periods seem relatively short, the Jamaican Broadcasting Corporation transmitted literally thousands of items (programmes, news, advertisements, etc.) during these times. Despite these limitations, it is a sad comment on the state of the art that we can make the claim that this small study nevertheless represents the most detailed analysis of television programmes ever made in a Third World country (Gould and Lyew-Ayee, 1981).

Jamaican Television 1980

When we consider the structure of 180 main programmes described on 206 terms at the N+1 level, we can think of looking at the structure through a series of spectacles whose lenses allow us to see programmes of successively lower dimensionality. With the highest dimension lenses in place, four programmes come into view: *Spiderman*, two *Kojak* programmes, and *API Insight*. Three of these are from the United States, including the children's programme *Spiderman*, a cartoon in which an enormous amount of action takes place, such as <Violent Anti-Person Crime, Violent Anti-Property Crime, Crime Combat, Superhuman Beings, Violence Infliction, Individual-Group Conflict ... >. The other two programmes are both *Kojak*, a similar 'action packed' TV movie made for adults with <Violent Anti-Person Crime, Violent Anti-Property Crime, Crime Combat, Violence Infliction, Individual-Group Conflict ... > - the 8-dimensional polyhedron is familiar to many people around the world.

What is not familiar, except to Jamaican viewers, is the programme *API Insight*, quickly joined by other API programmes at only slightly lower dimensional levels. These are approximately half-hour programmes put out by the Agency for Public Information, and they contain a wide variety of different subjects - perhaps a local steel band, something about fishing, a look at new buildings in Kingston, and bit about the bauxite industry, how tourism is faring, and so on. Frequently they will take such traffic as SERIOUS MAGAZINE and CURRENT AFFAIRS at level N, INFORMATION ELABORATION at N+1, and INFORM at N+2. In brief, they are informative programmes made up of different bits and pieces, and they tend to be interesting, high-variety productions with perhaps 'something for everyone'. Technically, such programmes made up of different pieces 'packaged' together are coded in special ways called *prisms*, because the total transmission times cannot be allocated to each piece, but must be carefully apportioned out. Since the equivalent of the American Nielsen Ratings or British TAM Ratings (based on the numbers of viewers watching a programme at a particular time), is not available in Jamaica, we have no hard data about dimensions and corresponding viewer traffic, but our local knowledge of Jamaica TV tells us that these API programmes are quite popular and watched by many at the beginning of the evening.

American programmes tend to be high dimensional, and over half viewing time(50.3 per cent) was devoted to those from the United States the rest being Jamaican (36.5 per cent), United Kingdom (5.7 per cent), West Germany (3.2 per cent of 'fillers'), and Unknown (3.7per cent). However, the American programmes tended to be rather the same type - in a sense they are quite predictable - in that they had low eccentricities, where the idea of *eccentricity* has the common meaning of being 'different from the rest'. This is a concept that can be made mathematically, and therefore structurally, precise, and refers to the proportion of vertices or descriptive terms that a programme has unique to itself. For example, a programme not sharing any characteristics with others would not be connected to the rest of the programming structure at all, and would be totally unique, or infinitely eccentric. Another programme, sharing all its terms with other programmes already in a programming structure at some dimensional level, would have zero eccentricity. Some of the highest eccentricities were characteristic of the API programmes, as well as *A Sense of Place*, a documentary set in Third World countries emphasising such things as shelter, housing and poverty. In a very real sense, this unusual programme stuck out of the general programming structure 'like a sore thumb', and perhaps attracted viewers as something quite different from the normal sort of transmission.

At this N + 1 level, we can also 'turn things around' and look at the structures created by the way the N + 1 descriptive terms connect over the programmes. The most common (highest dimensional) term is Individual-Individual Relations, hardly surprising since we, as individual human beings, are interested in relations between other individual human beings. However, at lower dimensional levels we see a distinctive 'Violence Infliction-Conflict-Human Relations' component, a distinctive and quite separate piece of the programming structure in which all of these things are tightly connected together. As shown in the 1st diagram on page 46.

At the centre is the very high dimensional polyhedron or simplex Individual-Individual Relations, a 66-dimensional 'object' in the structure. Going back to our spectacle analogy, if we were wearing 66-dimensional lenses this is all we would be able to see, but as we change to lenses of lower dimensionality other bits of the structure, as well as the connecting faces, begin to appear. For example, Violence Infliction is connected to Individual-Individual Relations, Individual-Group Relations and Crime Combat, but not to Intrafamily Relations at this level. Many programmes show violence

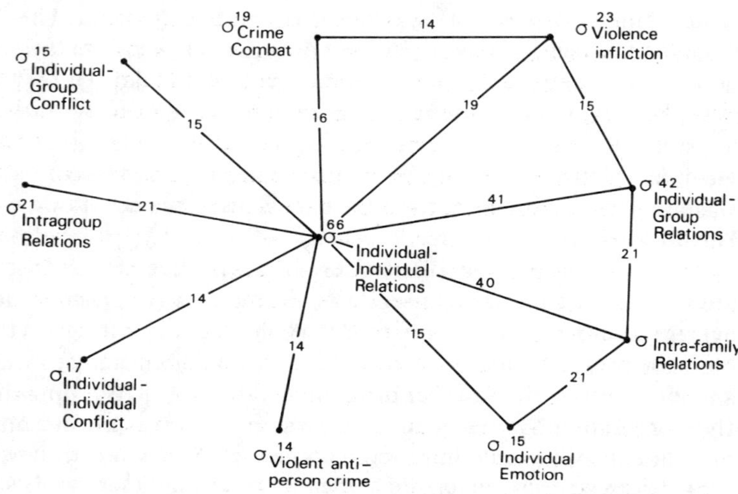

being inflicted between people (*Police Woman, Kojak, Quincy, Captain and the Kings, Nakia, Rockford Files,* and so on), but not very often as part of an Intrafamily affair.

At the more general N+2 level, there is also a large 'US Crime-Conflict-Violence' component, and we can see how the 20 US imports 'live' on this part of the N+2 structure as the one-, two-, or three-dimensional faces of a rather strange 'programme crystal' made up of three tetrahedrons joined by a common face:

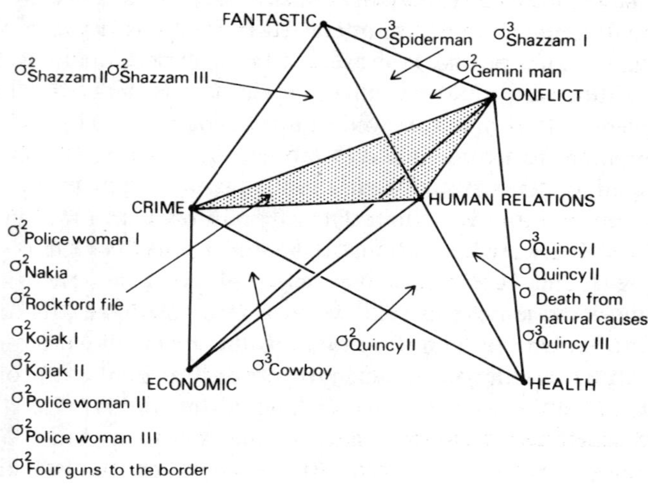

Spiderman and *Shazzam I* are the tetrahedron <Fantastic, Crime, Conflict, Human Relations>, while *Shazzam II* and *III* are the two-dimensional face <Fantastic, Crime, Human Relations>. The movie *Death From Natural Causes* is another tetrahedron in the 'crystal', described by <Crime, Conflict, Human Relations, Health>. The vertex <Health> appears since the subject of Death was an integral part of the story, and this aspect aggregates up to Health from the N + 1 level.

At this more generalised level most of the programme eccentricities are zero: if we want to describe programmes in more general, highly aggregated terms, we should not be too surprised if the distinctions blur, and programmes become more alike, lose their individuality, and so become less eccentric. Interestingly, four programmes taking INFORM traffic still stand out - two API programmes, a programme on agricultural education, and the *Busy Street Basic School* programmes (educational programmes for young children).

News programmes tend to be of particular interest to policy makers since, by definition, they represent flows of current information into a country from the 'outside world'. They are the focus of particular concern today as calls for a New Information Order are made at the international level, calls which reflect both a dissatisfaction with existing news channels and sources of supply, as well as distinct disquiet over possible constraints being placed upon a foreign correspondent's traditional and well-established freedom to report.

In the three-week period of 1980, there were 359 main news items broadcast (roughly 17 each evening). As we might expect, International Politics was the most prominent part of the structure, with Group-State conflict next. These are the first two subjects to connect at lower dimensional levels, a simple, but sad statement about the world we live in, and what is considered newsworthy. Of particular interest is the high visibility of Management-Labour Organization in the structure, a reflection of many of the difficulties Jamaica itself was experiencing in February-March 1980. National Economic Structure was also in the news, as grave problems of foreign exchange and capital investment created additional domestic worries. National Politics and Elections often tend to carry NEWS traffic, but these remain disconnected until much lower dimensional structures are seen: elections were not immediately pending in Jamaica at the time, and many of the Election items came from overseas, especially Rhodesia-Zimbabwe, where they were often connected with Group-State Conflict and Violence Infliction. Again, we must be careful in our interpretations and consider both the backcloth *and* the traffic (in this case, the geographic traffic particularly) before we can grasp what is going on.

Most of the main news items were generated by Jamaica itself (Table 2.1) with news from the immediate Caribbean area next. News items from Africa were third, reflecting both local interest in this continent, as well as the considerable generation of items considered newsworthy during this period. Zimbabwe alone generated nearly 60 per cent of the items from Africa, but news also flowed from South Africa, Ethiopia, Zambia, Nigeria, and the Central African Republic. Of course, we must keep in mind that these flows were generated over a particular three-week peiod in early 1980, and the statements we make are limited to the data set. Once again, however, this points up the crucial necessity of constantly monitoring the programme structure so that we can make more detailed and firmer statements about these important aspects of broadcasting.

Table 2.1: Jamaican Television, 1980: Aggregate Flows of Main News Items

Region of Origin	Per cent
Jamaica	59.4
Rest of Caribbean	13.6
Africa	8.8
Latin America	5.7
Middle East	4.1
North America	3.6
Europe	2.9
India-Far East	1.3
USSR	0.5

During the same three-week period of broadcasting on a single national channel, from approximately 6.00pm to midnight every evening, Jamaican viewers were able to watch 924 advertisements. These tended to be low-dimensional, generally concentrating on one or two things 'to get the message across', and they form a not-insignificant part of the fabric of television broadcasting. We also remind you that these form the sole source of revenue for the Jamaica Broadcasting Corporation.

At the N+1 level, Food-Drink-Cooking is the most prominent subject, quickly followed by exhortations to purchase products for Personal Grooming. At a somewhat lower level Alcohol connects immediately with Food-Drink, followed by Personal Health Care, Clothes, Repair Maintenance, and Cleaning. As we might expect, advertisements hold up a commercial mirror to a part of the human condition, dealing with everyday things in many people's lives - for instance, food and drink, appearance and health, and clothes. Of special interest is the relatively high dimensionality of Repair-Maintenance and Cleaning, particularly when we come to compare these items to those of 1981, in which they almost disappear. Holidays-Vacations were usually connected to Air Transport, but the connections must have been difficult for many viewers to make in the light of foreign exchange and travel difficulties during those days.

Jamaican Television 1981: Structures and Comparisons

In the interval between the two three-week periods in February-March 1980 and 1981, Jamaica experienced considerable change in its political life. It also experienced changes in its television broadcasting. Some of these may have been due to deliberate policy decisions within the Jamaica Broadcasting Corporation, others to outside circumstances over which it had little or no control. Our concern is to record the structures of television in 1981, and compare them with those of a year earlier. These examples will illustrate the sort of changes that can occur, and how these can be recorded and examined in some detail. As we have noted several times before, the recording of such detailed change is not carried out by any broadcasting system today, although the monitoring system is now available. We shall see, in a few illustrative comparisons, how such changes, recorded in hard and well-defined terms, are pertinent for the task of monitoring and steering - i.e. policy making.

The first impression we have is that the structure of television programming at the N+1 level has changed very little: in a sense, it has the same 'feel' to it. High-dimensional American imports (the ubiquitous *Police Woman, Nakia* and *Shazzam*), were still going strong, while at lower dimensions there was still a large 'US Entertainment' component, together with a piece of the structure that announced the arrival of the rather eccentric *The Muppets* in Jamaica. One marked difference, however, is that the API programmes, which were so high-dimensional in 1980, have been reduced in dimensionality. What sort of forces have acted on the structure to produce such a change? Has viewer traffic been affected? These are the sorts of questions that might easily arise out of a concern for policy making.

Nevertheless, and with the exception of the dimensional reduction in API programmes, the initial impression is that not too much has happened over the past year. This is where we have to be very careful, however, and try to avoid 'off-the-cuff' generalisations about television programming unless our statements are really rooted in hard data and careful structural analysis. When we look at the structure of N+1 level terms over the programmes, we begin to see some quite remarkable changes between the two years. Individual-Individual Relations is still the most prominent piece of the structure, although it has been reduced considerably in dimensionality, while another thing we notice immediately is the quite extraordinary decline in the subject Violence Infliction. Despite our initial impressions, the *structure*, the connective tissue that actually *is* television programming, has undergone some jolting changes. Moreover, when we talk about structural change we mean that things are connecting up differently. If we go to dimensional levels in 1981 that are only *half* of those in 1980, we now see a 'Human Relations' component that has *no* conflict such as Violence Infliction, and *no* crime such as Violent Anti-Person Crime attached to it at all. In contrast, a number of other things, such as Music, Personified Animals (the Muppets!), Plant-Animal Environment, and Physical Health have risen to higher dimensional levels in the structure.

What has been going on here? What forces have been at work between 1980 and 1981 to produce such changes? Perhaps we can get a hint when we look at how programme origins have altered between the two years (Table 2.2). There has been a massive decline in the proportion of the American programme shown, the 'gaps' being filled by Jamaica, the United Kingdom, and three other Commonwealth countries. We shall see that the decline in violence and conflict is due almost entirely to these changes, but we shall examine such questions in much greater detail below.

The question of change can be examined with great precision once computerised data bases are available, and it is worth considering with a concrete example the sort of interrogations we can make of these structural descriptions. Suppose we had to answer a question from a Parliamentary Commission, or respond to a rather aggressive,

Table 2.2: Jamaican Television 1980 and 1981: National Origins of Programmes Broadcast

Country of Origin	1980	1981		1981-80 Percent Change*
Jamaica	36.5	38.0	(45.1)	+8.6
United States	50.9	31.5	(27.9)	-23.0
United Kingdom	5.7	13.3	(11.7)	+6.0
West Germany	3.2	2.4	(2.1)	-1.1
Australia	-	0.7	(0.6)	+0.6
Canada	-	0.5	(0.5)	+0.5
Hong Kong	-	1.3	(1.1)	+1.1
Unknown	3.7	12.4	(11.0)	+7.3

*Percentage when Eduational Television Broadcasts (not transmitted during the same period in 1980) are excluded for comparative purposes.

off-the-top-of-the-head statement from a viewer, about the portrayal of the subject Sexual Relations on Jamaican television. Suppose the claims were made that 'There's too much ...', or 'It's much worse [better?] than a year ago ...', or simply the less value-laden question 'Has there been any change?' Now there are, in fact, many interesting ways that these sorts of questions might be posed to the computer data system. We might like to know what the vertex <Sexual Relations> was connected to; or how it was *treated* (and at what level?); or perhaps the amount of time it was treated in a certain way at a certain level.

One of the ways we can examine this question is by looking at specific backcloth and traffic combinations, and the numbers of minutes of broadcasting time devoted to this subject. Perhaps like this:

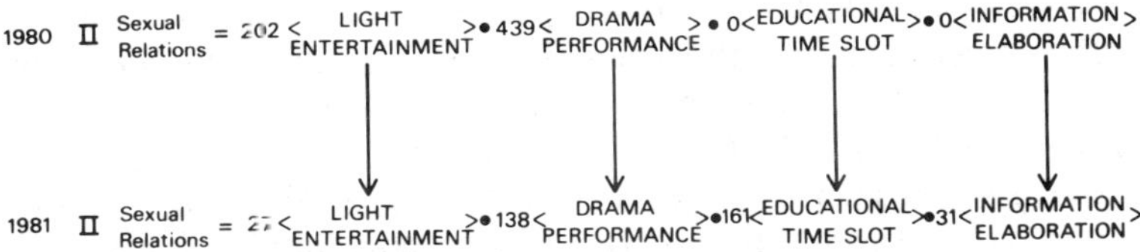

Formally, these are pieces of pattern polynomials, algebraic expressions of our backcloth-traffic structures that are a result of a

Sexual Relations 'mapping'. We see immediately some considerable change at this detailed level. In 1980, Sexual Relations carried 202 minutes of LIGHT ENTERTAINMENT (most cultures can laugh at sex, and with the long English tradition since Chaucer meeting in Jamaica the even longer tradition of West African folktales, we can understand this quite easily), but it also carried 439 minutes of DRAMA PERFORMANCE (most cultures find sex serious too, and a subject tending to produce dramatic situations). In the intervening year, however, forces have been working on these details of the backcloth. By 1981, Sexual Relations are down 45 per/cent, and strong forces of repulsion have shifted the treatment away from LIGHT ENTERTAINMENT and DRAMA PERFORMANCE, and attracted it to EDUCATIONAL TIME SLOT and INFORMATION ELABORATION. The small amount of DRAMA PERFORMANCE is still due, a year later, to *Return to Peyton Place*. Viewers with different value structures will welcome or regret such changes, and perhaps be attracted or repulsed by accordingly switching their television sets on or off.

We are also aware of considerable structural change in the entire backcloth at the N+1 level. The subjects Conflict and Crime have been greatly reduced, and in a sense they have been cut in half as the terms Art, Environment and Fantastic rise in dimensionality to take their place. As for traffic changes, a distinct 'Cops and Robbers' component has been replaced by 'Cousteau-Environmental Concern', together with a disconnected 'Political Broadcast' component. The latter is due to the fact that the three-week period in 1981 included the day for elections to local Parish Councils, and both major political parties were allotted identical 15-minute slots by the Jamaica Broadcasting Corporation to get their message to the viewers on any set of subjects they considered important. Since these political messages carried the N level traffic term POLITICAL GUIDANCE, they appear as a separate, disconnected part of the structure. At the lower dimensional level a very large 'Educational' component appears, and this is confirmed by such traffic terms as CHILD EDUCATIONAL TIME SLOT.

When we consider the programmes carrying NEWS traffic, the first thing we notice about the structure of 1981 compared to 1980 is that powerful forces have been at work. Whereas 359 main news items were broadcast in the same period in 1980, now only 182 were available to viewers, and no summary news headlines were given in the early and late evening times. News broadcasts were also shorter, and programmes tended to have less coverage, so that the news may have appeared to viewers as somewhat more 'spotty', disconnected, and fragmentary. This impression is precisely confirmed by the fact that at roughly comparable dimensional levels, the structure of the backcloth carrying NEWS traffic in 1981 was much more highly fragmented compared to 1980. Many people in Jamaica were aware that 'something has happened to the news', perhaps indicating some intuitively felt notion of the disconnection and fragmentation that had occurred by not treating news items in such depth as before. The sense of disconnection was even more remarkable when we realise that there were some rather rich (high-dimensional) news items in 1981, items which we may expect to have a strong effect in connecting up the structure.

There were also some changes in the origins of news programmes (Table 2.3) and, while we must be conservative in our interpretation since news events around the world vary considerably from one time to another, it is remarkable how the news coverage of North America rose from 3.6 per cent (Table 2.1) to 14.1 per cent (Table 2.3), an increase of 10.5 per cent.Europe has also risen slightly, but news from Africa has declined, along with items about the Caribbean. The decline in news originating from Africa is partly due to the prominence of the Zimbabwe elections in 1980, but actual geographic coverage was also much reduced in 1981.

Table 2.3: Jamaican Television, 1981: Aggregate Flows of Main News Items and Changes over 1980

Region of Origin	Percentage	Change since 1980
Jamaica	62.2	+2.8
North America	14.1	+10.5
Caribbean	9.2	-4.4
Europe	6.5	+3.6
India-Far East	3.2	+1.9
Africa	3.2	-5.6
Middle East	2.2	-1.9
Latin America	1.6	-5.1
USSR	0.0	<0.5

At the N+1 level, the structure of the news showed some marked changes. The subject Management-Labour Organization declined and it was much less well connected to Group-State conflict. In fact, nearly half the occasions that this latter term was used to code news items in 1980 was generated by Jamaica itself (Table 2.4).

For example, news programmes in 1980 reported such things as: dissatisfaction, negotiations, and strikes by prison officers, school teachers, school staffs, women, power supply workers, water supply workers, aircraft maintenance workers, nurses, civil servants, marine pilots, telecommunications service workers, and such other things as the arrests of fishermen protesting on the Pedro Banks. In 1981, there were only a couple of demonstrations against police, a demand by university students for bigger allowances, and a news report on a Supreme Court case about a suit brought by former (1980) members of the newsroom staff at the Jamaica Broadcasting Corporation contesting their dismissal!

Table 2.4: Jamaican Television, Geographical Origins of News Programmes 1980-81 containing the Vertex <Group-State Conflict>

Country	1980	1981	Country	1980	1981
Jamaica	21	5	France	1	0
			United Kingdom	0	2
Guyana	4	0	Poland	0	1
Surinam	4	0			
St Kitts-Nevis	1	0	Israel	1	0
Colombia	6	0	Lebanon	0	1
Guatemala	1	0	Afghanistan	4	2
Panama	1	0			
Dominica	0	5	Chad	0	1
Cuba	0	1	South Africa	1	0
Antigua	0	1	Ethiopia	1	0
			Zimbabwe	0	2
El Salvador	0	1			
			Totals	46	22

Sports play a very important role in Jamaican life, and it should come as no surprise to learn that between 16 February and 17 March 1981 inclusive, 200 news items were broadcast over JBC, originating from all over the world (Figure 2.1). Those who have witnessed the way in which a still hush descends on the English-speaking Caribbean during an important Test Match will understand the prominence of cricket over all other sports (Table 2.5). Nor is this merely hyperbole:

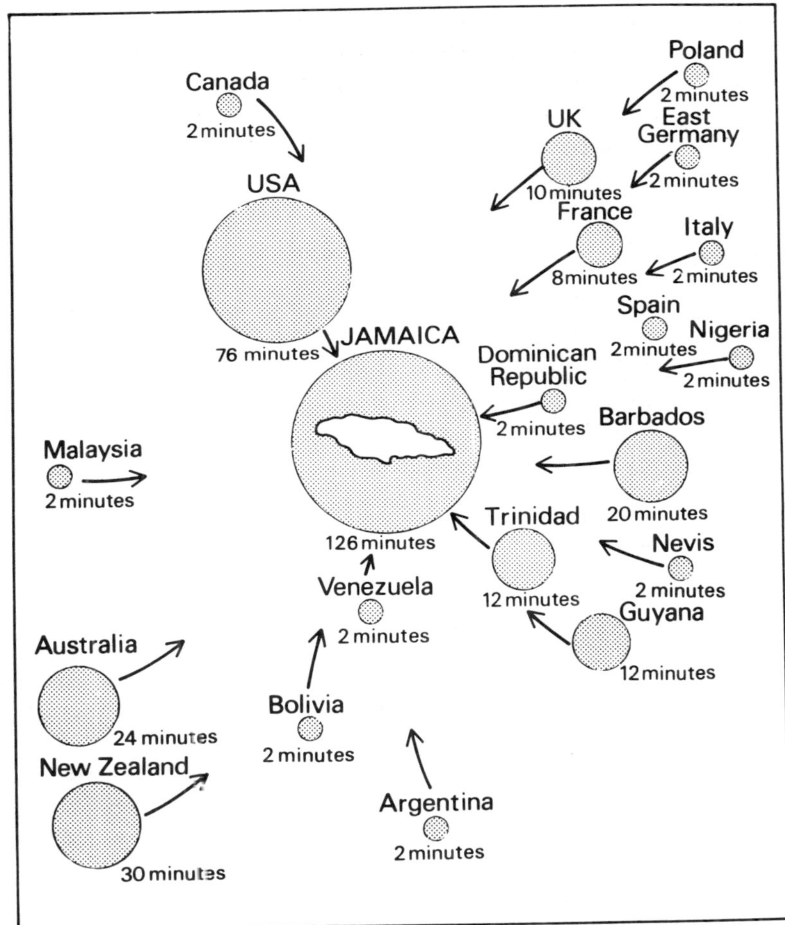

Fig. 2.1

we have both witnessed the effects, quite extraordinary to an 'outsider', of Test cricket on the fabric of life in Jamaica and Trinidad, and it is rumoured that in Guyana and Barbados people take it even more seriously. Work literally comes to a halt: shops are closed, school classes do not exist in any meaningful pedagogic sense, Parliaments find it strangely necessary to recess at such opportune times, crime seems to disappear temporarily, the streets are virtually deserted, and taxis become almost unavailable at airports. Europeans

Table 2.5: Jamaican Television Sports News, 1981: Individual Items 16 February - 7 March 1981

Cricket	58
Tennis	32
Football	28
Athletics	16
Golf	12
Boxing	11
Horse Racing	9
Basketball	8
Squash	6
Table Tennis	3
Field Hockey	3
Netball	3
Badminton	2
Cycling	2
Volleyball	2
Rifle Shooting	1
Motor Racing	1
Rugby	1
Swimming	1
Darts	1
Motor Cycling	1

with their football Cup Finals, and the Americans with their baseball World Series, appear incapable of understanding what total social devotion to sports really means. For many Jamaicans, cricket is not just a sport, but an activity which absorbs the attention of the individual totally, and lifts him up the hierarchy to the level of his local team, nation, or even larger international confederations (*the* West Indies cricket team). Tennis news is also popular, together with football (primarily the soccer results from overseas). Other reports are much less prominent, although there is a strong, and traditional, interest in athletics, boxing and horse racing. Golf reports originate almost entirely from the United States.

Advertising structures in 1981 generally reflect small changes, except for a strong decline in Alcohol and Health Care, and a sharp rise in Clothes. These changes are clearly the result of forces on a certain part of the advertising backcloth, as sponsors of some products shift away, and others take their place - although only in part. The total number of advertisements was down to 806, compared to 924 the previous year, and we must recall that the Jamaica Broadcasting Corporation depends upon advertising as its sole source of revenue. These shifts in revenue are the result of certain forces acting on the structure of Jamaican television, and it is worth thinking about what these might be and where they originate.

Every change that takes place is the result of certain decisions, and these decisions may well be the result of other forces in the larger environment of which Jamaican television is a part. Rather dramatic structural changes from one time to another direct our thinking to the forces at work, and one of the main advantages of monitoring a system for policy purposes is that we can begin to see how structural changes in backcloth and traffic point towards other changes in the larger society. When we interrogate these structures of television, to what extent are we interrogating the larger structures of society of which television itself is a part?

For example, we might like to pick out a particular subject, say Violent Anti-Person Crime at level N+1, and ask: What sort of N level traffic treatment did it receive, and what have the changes been over the course of year? Our data system immediately tells us that in 1980 this subject took 22 minutes of CARTOON traffic, 22 minutes of CHILD traffic, 625 minutes of TV MOVIE, and 625 minutes of SERIOUS PERFORMANCE. In other words, nearly 11 *hours* of this subject were shown over a three-week period, most of it transmitted for general adult audiences.

What about 1981? Here we see a big change, a change we might ascribe to strong forces of repulsion pushing transmitting time (and audience?) away. Now there were 0 minutes of CARTOON and CHILD traffic, and only 159 minutes of TV MOVIE and SERIOUS PERFORMANCE - a reduction of just over 75 per cent. Has this 'just happened'? Or have there been deliberate policy changes shaping the structure of television?

Suppose we wanted to go the other way, asking what a particular treatment, at a particular level, went to in terms of subject matter. For example, how is ETHICAL CONCERN 'mapped on to' particular N+1 level subjects (either singly or in combination)? In 1980, only two connected vertices <Christian Beliefs, Morals-Ethics> received 16 minutes of ETHICAL CONCERN, while in 1981 this same treatment went to 18 minutes of <Christian Beliefs, Morals-Ethics>, 29 minutes went to <Plant-Animal Environment, Wild Environment>, and 106 went to <Plant-Animal Environment, Water-Sea Environment>. As we saw before, the N+2 level subject Environment was much more prominent in 1981, and we now see that this subject often raised ethical issues - our responsibility to the sea and to sea animals such as whales, porpoises, and sea birds, as well as our care for the terrestrial world and its fauna and flora.

Or we might like to bring our questions 'closer to home', and ask how many items in 1980 and 1981 containing the N+1 level subject Man-Labour Organization, *in combination with any other* N+1 level 'conflict' subject, went to the *combined* N level treatments NEWS and JAMAICA. This is the same as asking how many news items there were about labour troubles in Jamaica. The answer was 34 items in 1980, compared to only four in 1981, and we can see how forces in the larger environment in which television is embedded shape these particular pieces of the structure carrying NEWS traffic.

These are simple and straightfoward answers to questions that a policymaker might pose, but sometimes the answers are a bit more complex. Suppose we ask what backcloth subjects at the more general N+2 level during 1980 and 1981 took the N+1 level treatment DRAMA PERFORMANCE? Many things receive dramatic treatment, because we are all so often ENTERTAIN-ed (N+2 traffic!) by dramatisations (Table 2.6). By far the most important subject in 1980 was Human Relations, for it comes as no surprise that human beings are fascinated by dramatisations of relationships between human beings. Yet notice how Conflict is also extremely prominent (over 27¼ *hours* in three weeks), often linked to Crime. Much further down the list are such subjects as Health, Economics, Politics, and Sports.

Turning to 1981, one may ask whether this part of the structure has maintained itself. It is here that we see that powerful forces of repulsion have been at work (Table 2.7). Virtually every subject receives less dramatic treatment, the largest losses being Conflict, Human Relations and Crime, often in combination with one another. Notice, too, how the overall dimensions of the programmes have fallen. What has been going on here? We get a clue when the computer gives us an answer to our next question: What were the N+2 level subjects generated by programmes imported from the United States? Here we are clipping out that piece of the N+2 level backcloth that carried USA traffic (Table 2.8). In 1980, there was a strong flow from the United States to Jamaica of Human Relations, Conflict and Crime, usually carried by quite high-dimensional programmes. But by the following year (Table 2.9) nearly all the subject had radically changed: Human Relations, Conflict and Crime were all down by 16 or more *hours*, and the only real increases were in Environment, Art and Communications.

Table 2.6: Jamaican Television, 1980: Subjects at the N + 2 Level treated in a dramatic way

	Dimensionality of Programme				
Subjects at N − 2 Level	0	1	2	3	Total Time (Minutes)
Human Relations	479	1248	837	383	2047
Conflict		578	678	383	1639
Crime		155	541	383	1079
Health				265	265
Economic		144		118	232
Politics		110	86		196
Sports		130	59		189
Transport		102	59		161
Day-to-day	94				94
Technical		59			59
Fantastic			51		51
	573	2496	2311	1532	

Table 2.7 : Jamaican Television, 1981 : Subjects at the N + 2 Level treated in a dramatic way

	Dimensionality of Programmes					
Subjects at N + 2 Level	0	1	2	3	Total Time (Minutes)	Change: 1981-80
Human Relations	374	984	377	60	1795	-767
Conflict		440	377		817	-822
Crime		75	273		348	-731
Health		175		60	235	-30
Economic					0	-232
Politics		164			164	-32
Sports			104		104	-85
Transport				60	60	-161
Day-to-day				60	60	-34
Technical					0	-59
Fantastic	73				73	+22
Communi-cations		130>		60	190	+190
	447	1968	1131	240		

It is not our concern to speculate here what policy decisions led to these massive changes, but we should realise that in 1980 programmers faced grave difficulties. Foreign exchange was almost impossible to obtain for the purchase of programmes, and costs of making domestic programmes were not only four times as high, but it was almost impossible to obtain working equipment, cameras and film. Under such circumstances, and given the responsibility of filling air time each evening, what could people do but 'reach up to the shelf' and pull down the old 'Cops and Robbers'? For all practical purposes, it was a case of that or nothing.

This examples raises a very important question for many Third World countries once 'someone', almost certainly innocently and unwittingly, has decreed that National System X *will* broadcast between the hours of Y and Z. Without a well-developed production system (and without much money for cameras, film and equipment), what *can* a country do to fill the transmitting time except rely on a stream of relatively cheap foreign programmes whose original costs were probably recovered many times over a decade before? Furthermore, once a small country gets locked into a supply system, and the viewers are used to the sort of programmes shown, how easy is it to change - even if one wants to?

A great deal has been written during the last decade about the preponderance of certain types of programming, and all sorts of blanket statements have been made about 'Cultural Imperialism'. Although there are certainly well-documented cases of strong influences at work on the international television scene (forces of repulsion and attraction again - but on what backcloth?), we feel that blanket charges of cultural and economic imperialism are quite dysfunctional, and may actually obscure with rhetoric more than they reveal. There are certainly cases where commercial and political pressures combine to produce forces that a small Third World country finds difficult to resist. Yet it is equally clear that relatively high degrees of dominance can also occur simply because time has got to be filled, and lots of cheap programmes are there to plug the gap if they happen to be chosen. We should avoid the cliches so increasingly prevalent in this area, and examine in terms of hard, well-defined data sets the *actual* structures, and the *actual* problems.

As we have seen, this can be done today to provide a firm basis for those acts of policy making that always represent attempts to steer a complex system from where it is now, to where people would like it to be. With a well-tried coding system tested in over a dozen countries,

Table 2.8 : Jamaican Television, 1980: Subjects at the N + 2 Level generated by Programmes imported from the United States

Subjects at N − 2 Level	Dimensionality of Programme 0	1	2	3	Total Times (Minutes)
Human Relations	895	671	1341	447	3354
Conflict	86		1177	447	1710
Crime		155	586	447	1188
Sports	325	130	85		540
Fantastic	184	27	122	64	397
Transport		92	183		275
Health				265	265
Economic		114		118	232
Day-to-day		94	124		218
Environment	72				72
Technical		59			59
	1562	1342	3618	1788	

Table 2.9 : Jamaican Television, 1981: Subjects at the N + 2 Level generated by Programmes imported from the United States

Subjects at N + 2 Level	Dimensionality of Programmes 0	1	2	3	Total Time (Minutes)	Change: 1981 - 1980
Human Relations	619	727	317	60	1723	-1631
Conflict		347	383		730	-908
Crime			225		225	-963
Sports			104		104 >	-436
Fantastic	218	75	66		359	-38
Transport					0	-275
Health		228		60	288	+23
Economic					0	-232
Day-to-day				60	60	-158
Environment	296				296	+224
Technical		53			53 >	-6
Communi-cations		130		60	190	+190
Politics			54		54	+54
Art	191				191	+191
	1324	1560	1149	240		

with coders well trained by those who have developed the system, and with microcomputers dedicated to the specialised tasks of data formation and analysis, *any* broadcasting system today can make policy on such a firm basis for perhaps less than one per cent of its annual costs. It hardly seems a high price to pay to know where you have been, where you are now, and where you might want to be in the future.

CHAPTER 3: THE CHANGING CONCEPT OF PLACE IN THE NEWS

Susan R. Brooker-Gross

MEMPHIS

DROWNED

Memphis, February 9. - Nick Dupont, a fisherman of Helena, Arkansas, was accidentally drowned on Saturday.

MURDER TRIAL

The trial of Doran, for the murder of Captain Ed. Whitfield, commenced today.

PEDDLER MURDERED BY A BOY

An unknown peddler was murdered in McNair County, a few days since, by a boy named Quill, only fourteen years old. The boy was arrested, and confessed his guilt.

THE SLEEPY DETECTIVE

The *Avalanche* believes that the detective from whom Wells escaped a few days ago was Barmere, the missing Nashville detective.

From *The Cincinnati Daily Enquirer*
20 Feb. 1869

Such news stories could only have come from the mid-nineteenth century. Earlier a newspaper would not have had access to such timely details of events in a distant city. Later, I contend, no-one would have cared.

The premise of this paper is that the means of communication affect the amount and quality of public information that a particular society received from other places. If such means of communication are slow and bound to a local area, there is little potential for learning about distant places. Conversely, it is argued that the availability of rapid and global means of communication will not necessarily mean that public information about 'elsewhere' is abundant. Rather, advanced technologies for communication can render elsewhere so commonplace and routine as to erode interest.

To assert that interest in elsewhere can be moulded by communications technology resembles Marshall McLuhan's statement that 'the medium is the message' (McLuhan, 1964, p23). McLuhan believed that the involvement of human sensory perception with communications technology framed any content carried by the medium. His approach contrasted with, yet was derived from, the more cultural approach of Harold A. Innis (Carey, 1967). Innis, too, believed that communications media influenced society, but focused on social structure rather than on sensory perception (Innis, 1951, 1952; Carey, 1975). Since information about, and interest in, other places is more a social than a sensory question, it will be Innis's ideas that will be used to explore the relationship between place orientation and communications technologies.

This paper contains two major elements. First, orientation to place is investigated by means of content analysis of a newspaper, the *Cincinnati Enquirer*, through the nineteenth and twentieth centuries. Rather than analysing the places that are mentioned in the news, as done in previous research (e.g. Cole and Whysall, 1968; Cole, 1969; Kariel, 1978; Kariel and Rosenvall, 1978; Walmsley, 1980, Brooker-Gross, 1983), this study examines the quality and quantity of news from all non-local places. Interest in other places in general can be gauged from this approach. The second section of this paper, using the arguments of Innis, connects interest and disinterest in places to the dominant mode of news-gathering communication.

News

News-gathering in the early 1800s was severely constrained by transport technology. News had to be transported physically in the same way as any other commodity, whether in the form of newspapers, letters, or other written documents, or even in the minds of travellers. While such innovations in transport media as road, canal and steamboat improvements facilitated more rapid and more extensive communication, it was not until the 1840s that communications started to become distinct from physical transportation. The electronic era began with the invention and spread of the telegraph, and was consolidated by further advances in telegraphy, including transoceanic cables, and by other developments dating from the last quarter of the nineteeenth century, such as the telephone. These technological changes in the ability to gather news were mirrored in the manner of presentation of the news, as well as the quantity of news carried in the newspaper.

The news content of the *Cincinnati Enquirer*, thus, is analysed for both the manner of presentation and quantity of news. The *Enquirer* was chosen deliberately to avoid both the newspapers of small towns and the 'elite' newspapers of major east coast cities, being a long-established major circulation newspaper in a medium-sized city. As such, it has the advantage of having looked to larger cities for news and standards of journalism, as well as setting standards within its region.

The sample of this newspaper that was taken comprised four complete issues from every tenth year between 1839 and 1929, and of four issues from both 1949 and 1969. The four issues in all years sampled were the first Tuesday and Wednesday, and the second Thursday and Friday in February. Analysis of these newspapers was in two parts. First, the grouping or presentation of news items were analysed qualitatively, looking at whether place of occurrence or the occurrence itself was given greater emphasis. Secondly, a quantitative analysis counted the total number of non-local news stories and the number of different places in which those stories took place. A ratio of items-to-places was calculated to give a relative measure of news interest in other places.

Qualitative analysis

Early in the nineteenth century the necessity for physical transportation of news items was evident in the presentation in the newspaper itself, resulting in a technique of news-writing that is termed here *geographic bundling*. News from Europe literally came in bundles, usually packages of English newspapers brought by ship. The bundle would be re-created in the port city newspaper, with the news typically of the format: (a) a ship arrived from London; and (b) here is the news it brought. A similar pattern persisted in the interior, with gateway cities assuming the role of port cities. One day's mail brought newspapers from other cities and that news was reprinted locally. In both cases the news from the gateway city's hinterland was bundled together, such that 'all the news from ...' was printed together in the newspaper. These bundles emphasised the place of news occurrence and presented a varied picture of both routine and extraordinary news from a given place.

To take an example, the 8 February 1839 issue carried a column detailing the available news from a major winter storm (see Extract 1,

Appendix). The available news was relatively sparse and the storm itself must have served to disrupt communications. While news is present from a variety of places, the technique of geographic bundling is evident, particularly in reprinting items from the Germantown newspaper. Another, more common example is the presentation of foreign news, with news from all parts of Europe and even Asia bundled together under the headline 'England'.

To the modern reader, the news appears jumbled and disorganised. This method of news presentation reproduced a distant source with little, if any, editorial filtering. Channels of communication directly moulded the presentation of news. Treatment of news was analogous to handling of tangible cargo - picked up from one location, deposited at another. The directness of the transportation route determined the emphasis on place. News of events in New York or Philadelphia might have been directly reprinted from a New York or Philadelphia newspaper, giving the Cincinnati reader a feel for the diversity of life in those other cities. If the news events were further removed, say, from Europe, the Cincinnati news accounts were effectively reprinting material that was already reprinted, possibly many times over. Thus diverse event locations were brought together in one geographic bundle, as frequently was the case for European news.

The interest in elsewhere at this time stemmed in large part from the scarcity of information about other places. The combination of the desire to hear news of Europe or east coast locations, plus the slow and uncertain conditions for receiving such news, produced an emphasis on the route or mode of communication. Editors often lamented disruption of mail services from the interior, whether attributed to difficult weather or incompetent authorities, and news-story presentation almost always stated or implied a method of transmission. Emphasis on the editor's accessibility served to make news from *anywhere* noteworthy, if only for the fact that it had been successfully procured. Consequently, all available information was newsworthy, regardless of place and any presumed inherent newsworthiness of the event.

For Cincinnati and other river towns, the waterways were the usual means by which other cities' newspapers arrived. One could find columns of news from other river-town newspapers reprinted fairly quickly after initial publication. To the extent that a display of speediness was becoming important in journalism, other river towns were good news producers. To merchants and farmers, other river towns were not only familiar but also economically important, since the river transported their merchandise and produce. Regardless of the economic importance of a given event, however, the easily accessible river towns became newsworthy.

Quickly, the river itself became news too. Instead of 'here is all the news from Pittsburgh', the newspaper began sorting news topically as it pertained to the travel conditions and events of the river. A 'River News' column was begun, bringing together titbits of river information from diverse locations along the river. A shift occurred here from geographic bundling to topical sorting. Yet even for such a straightforward topic, the newspaper had to be assured of enough routine information from diverse points along the river to fill such a column. Hence the enlargement of river traffic insured that river conditions for more than one place would be available for any given day's edition of the newspaper.

Telegraphic reports added to the assurance of river news after the late 1840s, as indeed telegraphic reports made easier a 'market column'. By 1849 both market and river conditions had their own columns, bringing together similar items from diverse locations, with place being much less relevant than previously. Although the conditions of the river and prices of commodities were still firmly fixed in a location, these columns eliminated the diverse mixture of topics and events in the locations from which they emanated. A major step was taken toward event-orientation and away from place-orientation.

For some time, topical collections of news items from diverse locations remained limited to predictable and routine events: for the most part, to river conditions, river traffic and market prices. Meanwhile geographic bundling persisted, changing with new communication routes only in the origin of the bundle. As new territories in the western United States were settled and as postal and telegraphic connections became established, new gateway cities became the collection points. A *Cincinnati Enquirer* news story in the late 1850s and 1860s might have had a western gateway city dateline, followed by a collection of news from the far-flung hinterland of that city. St Louis, for example, was a major western gateway, as the diverse 1859 column from the overland mail route indicates (Extract 2). Back east, the port cities, especially New York, maintained their collection point status for trans-Atlantic news.

By 1869, geographical bundling had changed in character. Whereas a gateway city had previously acted as a collection point for its hinterland, the cities themselves were now the news locations. A diverse column of news from Chicago, for example, carried no news from places beyond Chicago (Extract 3). As previously, both major and minor events of the city were included with, if anything, the addition of even more minor events - a result of an increasing ability to transmit information from Chicago to Cincinnati. It also seems to be presumed that the Cincinnati reader followed the news in other cities. For instance, the item in the Louisville column about the condition of Charles Young, 'injured boat-builder', appears to imply that Cincinnati readers knew that he had been injured some time ago. The 1869 issues, then, give a variegated image of specific other places; places that the Cincinnati reader is presumed to be interested in for their own sake.

There is relatively little editing in any of these news items. Acquisition of 'special despatches' may be considered the most significant editorial influence. News acquired speedily from other sources, (which at this time largely meant news wire-services' copy), tended to be reprinted directly and in full. As a result, the Cincinnati reader could have gained an impression of life in Louisville or Chicago or any other place that would be similar, if less complete, to the news available to the Louisvillian or Chicagoan in his own city. This similarity lies not in quantity of news, but in the indiscriminate mixture of news with varying degrees of significance outside the local area. To an extent, this lack of discrimination in news events may be taken to represent an interest in these places for their own sakes.

By the 1880s, collection of events by topic was often extended beyond markets and river reports. Events, rather than place, formed the headline and the interest. The 13 February 1889 issue was typical in its bundling together of news on fires in diverse places (Extract 4). Fires, a subject of clear concern in cities of the late nineteenth century, were reported from various locations around the midwest. This arrangement of news stories is strikingly different from a presentation which focused on diverse events in a given place.

For a time both geographical bundling and topical headings coexisted. In the 1899 issue (Extract 5), one page exhibits topical bundling of deaths ('Grim Reaper'). From the same page was to be found topical bundling of steamship movements from New York City, Bremen, Marseilles and Rotterdam (not reprinted here). Many other items stand alone, with the items following 'Grim Reaper' being but two examples. Geographical bundling appears, but in a modified form. Events are grouped by state, but were not originally a part of a true bundle; that is, these items did not arrive at the newspaper (or wire service) office together from a common origin.

By the turn of the century collection of diverse items around a common topic included not only the original market and river reports but also fires, deaths, occasional *ad hoc* collections and, later, sports. Earlier scarcity of news would have precluded these topical collections, but as news quantity increased it became possible to organise news thematically. Items not falling into any common theme stood alone. By 1904, geographic bundling was rare, and no longer was equal emphasis given to both important and less important items from a particular location (Extract 6). Editorial selection and filtering of news items greatly increased at all news-collection points. Only when war and other prolonged calamities focused extended attention on a specific locale did geographic bundling reappear. More abundant news and increasing sophistication of editors led to reduced orientation to place, not through any conscious strategy to obliterate interest in places, but rather as a by-product of eliminating the 'unimportant' news.

Quantitative measures

Counts of news items and news places yield a similar picture: an increasing focus on places as technological capabilities expanded, followed by decreasing emphasis as the less important events were sifted out of the news.

Throughout the nineteenth century the quantity of news contained in the *Cincinnati Enquirer* multiplied in terms of both absolute number of news items and column inches of printed news. The number of items rose substantially between 1869-79, grew moderately thereafter and declined after 1919 . The diversity of places in the news followed a similar trend, rising sharply just before 1879. This high level is maintained for several years, but place diversity dramatically diminished after the 1920s . Relative intensity of place orientation can be indicated by the average number of news items per place. Prior to 1879, this index also rose and continued to rise after the number of places had levelled off, peaking in the early twentieth century.

The period from 1870 to the early 1900s, therefore, was an era of high place-orientation. Earlier, news was not abundant and few places were reported. After the 1920s, news from diverse places was still technologically available, but orientation to place diminished, replaced by an orientation to event. From the 1870s to 1920s we might tentatively identify a transition to a high awareness of elsewhere. By the 1920s, a relatively placeless newspaper had emerged, reflecting little of the diversity of life in other locations.

Communications Systems and Orientation to Place

I have purposely not examined the issue of which places occupied prominence in the sample newspapers for fear of distracting attention from the broader issue of whether places in general took prominence over the nature of the events reported. My argument is that limited means of communication coincided with the importance of place but relatively little news, and that rapid and spatially extensive communications with a potential abundance of news, led to a small selection of news items based on event and not place of occurrence. This evidence supports a broader relationship between the means of communication and orientation to place.

If a society ascribes importance to other places it may be said to have a 'sense of place': a term used to mean a conscious understanding of locations and their present and historical significance (Tuan, 1980). In the newspaper data only that era between the 1870s and 1900 combines an interest in place-based information and the ability to gather it quickly. After the early 1900s the importance of place diminished and a relatively 'placeless' picture results. Before 1870 few places could be reported one at a time, but the detail of news from a given place gave a fuller impression of life in that place.

Time-based society

In Innis's terminology, the era of constrained but place-oriented news-gathering before the late 1800s was relatively 'time-biased'. A time-biased society is characterised by its unity with past and future, combined with powerful ties to a given locale. Innis used time-bias to describe societies whose communications technology emphasised durability and continuity rather than spatial accessibility or portability. Thus writing was more time-biased than the printing press, stylus on clay was more time-biased than ink on papyrus, and oral communications were most time-biased of all. To the degree that transportation and communications were limited in speed of spatial transmission in the pre- and early telegraphic era, the society was relatively time-biased. Extension to the archetype of time-biased society - an oral society - clarifies the relationship between communications systems and orientation to place.

An oral society is characterised by continuity (Havelock, 1963; Ong, 1967). Continuity is achieved by continual re-creation of traditions, stories and practices. Since the past is not separate from the present, there can be no history as such. Indeed, there is little curiosity about a separate past or future, since past and future co-exist with the present. Ruth Finnegan (1973), a scholar of oral poetry, suspects that a minstrel beginning a story with the words "We know from the ancients that ..." is using a distancing device, in order that the intimacy of oral communication does not become overly intense. The introduction does not necessarily imply that the story *is* ancient. The durability of the oral communication comes not so much from verbatim reproduction of ballads and tales, but from continuing re-creation of the experience in the telling.

The minimal portability of oral communication stems from two sources: the lack of more rapid means of transportation and the inherent irreproducibility of an oral communication. The latter stems from the fact that it is the performance rather than the message that is the real event. Audience and speaker, or mutual conversors, are bound together in an intimate experience that will not be the same with a different group of people. Only rarely does the written word share this characteristic. Writing itself is immutable and readers strive, with varying degrees of success, to understand what the author meant at the time of writing. Only rarely, as sometimes happens in poetry or religious works, are we exhorted to let the passages speak to us today, to accept the significance of 'The Word' here and now.

Without explicit knowledge of other places, a time-biased society has no contrast to bring the characteristics of home place into focus. Place is taken for granted. In an oral society, all time is held within this place. Relative time-bias existed in the limited communications technologies of the early 1800s and before, and may continue to exist despite the presence of advanced communication technologies if there is little inclination to use those technologies. Geographers and others have characterised such societies as 'rooted' (Tuan, 1980), or as inhabiting 'magical space' which is controlled by benign and demonic spirits (Cox, 1968, p424), or as occupying 'mythic space', in which personal introspection overshadows any recognition of places, here or elsewhere (Houston, 1978, p233). Individuals exhibiting this taken-for-granted acceptance of place are said to possess 'existential insideness' (Relph, 1976, p55).

The pre- and early telegraphic communications of the newspaper signify a society that was relatively time-biased. Place presentation, as indicated by the definition of what is regarded as 'news', was not confined to the locality of publication. A catastropic flood in Philadelphia, for example, was no less catastrophic to the Cincinnati reader by virtue of being reported days afterwards. A sinking ship was no less newsworthy, even if news took months before being reported in the newspaper. Some news could not be gathered rapidly due to the slow and spatially limited communications technologies, but other news simply was not gathered quickly. The attitude of news-workers was more leisurely than its present-day equivalent. The written history of journalism, typically elite in its view, gives anecdotes of prominent journalists who created greater timeliness or immediacy in news. These leaders are portrayed as going against the trends of the time, whether scooping their competitors by all-night stints of editing (Curl, 1966, p222) or asking permission (and being denied) to ride to a nearby town to get quicker publication of a Presidential address (Mott, 1941, p218). We know less about the attitudes of the ordinary news-worker (see the essay by Catherine and John Silk, this volume, for interesting parallels here).

From the mid-century, however, the lead of prominent journalists could be more easily emulated. Improved and spatially diffusing telegraphy systems, coupled later with the newer telephone, made news-gathering easier. News wire services emerged with a vested interest in selling the idea of rapid news acquisition to editors and publishers and in selling them memberships and services. These forces began to move the newspaper out of a time-biased into a space-biased world.

Space-biased society

The countervailing force to time-bias is space-bias - a tendency to bring places together in space at a single time. Space is unified; time is divided into different dimensions, and the past is irretrievable (Table 3.1). Space-biased society is one of exploration, conquest and colonialism. Western society generally has a history of space-bias, as innovations have provided better means to conquer distance. In an absolute sense, all eras of the newspaper in western culture (and hence all issues of the *Cincinnati Enquirer*) emerge from a space-biased world. Relative terms, however, may be employed to mark the proliferation of more rapid and extensive news-gathering apparatus, to note a more space-biased presentation of news towards the end of the study period. To date, the electronic era provides the model of space-biased society, having produced technologies capable of near-instantaneous global communication and attitudes which have made yesterday and its newspaper obsolete.

The emergence of this space-biased society is closely related to the emergence of a 'placeless' society, since all locations approach identical information and tend toward homogeneity. A truly placeless society is associated with alienation. Houston typified it as the post-nuclear desert, 'devastated space' (Houston, 1978); to Cox (1968, p424), placeless 'secularist space' was 'monochrome and lack-lustre'; and individuals who belong nowhere experience 'existential outsideness' (Relph, 1976). Place itself is obliterated, leaving undifferentiated space. It would be difficult to argue that absolute placelessness exists, but modern society has trivialised many of the remaining differentiations in space and has made place effectively 'commonplace' (Jakle, 1982). It is not so much that the news of the twentieth century is placeless, but rather that place has become simply irrelevant. In the *Cincinnati Enquirer* the place of occurrence of fires became incidental to the inherent newsworthiness of the event. Today's news stories cover predictable themes, with place of occurrence a 'fill-in-the blank exercise'.

Table 6.1: Communications - Time and Space

	Time-biased Society	Balanced time and space-bias	Space-biased society
Space	Only here	Aware sense of place	Unified and uniform
Time	Unified and uniform	Aware sense of history	Only now
Model	Oral, sedentary society		Electronic mass society

It is difficult to speak of placelessness (or even 'commonplaceness') without emotion ranging from outrage to resigned resentment. Yet a bias toward space is not any more negative than is a bias toward time. Attachment to place can fetter as well as unite (Porteous, 1978; Tuan, 1980). Space unified can imply freedom, equality and opportunity. Innis saw tension between the two biases with the oscillating dominance of first one, then the other. Often, in Innis's views, swings of dominance were accomplished by an underclass gaining access to a new means of communication. From the perspective of a space-biased culture, it is not difficult to see why space-bias gains the upper hand. Many time-biased societies have had little choice in becoming more space-biased after their conquest by space-biased societies. Examples of such conquests abound in eighteenth and nineteenth century colonialism, while twentieth-century conquests make explicit the hegemony of space-bias over time-bias, from infiltration of Third World cultures by First World television, to destruction of an urban village to build a new expressway. Perhaps the proliferation of individual instead of mass communications will presage an alternative swing (Gumpert, 1970; Abler, 1973), but this remains merely a conjecture.

The loss of place importance is clear in the *Cincinnati Enquirer*. The number of both news items and news places diminishes after the turn of the century. News presentation by the end of the 1800s emphasised event, not place. The abundant means of communication reduced the self-promotion about a newspaper's ability to get news from exotic as well as familiar places. The news reported was better organised, yet the emerging professional norms of journalism lumped the 'where' in the 'who, what, when, where, how and why', as an incidental descriptor. Events took prominence, either standing on their own or being grouped together with similar events. The emerging professional attitudes towards news were clearly space-biased.

Sense of place

The transition from relative time-bias to clear space-bias which occurred between the 1870s and the 1920s represents a period qualitatively different from what came before or after. In this era high place diversity and plentiful news balance time and space-bias. The term 'sense of place' may best apply to this transition era (Table 3.1). An aware and informed appreciation of place and the historical accumulation of a place's significance is a great deal to expect from an individual, let alone an entire society. Yet the interest in other places evident in the late-nineteenth-century newspaper is a mundane example of a fleeting balance between time and space-bias. The advantages of new, rapid communications were exploited, while the less praiseworthy trait of commonplaceness had yet to erode curiosity about elsewhere.

Innis pleaded for a balance between space and time-bias. This period of transition fills the prescription, but was merely a passing stage. It falls short of ideals set forth by Cox, Houston and Relph. Cox imagined a 'humanized space', free from the domination of place, yet enjoying the variety of place (Cox, 1968, p424). Houston's 'lived space' was 'desacralized but not desecrated' (Houston, 1978, p233). Relph's equivalent described an individual's deliberate perception of the symbols and significance of place (Relph, 1976, p54). In the news transition era, openness to place information from elsewhere was not so much deliberate as incidental to the newness of innovations in communications technologies.

It is difficult to predict whether this transition period is a singular phenomenon, or whether, as in Innis's predictions, we are likely to experience yet another swing of the pendulum, perhaps with a similar transition period. The pathetic state of 'geographical literacy' has been given recent lip-service in the USA yet remedying this illiteracy seems an enormous if not impossible task. In journalism, laments are interspersed with documentation of the relatively few places from which Americans get their news (Dominick, 1977; Gerbner and Marvanyi, 1977; Lent, 1977; Hester, 1978; Kaplan, 1979; Larson, 1979). While the distribution or quantity of news remaining in the typical newspaper remains unchanged, the emergence of 'precision news' may report events in greater depth, and hence somewhat greater place orientation (McCombs *et al*, 1981). If the litany of woes gives rise to greater understanding of other places, then at least we may hope for a temporary, transitional 'sense of place', including other places; at best, a permanent, intentional balance of time and space-bias.

Nonetheless, the current provincialism of the American press is unmistakable. This provincialism may stem less from the arrogant belief that other places are unimportant and more from the notion that they are simply similar to our own locale. One critic summarised this attitude among news-workers as 'that cosmopolitanism that treats every event in the modern world as if it were happening three blocks from the White House' (Karp, 1982). The lack of information about places in the post-1920s newspaper, in the most practical analysis, resulted from elimination of 'unimportant' news. Yet those unimportant details of routine life often differentiate places one from another. When only those events which some national or international consensus deems important are newsworthy, there is homogenisation of the type of information which becomes news. As a consequence, place differences are discounted and space becomes unified in perception - in the news - if not in fact.

APPENDIX

Extract 1: *Cincinnati Enquirer* 1839

8 February 1839

INCIDENTS OF THE STORM

The papers from the interior come to us teeming with accounts of the devastations of the storm, so as to render it impossible to make anything like a record of the rain caused by the winds and floods of Saturday last. We subjoin, however, notices of several striking incidents ...

The Norristown Register has the following:

The Lock House on the Schuykill Canal ... occupied by a widow and three children ...

A dwelling on French Creek, together with the family, was carried away by the freshet, and in passing down the Schuykill, near Lamberville, struck a tree and broke a hole in the roof, through which the man (we have not learned his name) escaped upon the tree, but only to perish ...

The Reading Democrat says:

Owing to the goodness of Providence, no lives were lost in the vicinity, although some persons were rescued from imminent peril ...

THE STORM

The Germantown Telegraph, in speaking of the late destructive storm, says:

The quantity of rain fallen, as indicated by an established gauge in this place, was three and a half inches.

According to the diary of Mr Jonathan Roberson, the Schuykill was four feet higher than in 1822 ...

Letters from Easton and Bethlehem give detailed accounts of the damage sustained on the Lehigh company's works ...

12 February 1839

FOREIGN

Further extracts from European news, per Packet ship Philadelphia. London dates to the 24th Dec.

ENGLAND

The steamship Liverpool performed her voyage in fourteen days ...

Considerable uneasiness prevails with respect to Belgium ...

Dispatches from India had been received in London to the 21st, declaring the intention of the Governor-General to assemble a British force for service across the Indus ...

The supply of grain in the London market is short ...

FROM THE N.O. COURIER, 28 JANUARY: LATEST FROM MEXICO

To the politeness of one of the passengers in the schooner Eliza Ann, which vessel left Metamoras on the 18th inst. we are indebted for the following information from Mexico ...

Extract 2: *Cincinnati Enquirer* 1859

8 February 1859

ADDITIONAL BY THE OVERLAND MAIL

St Louis, Monday 7 February

Major Dodge, who has just returned from Pyramid Lake, reports the weather intensely cold, and great suffering among the Indians for want of food and clothing.

Fifteen Indians who had stolen some horses, were killed by a party of whites in Eden Valley on the 26th of December ...

That portion of the President's message treating of Kansas was not favourably received in Oregon ..

The Legislature of Washington Territory had passed resolutions instructing the Delegate in Congress to urge the necessity of establishing a line of military posts from Walla Walla, via the South Pass, to the Missouri River.

Passengers report that the Gila Mines were almost entirely deserted.

The Mexican Boundary Commissioners were at Fort Fillmore ...

The Indians had again obstructed the road with rocks at Devils Canyon ...

By the Tehuantepec Route

SIX DAYS LATER FROM CALIFORNIA

New Orleans, 6 February

The steamship Quaker City with Dates from San Francisco to the 20th ult., has arrived here ...

The steamer Sonora takes over $1,500,000 in specie and one hundred and ten passengers via Panama: $1,296,839 of the treasure goes to New York.

The whaling brig Emma was wrecked near Honolulu on the 10th of December. The crew were saved.

Richmond Flour was dull ...

The weather for mining purposes was favourable.

The French had taken possession of Clipperton, a guano island.

The Quaker City brings dates from the city of Mexico to the 28 ult. ...

ONE WEEK LATER FROM EUROPE: ARRIVAL OF THE ASIA

Continent Affairs Gloomy - Reported Death of the King of Naples - New Austrian Loan

New York, Monday 7 February

The royal mail steamship Asia ... arrived at this port this evening ...

There was less confidence felt in the state of affairs on the continent ...

The death of the King of Naples was reported, but the report was discredited ...

It is reported that Parliament ...

Accounts from Lombardy ...

The latest Continental correspondence says ...

FRANCE ...
ITALY ...
AUSTRIA ...
SWITZERLAND ...
INDIA ...
CHINA ...

RIVER NEWS

St Louis, Monday 7 February

River falling at the rate of half an inch an hour, and considerable heavy ice running. Nothing new from the upper streams. Weather clear and moderating.

Pittsburg, Monday 7 February

River six feet three inches by the pier-mark and falling. Weather clear and cool. Arrived - Commerice and General Pike. No departures.

Pittsburg, Monday 7 February

River six feet two inches by the pier-mark and falling. Weather moderating. Departed - Glenwood, for Nashville.

Louisville, Monday 7 February

River falling, with eight feet water in the canal, six feet on the Pass, and five feet two inches over the rocks.

Weather clear. Mercury 28.

Extract 3: *Cincinnati Enquirer* 1869

4 February 1869

CHICAGO

Special Dispatch to the Enquirer:

Chicago, 3 February 1869

CHICAGO AND NORTH-WESTERN RAILROAD

The earnings of the Chicago and Northwestern Railroad for January were $871,218, an increase of $158,272 over the same month of last year.

FIRE

A fire tonight at No 447 Randolph Street ...

SUIT AGAINST MAX STRAKOSCH ...

THE NEWBERRY ESTATE ...

PARK PROJECTS ...

DIDN'T 'COME ON TIME'

Enssey failed to appear tonight to put up a deposit in his pugilistic match with Donovan ...

ELOPEMENT AND DESERTION

10 February 1869

ST LOUIS

Special Dispatch to the Enquirer:

St Louis, 9 February 1869

FROM CHICAGO TO NEW ORLEANS

A rumour is current here that the Illinois Central Railroad has purchased or leased the Mobile and Ohio Railroad, and the line will be operated as one continuous whole from Chicago to New Orleans.

THE MURDER OF GENERAL M'CONNEL

General Murray McConnell, known as an author and distinguished as an Illinois Legislator, was assassinated at his residence at Jacksonville, Illinois, at nine o'clock this morning ...

LIBEL SUIT

School Director Miller has sued architect Manrice for $10,000 damages for libel ...

RADICAL STEALING ...
CATTLE MARKET ...

To the Associated Press

OUR LEVEE

St Louis, 9 February - At a meeting of the Board of Trade this evening, resolutions were offered providing for a Committee to inquire into the feasibility, practicability and cost of changing the present levee from an inclined plane to a level quay or mole ...

SUICIDE OF A DISCHARGED SOLDIER ...
ANOTHER STAGE LINE ON THE PLAINS ...

To the Associated Press

ARRIVAL - CREW WOUNDED

New York, 9 February - The steamship Queen from London arrived. Eight of her crew were badly wounded on the passage by a heavy sea.

INDIAN PEACE POLICY ...
EXPECTED RESIGNATION ...
INVESTMENT IN AMERICAN BONDS ...
SPECIE TAKES OUT ...
DEATH OF JAMES T. BRADY ...
HEAVY FAILURE IN ENGLAND ...
THE ERIE LITIGATIONS ...

INDIANAPOLIS

Special Dispatch to the Enquirer

Indianapolis, 9 February 1869

INDICTMENTS ...
INFANTICIDE ...
THE SECOND TRIAL OF MRS CLEM ...

MEMPHIS

DROWNED ...
MURDER TRIAL ...
PEDDLER MURDERED BY A BOY ...
THE SLEEPY DETECTIVE ...

6 February 1889

LOUISVILLE

SPECIALLY REPORTED FOR THE ENQUIRER

The United States Grand Jury will be impaneled at ten o'clock this morning.
Addrian S. Kendall was yesterday sworn as an attorney to practice in the Chancery Court.
There are now hopes that Charles Young, the injured boat-builder, who has been lying at the Hospital in a precarious position for some time, may recover.
It is said that the special Committee appointed to examine the eligibility of L.B. Kean to his seat as Councilman from the Eighth Ward, contested by W.R. Harrig, will report in Kean's favour ...

Extract 4: *Cincinnati Enquirer* 1889

13 February 1889

FIRES

Special Dispatches to the Enquirer:

LUMBER BURNS

Chicago, 12 February - Fire this morning destroyed about [$] worth of hardware, and the dry kiln of A.H. Andrews and Co., manufacturers of furniture in the south-western portion of the city.

AT DEFIANCE

Defiance, 12 February - L.E. Beardsley's photograph gallery was destroyed by fire this morning ...

ELEVATOR BADLY WRECKED

Indianapolis, Ind., 12 February - Elevator 'It' owned by Matchner, Higgins, and Co., was badly wrecked by fire tonight ...

BLAZE AMONG WALNUT LUMBER

Logan, Ohio, 12 February - One of the dry houses filled with fine black walnut lumber belonging to the Logan Manufacturing Company, burned this evening. The building is a total loss, but a proportion of the lumber was saved ...

Extract 5: *Cincinnati Enquirer* 1899

3 February 1899

GRIM REAPER

Buchanan's Housekeeper

Lancaster, Penn., 2 February - Miss Hester Parker, who was housekeeper for President Buchanan here and at Washington during his Administration, died this morning from old age. She was in her ninety-fourth year.

Major W.G. Beatty

Special Dispatch to the Enquirer:

Columbus, Ohio, 2 February - General John Beatty, of this city, received word today that his brother, Major W.G. Beatty, died this morning at Cripple Creek, Colo., where he was superintending the development of valuable mining property he owned. Major Beatty was well known in this state as a politician.

COST HIM A THOUSAND

Special Dispatch to the Enquirer

Toledo, Ohio, 2 February - The only person in Toledo who appears to mourn the departure of Marie Cicotte Wilson and her mother is Louis Hirschey, who went on Marie's bail bond for $1,000 in order to secure her release. The bond has been declared forfeited, on account of the Cicotte woman's refusal to appear in court for a hearing on the charge of perjury, and now Mr Hirschey is out a cold $1,000 on account of his sympathy for the adventuress.

PRISONER RETURNED TO JAIL

Special Dispatch to the Enquirer

Cynthiana, Ky., 2 February - George Lanan, who murdered 'Doc' Caldwell last August, and who escaped from jail a few days ago, returned this morning and was almost frozen to death. All the prisoners were captured.

DROPS

From an Ocean of News

Clear, Sparkling and Refreshing to Those Who Partake

Ohio Valley Items, Boiled, Filtered and Free from Even a Germ of Verbiage

OHIO

Toledo, 2 February - Karg and Andrews Bros., contractors of Fostoria, were awarded the contract yesterday for the new Good Shepherd Church ...

Lima, 2 February - After a long fight in the Council in which serious charges were talked of, the Columbia Construction Company of Rochester, N.Y., was given the contract of paving West North Street with asphalt ...

Chillicothe, 2 February - Mr and Mrs W. W. Woodward and two children had a narrow escape from death last night from ptomaine poisoning ..

McArthur, 2 February - Three men who burglarized the store of Wilkers and Dye at Hamden Tuesday night were arrested ...

Lorain, 2 February -

Bellefontaine, 2 February -

Extract 6: *Cincinnati Enquirer* 1904

4 February 1904

PLUCKY WIDOW

Awarded Judgment for $24,000 Against Kentuckians

Special Dispatch to the Enquirer
New York, 3 February - There was awarded by a Queens County Jury today a verdict of $24,690.15 to Mrs Rose Hermann, widow of the late Henry Hermann who for many years was the head of the Hermann Furniture Company doing business in this city. The defendants in the action were Floyd Day and James Swan, lumbermen in Kentucky.

Mrs Hermann sued Day and Swan to recover $26,000 which she claimed to be due to her on the sale to the defendants of 23,000 poplar trees in Kentucky.

It was developed that Mrs Hermann went personally to the Kentucky mountains and traveled horseback through the roughest country to summon mountaineer witnesses to her relief. Even while the trial was in progress, covering a period of 10 days, Mrs Hermann assumed charge of the welfare of the husky backwoodsmen who responded to her call.

BRIDE DEFIED

Truant Officer After She Was Married to the Boy Bridegroom

Special Dispatch to the Enquirer

Toledo, Ohio, 3 February - Just as Mr Jennings of the City Mission was commencing the ceremony which made George Williams and Miss Florence Edwards man and wife, Truant Officer Wonifert appeared at the mission. The bride turned to the Truant Officer with an air of commingled pride and defiance and remarked:

"There, now, Mr Wonifert, you can't chase me to school any more."

Both of the contracting parties were under age, but the parents were present to give their consent.

BABE LEFT

But the Mother and Father Are Both in the Great Beyond

Philadelphia, 3 February - Williams Anderson, a young married man of this city committed suicide today under pathetic circumstances. He was informed by a physician that his wife who had given birth to a daughter was dying. He immediately picked up a revolver and saying, "If she goes I'm going too ", shot himself through the head. His wife died a few minutes after the shooting and he passed away late tonight. Besides the baby they have a four year old daughter.

LYNCHERS

Searching for the Colored Slayer of a Mississippi Planter

Doddsville, Miss., 3 February - John Eastland, a wealthy plantation owner, and Albert Carr, a negro tenant, were killed by Luther Holbert, a negro, in a shooting scrape which grew out of a difficulty between Eastland and Holbert.

Holbert escaped, and possees from Greenville, Indianapolis, Cleveland, and other points are searching for him and two other negroes, who, it is charged, were implicated with him in the killing of Eastland. The negroes will probably be lynched if captured.

BARRED

From Naval Libraries

Is the Book Written and Lately Published by Former Secretary Long

Special Dispatch to the Enquirer

New York, 3 February - A Washington dispatch to the Herald is as follows: John D. Long's latest book, 'The New American Navy', which he wrote after having served five years as Secretary of the Navy, and which attracted attention through certain references to President Roosevelt, will not find a place in the libraries of American warships.

MOTHER

Says That She Killed the Devil When She Choked to Death Her Own Daughter

Special Dispatch to the Enquirer

Columbia, S.C., 3 February - Mrs Patsy Eiyan, living on a plantation near Walterboro, went to the bedroom of her seventeen-year-old daughter Anita at 4 o'clock yesterday morning and without apparent cause choked her to death. The other daughters of the woman were in the room at the time of the tragedy, but say they knew little of its details except that they assisted in removing the body to an adjoining room at their mother's command.

CHAPTER 4: NATURAL HAZARDS IN NOVELS AND FILMS: IMPLICATIONS FOR HAZARD PERCEPTION AND BEHAVIOUR

Diana M. Liverman and Douglas J. Sherman

The natural environment poses many hazards to life and property through events such as earthquakes and hurricanes. The threat can often be reduced by understanding and controlling the causes of disaster, predicting their timing and location, and ensuring a fast and appropriate response to them. With their subject bridging the physical and social sciences, geographers have made many contributions to the study of natural hazards, led by the work of Gilbert White and his colleagues (e.g. White, 1974; Burton *et al*, 1978). Although physical geographers have made important contributions to understanding, predicting, and controlling floods, severe storms and earth movements, the predominant approach of natural hazards research in geography has been the behavioural model elaborated by Kates (1971) and White (1974). According to this perspective, hazards occur where society occupies locations subject to extreme natural events. The severity of the hazard depends on the magnitude and frequency of the natural event and on the vulnerability of the human population. Although it is seldom possible to eliminate risks completely, society adjusts and adapts to a hazardous environment by altering the natural events, for example, through flood control or by reducing the social consequences through evacuation, insurance and land-use planning.

One assumption of the behavioural approach is that the response to natural hazards depends on an individual's knowledge and experience of the event. This assumption has been tested in a large number of surveys, (see, for example, those reported in White, 1974 and Quarantelli, 1978), which have shown that the perception of a hazard correlates with education, income and previous hazard experience, and that these perceptions correspond with behaviour in disasters. A link has therefore been established between knowledge of a hazard and the response to the threat. Hazard awareness also enhances support for hazard prevention and emergency planning programmes. Hence, several attempts have been made to increase hazard awareness through public information programmes funded by local, state, and national governments. In Texas, efforts to improve hurricane awareness include the distribution of maps and brochures, and information broadcasts on radio and television (Ruch, 1980). Many local authorities in North America and Britain provide citizens with flood maps and information leaflets. However, people also gain hazard information from many non-official sources, including personal experiences, friends, school and the mass media. Most people have some image of natural disasters although very few people have actually experienced a severe earthquake or tornado. Therefore many people must obtain images of natural hazards from sources other than personal experience, and some of these sources may be less accurate than government publications. Inaccurate information may result in misperception of risk, poor responses and greater losses from diasters.

Researchers have attempted to evaluate the importance and credibility of different information sources. Ruch (1980) found that exposure to information brochures improved hazard awareness more than exposure to television or radio bulletins. The National Academy of Sciences (1980) and Scanlon (1978) have discussed the credibility and accuracy of disaster reporting in newspapers and in the broadcasting media. Yet within the category of the mass media we should include not only television, radio, and newspapers, but also novels and films. Whereas the first three sources tend to report actual events, the latter two provide us with fictional accounts of disaster. All of these information sources can improve hazard awareness, although there is little evidence, one way or another, that this information then leads to more appropriate behaviour and a reduction in disaster damages.

Nevertheless, we can draw upon the wider literature about the influence of the mass media on popular culture and social activity when discussing the relationship between the mass media, hazard awareness and behavioural response. Among others, Klapper (1960) suggests that the mass media can create and convert opinion. He reports on studies that link television portrayal of crime and violence to delinquency, that examine the reinforcement of anti-social behavioural tendencies, and that consider the impact of escapist and erotic television material, concluding that there is not enough evidence to correlate escapism with immaturity, addiction and apathy, nor eroticism with sexual assault. Although discussions of disasters and the mass media exist, they do not link the content of disaster films and books to the question of hazard awareness and response. Until recently, only Quarantelli (1980) had raised some preliminary questions about the impact of disaster movies on the public. However, a recent US television drama *The Day After*, dealing with the immediate impacts of a nuclear attack, stimulated a debate concerning possible changes to viewers' attitudes on the nuclear arms debate, the psychological stress which might result from seeing the programme, and the need to provide information about the appropriate responses to a nuclear attack. Both pro- and anti-nuclear groups hoped that the information in the movie would rally support for their causes (*New York Times*, 20 Nov. 1983, p2:1). In certain cases newspapers sought to add to or contradict the movie. For example, some articles claimed that the environmental effects of nuclear war as shown in the film were mild compared to the major fires, weather disturbances, and climate change that would actually occur (*US News and World Report*, 28 Nov. 1983, p85; *Chicago Tribune*, 21 Nov. 1983, p11). The Federal Emergency Management Administration hired extra staff to deal with the telephone calls they anticipated with questions about the film's content (*Newsweek*, 5 Dec. 1983, p62). However, early opinion polls indicated little change in attitudes as a result of viewing the film (*Newsweek*, 5 Dec. 1983, p62) and suggested that *The Day After* inspired fear and apathy rather than any constructive education or response (*Washington Post*, 22 Nov. 1983, p7). This television disaster movie strongly demonstrated the power of the mass media to attract attention to an issue, even if no attitudes were demonstrably changed.

Fictional disaster is big business in the mass media. The last ten years have seen a plethora of films and books with disaster themes. Novels about ice ages, meteors, floods, and epidemics have appeared with increasing frequency and apparent commercial success. Films like *Earthquake* and *The Poseidon Adventure* have ranked among the film industry's major financial triumphs. The financial success of disaster movies is an important measure of their popularity. *The Poseidon Adventure* was the world's most profitable film in 1973 (Quarantelli, 1980) and the magazine *Variety* reports a gross income of 13.2 and 17.9 million dollars for *Earthquake* and *The Towering Inferno* in the first three months of 1975. More than 100 million people watched *The Day After* (*Washington Post*, 22 Nov. 1983, p1).[1] The novels are less popular than the films, and data on readership is difficult to obtain. A preliminary survey provided only a few sets of sales figures, partly because publishers are reluctant to give information which might be of use to their competitors. *Condominium* (hurricanes) sold 800,000 copies, *Twister* (tornadoes) 104,000, and *Heat* (climate change) 176,000. *The Fog*, *Earthquake*, and *Earthsound* respectively sold 262,000, 372,000 and 296,000 copies. The enormous number of novels with geophysical themes 2 itself suggests that publishers must find disaster novels commercially successful. In some cases the novel is popular because it parallels a popular film, in others the theme or title appeals to the wide audience for science fiction.

What are the reasons behind the extraordinary popularity of disaster films and books? Conrad (1978) sees the fascination with disaster as a safety valve for our hostility towards technology and nature. It may also reflect our alienation from each other and from the natural environment, and represents a feeling of powerlessness over our future and our lives (*Village Voice*, 1974). Lasch associates disaster in the media with a general unease: 'Storm warnings, portents, hints of catastrophe haunt our times ... impending disaster has become an everyday concern' (*Time*, 1975). 'Disastermania' has also been linked to the end of the millennium, fear of science, the atom bomb, and economic depression (*Time*, 1975). More practically, Gans (1973) and Kaplan (1975) see the genre following a traditionally escapist theme, with simple thrills and good special effects providing a relief from boredom to a wide audience. The films and books also appeal because they conform to traditional values. There are heroes, the bad guys get killed or repent, and good leadership saves the day. Finally there is the interest in the vicarious experience of disaster. In watching or reading about the unfortunate victims from a safe seat we can ponder at leisure how we would react and what we could do to save ourselves and others.

Gans (1975), Kaplan (1975), Shatzkin (1975), Conrad (1978) and Andrews (1980) review and discuss disaster novels and films as a particular category of popular culture. There is certainly a case for identifying a disaster genre, since the appropriate novels and films share many characteristics. They have short titles dramatising the hazard (*Earthquake, Hurricane*); employ many special effects or detailed descriptions of destruction; contain stereotyped plots and characters; and feature unusual narrative techniques, such as the use of weather bulletins to document the onset of disaster and to permit rapid switches of geographical location. Perhaps the most common element is a standard relationships between the progress of events and developments in the lives of the main characters. The romantic and sexual encounters are interspersed with warnings and descriptions of the hazard onset. Social and sexual tensions reach a peak at the same time as physical events reach a climax. The hurricane reaches land just as illicit affairs are consummated, corruption revealed, and loved ones found to be missing (*Condominium, Hurricane*). A hero must choose between saving his wife or his mistress (*Earthquake, Condominium, The Flood*). The emphasis is usually on the pre-disaster period and the actual event rather than on rescue and recovery. However *Lucifer's Hammer* (meteor) and *Earth Abides* (epidemic) do focus on the attempts to recover from disaster.

Within the genre there is variation by scale and type of disaster. For example, some are local dramas involving floods and landslides, others have regional or national disasters such as hurricanes and earthquakes, and yet others are global in scale, particularly those dealing with climatic change or epidemics. The films tend to incorporate short duration, sudden onset disasters like earthquakes, avalanches, tidal waves and meteors. There are a considerable number of biological disaster films such as *The Swarm* (bees), *The Andromeda Strain* (disease), and *Jaws* (sharks). The books focus on meteorological hazards including drought, major climatic change and weather modification. Other natural hazards in the novels include volcanoes, tornadoes, fire, disease epidemics and animal infestations. Thus, the mass media cover the full range of natural hazards and their impact on society, presenting the public with a vast array of images and information about the physical nature of disasters, possible individual and institutional responses, hazard causes and prevention measures.

Geographers concerned with natural hazards or with the influence of popular culture could profitably pursue a number of questions about disaster. In the remainder of this essay we undertake a preliminary assessment of natural hazards in films and novels. Although there is little evidence, as yet, that the films and books are altering attitudes and behaviour towards natural hazards, it is interesting to evaluate the nature and accuracy of the information that they provide. For if the information in these widely-viewed films and popular books is not accurate, then exposure to this type of media may lead to increased risk to life, and greater damage to property.

Images of Scientists and Officials

The way in which scientists and other officials are depicted in the films and novels might be of direct concern to emergency planners and natural hazards researchers. Many novels and films portray senior scientists as corrupt, ineffectual, selfish and cynical. In *Earthquake, Twister* and *Blizzard*, the senior scientists ignore warnings of disaster and try to undermine the credibility of younger colleagues who wish to make predictions. In *Jaws* and *Condominium* local officials are hesitant to provide warnings or require evacuations because of likely loss of tourist revenue and the possibility of panic. In *The Weathermakers, Weatherwar* and *White August* scientists and government officials are actually causing the disasters through weather modification. There is a contrast, however, between George Stewart's novels from the 1940s and more recent books. In *Storm* and *Fire* scientists and officials are objective and unselfishly dedicated, but in *Hurricane* (1977) a scientist who uses computer models for forecasting argues constantly with another who trusts instinct and qualitative indicators of hurricane approach. They contradict each other's forecasts and compete for the attention of the same female companion. The negative images of scientists and emergency officials perhaps indicate a reduction in the public's trust of authority and belief in scientific predictions.

Images of the Physical Event

Disaster novels often convey a sense of scientific accuracy. The prefaces to the books frequently contain acknowledgements to well-known scientists or government agencies who provided information and advice to the author. For example, in the preface to *Twister*, a novel about tornadoes, the author acknowledges Dr Fujita, the tornado expert, and the National Severe Storms Forecast Center. Moreover, some books are written by well-known scientists, such as *The Sixth Winter* by science writer John Gribbin, an expert on climatic change. This tends to lend an air of authenticity and credibility to the fictional accounts that follow, and may help to explain the accuracy of some of the descriptions and scientific commentary in the novels. In some cases references to scientific work are also found in the text. In *Icequake*, the characters refer to the works of glaciologists Hollin and Wilson on icesheet dynamics. An aura of authenticity is also added to the novels by the use of acronyms, some associated with genuine institutions. In *Heat*, there are references to ARPA, WMO, CRISES, NCAR, DPR, and NADWARN.

The disasters are usually shown to have natural causes. The approach of meteors and tornadoes and the onset of ice ages are Acts of God in *Meteor, Twister,* and *The Sixth Winter*.However, the books *Weatherwar, The Weathermakers, White August* and *Blizzard* have disasters caused by attempts to control weather. The earthquakes in *Goodbye California* and *The California Factor* are induced by terrorists. In other cases the impact of physical events is magnified by human action or inaction. In *Hurricane* and *Condominium*, poor land use planning, lax building codes and human greed increase the death toll. *The Wave, Goodbye Piccadilly* and *Dark Water* combine natural factors (heavy rain and landslides) with human corruption (poor dam construction, deliberate sabotage) to increase the force and magnitude of floods. Such an emphasis on the social factor in triggering disasters and increasing their impacts is realistic, and certainly natural hazards researchers have shown that socioeconomic and political mechanisms can increase the risk from natural events (Hewitt, 1983).

Most of the novels and films are reasonably accurate in their portrayal of specific physical events. The probabilities and magnitudes of events may be stretched, but the bounds of possibility are rarely exceeded. Meteors are unlikely to hit large urban centres like New York (the film *Meteor*) or Phoenix (*Fire in the Sky*). The storm surge in the film *Condominium* looks more like a tidal wave than a hurricane event, and the towering, breaking tidal wave in *The Poseidon Adventure* is very different from the long swell which characterises tsunamis in the deep ocean. The earthquake in *Superman* supports the myth that the ground opens with gaping holes to the planet's interior. Unbelievably short time scales are frequently given to events like climate change. In *Ice* the glaciers reach New York City in a matter of months following a series of intense snowstorms. In *Heat*, carbon dioxide feedbacks and associated climate changes bring drought, desertification, mass starvation and temperatures of 180 degrees Fahrenheit within a year.

Images of Human Response

The majority of the inaccuracies in both books and films arise from the description of human responses to disaster. In a 1972 article, Quarantelli and Dynes debunk a number of myths about disaster behaviour; myths which are perpetuated by the media's fictional versions of disaster. First, mass panic is suggested as a common response to flood in the book *Deluge*, to hurricanes in *Hurricane*, and to drought in *Heat*. In fact, as Quarantelli and Dynes report, mass panic is rarely observed or recorded in natural disasters. Secondly, there is the myth that victims of disaster are shocked, introverted and incapable. The characters described as 'rigid with fear' in *Flood* or *Deluge* might in reality have adrenalin pouring through their veins and would be showing great concern for helping others. Shock has been shown to be a delayed rather than an immediate response to disaster. Thirdly, Quarantelli and Dynes indicate that crime is less of a problem than commonly believed. In the novels *Ice* and *Felicia* looting is widespread. In *Dark Water* and *Goodbye Piccadilly* rapes and robberies occur. In fact, the predominant social behaviour during and after natural disaster has been observed as mutual aid and assistance. Crime is usually controlled by the police. Finally, Quarantelli and Dynes suggest that there is a tendency to exaggerate the numbers of dead and injured. In most cases actually disaster impacts are less than reported. In the book *Hurricane* 11,340 people are killed and 23,000 injured and in *The Wave* a flood contaminated with nuclear waste takes the lives of 185,000 people. In the climatic change novels, untold millions die or disappear. Some films show death resulting not from the actual physical event such as drowning or smoke asphyxiation, but from crime or the collapse of buildings. In real fires the majority of deaths are from suffocation, whereas in *The Towering Inferno* fatalities are from other causes. The films usually fail to portray the true nature or extent of injuries. People either die or suffer only minor injuries.

Other problems with the media's presentation of hazard responses include unrealistic assessments of vulnerable populations and official behaviour, and a failure to portray warning systems, rescue activity and recovery after the disaster. *Earthquake* occurs in Los Angeles, where we see no Hispanic characters in a city with a very large Hispanic population. Natural hazards research has also shown many times that it is the poor that suffer the greatest damages from disaster. In both books and films key characters tend to be white and middle class. The locations are predominantly in the Western world, whereas some of the most damaging disasters occur in developing countries. Officials are shown as unreliable. Scientists and officials in the novels put self before community, family before responsibility and sex before public duty. Yet studies of the behaviour of public officials during disasters generally show that they stay calm, remain at their posts, and even risk their lives, as in the case of the USGS geologist killed by the Mount St Helens volcanic eruption. The films and books rarely show official warning systems and do not indicate the role of rescue organisations like the Red Cross. Only the film *Avalanche* shows a well-organised search and rescue mission. In reality, warning and rescue are key components of natural hazard planning and response.

Conclusion

It is clear that disaster films and novels provide considerable information about natural hazards but that the information varies in accuracy. It may well be that authors and directors care less about the accuracy of their descriptions than to produce spectacle or excite the reader, although the acknowledgement of scientific advice in books suggest some concern for accuracy in describing physical events. Perhaps the authors and scriptwriters do not have easy access to research findings on the social response to natural hazards. Perhaps too the complexity of natural events and social responses to them is not readily adaptable to the media and the wide audience. At the same time, it is also apparent that the deficiencies in research linking hazard information to hazard response are such that it is difficult to prove that inaccurate information in films and books poses problems for emergency management. Nevertheless, these media do command attention. Geographers and others concerned with perception and response to natural hazards, should seriously consider popular culture, as expressed in novels and movies, as a potentially significant source of information about disaster.

Notes

[1]. Among those films that have reached mass audience would be included: *The Andromeda Strain* (epidemic), *Avalanche, Cassandra Crossing* (epidemic), *China*

Syndrome (nuclear meltdown), *Condominium* (hurricane), *The Day After* (nuclear war), *Earthquake, Fire in the Sky* (meteor), *Hurricane, Jaws* (sharks), *Krakatoa - East of Java* (volcano), *Meteor, The Poseidon Adventure* (tidal wave), *Superman* (earthquake), *The Swarm* (bees), *Testament* (nuclear war) and *Towering Inferno* (fire).

2. A sample of such novels would include (in alphabetical order of title): Hoyle (1957) *The Black Cloud* (climate change), Verner (1980) *The California Factor* (earthquake), MacDonald (1977) *Condominium* (hurricane), Updike (1978) *The Coup* (drought), Komatsu (1976) *Death of the Dragon* (earthquake), Doyle (1978) *Deluge* (flood), Ballard (1968) *The Drought*, Ballard (1962) *The Drowned World* (climate change), Stewart (1978) *Earth Abides* (epidemic), Fox (1976) *Earthquake*, Herzog (1975) *Earthsound* (earthquake), Jackson (1971) *Epicentre* (earthquake), Effinger (1976) *Felicia* (tornado), Stewart (1948) *Fire*, Cullen-Tanake (1980) *Fire Mountain* (volcano), Stern (1981) *Flood*, Young (1956) *The Flood*, Herbert (1979) *The Fog*, Maclean (1979) *Goodbye California* (earthquake), Barling (1981) *Goodbye Piccadilly* (flood), Herzog (1977) *Heat* (climate change), Davis (1977) *Hurricane*, Perry (1976) *Hurricane of Ice* (blizzard), Federbrush (1978) *Ice* (climate change), Killian (1974) *Icequake* (climate change/volcano), Niven and Pounelle (1977) *Lucifer's Hammer* (meteor), North and Coen (1979) *Meteor*, Christopher (1956) *No Blade of Grass* (drought), Browne (1976) *Slide* (landslide), Steward (1941) *Storm*, Maine (1958) *Thirst* (drought), Bickham (1976) *Twister* (tornado), Hyde (1980) *The Wave*, Bova (1966) *The Weathermakers* (weather modification), Leokum and Posnick (1978) *Weatherwar* (weather modification), Ballard (1962) *The Wind from Nowhere* (wind), and Ballard (1955) *White August* (blizzard).

CHAPTER 5: THE TRUTH IS ONLY KNOWN BY GUTTERSNIPES

Bob Jarvis

A record review from *New Musical Express*, an advertisement for CBS LP and two paragraphs from standard works on rock music sketch an imaginary landscape:

> Once more into the calloused heart of urban living, the city seen as a bubbling swampland, the graveyard of hope mouldering under the shadows of neon signs. *The Red and the Black* ... fantastically laughs "how does it feel to have lost your way" as the rhythm dances right off to oblivion' (Cook, 1981).

> the sound of surviving on the edge. A brilliant, brutal evocation. New York, New York so bad ... There are a thousand sides to a city like New York and as long as the city stands there will be street corner storytellers itching to feed the fantasies of anyone who'll listen with another anthem of cars and bars and subway crawls.

> (Chuck Berry) offered an urban slang - sophistication slicker than any city blues man before him. He offered cold and captivating use of cars, planes, highways, refrigerators, skyscrapers - he put love in an everyday metropolis, fast and cluttered as no-one had before. In Chuck Berry's cities real people - individuals - struggled and fretted and gave vent to ironic perceptions (Grey, 1973, p127).

> Rock and roll was perhaps the first form of popular culture to celebrate without reservation the characteristics of city life that have been criticised - cars, alleys, hotels, motels, freeways, stations, provided the context in which singers began to consider love (Gillet, 1970)

Rock music is rich in quotations that can easily be lifted by advertising copywriters or used to confer a guaranteed superficial street credibility on the urbanist. Theo Crosby's (1969) *Architecture: City Sense* and Robert Stern's (1981) *The Anglo-American Suburb* are two of many examples of urbanists who quote rock lyrics. It may well be that Charles Riech's claims for rock in *The Greening of America* now seem overstated:

> an understanding of the world, and of people's feelings, incredibility far in advance of what other media have been able to express ... a relevance, an ability to penetrate to the essence of what is wrong with society, a power to speak to man "in his condition" that is perhaps the deepest source of (the new music's) power (Riech, 1970, p208).

Fig. 5.1

Despite the hyperbole (e.g. Fig. 5.1), the figures suggest that rock music does pervade contemporary culture, especially for those under 25. In 1974 160 million records were pressed, with £160 million spent in the UK alone on records and tapes. In 1976 over 80 per cent of record buyers were under 30, with 75 per cent of sales to the 12-20 age group. In 1980 £146 million was spent on records and tapes by the 11-17 age group and £25 million was spent on advertising records and tapes in magazines, newspapers and television. [1]Moreover, studies have indicated the importance of rock music to those who listen to it, suggesting that rock music is much more than aural wallpaper. From an extended participant observation study among hippies and bike boys in the late sixties, Paul Willis found that music was important to both groups - to the bikers in their physical responses, to the hippies in its meanings. However, he rejected any analysis of music as cipher for social events; its relevance was in its culture, providing special resonance and relevance to present lives (Willis, 1978).

Simon Frith wrote of three groups of teenagers in Keighley in the early 1970s. Again, music served different functions; sixth formers with intellectual pretensions and eclectic musical tastes preferred rock that was 'apparently artistic - technically complex or lyrically poetic music was shouting a temporary "Fuck the world" . To unqualified fifth formers - 'itching to get out' - music in the rooms, clubs, juke-boxes and discos gave group identity; 'when they were in their group they had their music and they knew what it was without thinking too much'. The most telling use of rock was by the fourth formers who needed it to reinforce their identity. They would 'sit around the record player like it was Moses or something, bringing messages from on high'. For one of this group, who failed academically, 'not articulate enough to say what he really wanted but hearing it in the music', rock became 'a real boost from reality' (Frith, 1978, pp44-46).

Some aspects of rock music's environmental imagery can be traced from its lyrics. This exploratory analysis does not attempt to discuss the intentions of the composers, lyricists and performers or the environmental meanings and images that their work might have for any audience, but it does suggest that there are some coherent patterns which are worth following up in geographically-based research.

Analysis of lyrics alone is open to criticism. Denisoff and Levine (1971) described it as 'one dimensional', while Frith placed lyrics in their context:

> In naive days gone by, sociologists were quite happy to analyse the lyrical context of the top twenty and so chart changing cultural norms. We know too much to do this now. We know that genres have conventions and that pop has a history. We know that lyrics work as sung, not as written. We know that textual meaning can't be abstracted from the singer-song-audience relation (Frith, 1979, p723).

So that, as he commented on Gloria Gaynor's *I Will Survive*, 'Routine soul, a disco sound, but in the end it is always pop words like these that cut most sharply through the night - a source of dreams, and source of comfort and nothing to do with poetry at all' (Frith, 1979, p723). The lyrics themselves are often deliberately obscured or obscure. After discussing the varieties of tongue-in-cheek self-censorship, particularly of references to sex and drugs, and rock as a mystic speaking-in-tongues, Richard Meltzer (1970, p141) concluded: 'words are necessary - but even more crucially - they are replaceable'. Alexis Korner (1981), discussing the language used in blues and soul, has noted the importance of sustaining rhythm and rhyme and instinctive, intuitive means of getting across feelings rather than 'correct' use of language so that 'it twists you up inside, you remember it, what it did to you'. Many blues songs have origins in slavery or imprisonment where what cannot be said may be sung. Similar patterns have been traced in rock:

> there's often a deliberate artful fuzzing of words and effects, of making the message deliberately to get a cunningly embedded deeper layer of meaning under the surface texts. Some of this is gleeful mischief, but more of it is akin to the subtleties learned by journalist, writers and artists of an occupied country or one under rigid primitive censorship (Rossman, 1969).

Content analysis of the themes of Country and Western Music - one of the roots of modern rock - has been undertaken by Di Maggio and others in the context of wider research on mass communication and cultural patterns. Environmental themes such as 'home is where the heart is', 'these are not my people, this is not my home' have been identified (Di Maggio *et al*, 1972). Recently this work has been taken up in the context of American cultural geography particularly by Riley (1980) and by Sulzinger (1979), who has written about the landscape imagery of the Country and Western sub-genre of the trucking song - *Will there be any truck stops in Heaven?* A model for sympathetic discussion is Griel Marcus' *Mystery Train* (1975) which traces the cultural environment and imagery of The Band, Sly Stone, Randy Newman and Elvis Presley. Marcus's approach owes more to American social literary criticism than academic sociology and, like Richard Meltzer's *Aesthetics of Rock* (1970), it is written with commitment to and feeling for the music. These approaches suggest scope, direction and a starting point for environmentally-directed analysis.

The notion of rock music that is implied in the following analysis is, perhaps, white, male, English middle-class, middle-aged intellectual, but the range of music considered is generous historically and stylistically. Six environmental themes are discussed in detail - on the road, cars and girls, promised lands, rock music as an escape or transformation, the lure of the city, alienation and revolution - but others could have been developed. These would include isolation in a hostile urban environment (a theme hinted at by Carey, 1969), work and the routine it enforces, telephone songs and their inversions of time and distance, railroad songs, and the use of environmental sound, street noises and conversations to add a kind of authenticity to the song.

On the Road Again

'Their crime is in part their mobility' commented Martin Pawley (1970) on the conviction of one Anthony Gregson, of no fixed address, for 'wandering abroad and sleeping in the open air'; a comment intended to give an environmental explanation of the phenomena of the large outdoor rock festival that has since become an accepted feature of the summer landscape. The travelling song is one of the blues traditions, and has been easily absorbed into the rock genre. Griel Marcus (1975, p28) cited, among others, Robert Johnson's *Hell Hound on my Trail* as one of the most characteristic of American images:

> When Robert Johnson travelled ... he was tracing not only the miles on the road but the strength of its image. It was the ultimate American image of the flight from homelessness ... Sometimes the road was just the best place to be, free and friendly, a good way to put in the time (Marcus, 1975, p28).

The Road is a recurrent modern American theme, from Jack Kerouac through the Merry Pranksters (Wolfe, 1968a) to Fritz the Cat (Crumb, 1965). Leslie Fiedler (1964, p175) sums up literary aspects in this way:

> A final possibility is to go, as some of them like to say, "on the road" but the road leads to no place where they have not been before, and to remain perpetually in flight between nowhere and nowhere is not possible for very long, even for the very young.

> Perhaps this is why the generation of the Sixties characteristically attempts to escape to that other globe, their own head.'

Unlike many blues songs where travel and its heartaches are a matter of economic or psychological necessity, hard and gruelling, many rock lyrics celebrated mobility, especially in the mid-1960s. For example, the Beach Boys' *Get Around* observes: 'I get a bug driving up and down the same old strip/I gotta find a new place where the kids are hip'. This hedonistic flitting from one Southern Californian strip to another seemingly celebrates a mobility born of affluence: 'I'm a real cool head/earning lots of bread' (Wilson, 1964; Burlington Music). [2]The Who's *Anytime, Anyhow, Anywhere* is equally assertive: 'Well I can go anywhere/ without you/live anyhow/win or lose/go anywhere/for something new' (Townshend, Daltry, 1965; Fabulous Music, Essex Music).

When J.B. Jackson wrote, in *The Abstract World of the Hot-Rodder*:

> The man who interests me ... is already at home in the abstract preternatural landscape of wind, sun and motion. Because it is he, I think, who will eventually enrich our understanding of ourselves with a new poetry and a new nature mysticism. I would not go so far as to say that the Wordsworth of the second half of the twentieth century must be a graduate of the drag-strip or that a motor cycle is a necessary adjunct to any modern excursion, but I earnestly believe that whoever and whenever he appears he will have to express some of the uncommunicated but intensely felt joys of that part of American culture if he is to interpret completely our relationship to the world around us' (Jackson, 1957, p27).

it is unlikely that he conceived of such associations of music, bikes and the rebel stance that has been a long-standing aspect of rock music. Bikes and their riders are one of the modern folk devils (Cohen, 1972; Thompson, 1966). The film *The Wild One* (1953) popularised a cult, but before it acquired rock connotations via Hell's Angels, *The Leader of the Pack* and the like, there were underground homosexual connotations - a theme explicit in Kenneth Anger's experimental films (especially *Scorpio Rising*, 1963). Lyrics such as Steppenwolf's *Born to be Wild*: 'Get your motor running/head out on the highway/looking for adventure/and whatever comes our way' (Bonfire, 1969; Leeds Music, BIEM, NCB, Mecolico), and ten years after Def Leppard's *Ride into the Sun*: 'It's such an easy living with the wind in my hair/I'm burning up the rubber and I really don't care/cos I'm riding into the sun' are part of this tradition of the bike/road/freedom song. Bruce Springsteen's *Born to Run* transcended this idiom not only for its more precise, science fiction super-realist imagery, but also by the realism of its relating causes to myth:

> 'in the day we sweat it out in the streets of a runaway American dream/at night we ride through mansions of glory in suicide machines/ sprung from cages out on Highway 9/chrome-wheeled fuel-injected and stepping out over the line/Baby this town rips the bones from your back/it's a death trap, it's a suicide rap/we gotta get out while we're young

and its acknowledgement of the futility of trying to live out the highway myth in the modern urban world:

> ... the highways jammed with broken heroes/on a last chance power drive/everybody's out on the run/but there's no place left to hide (Springsteen, 1975; Laurel Canyon Music, ASCAP).

Another dimension of travel and freedom is found in the truck driving song, a recognised Country and Western idiom with its own 'fakelore', a narrative told in a language of 'dimes, Georgia overdrives, cups of coffee, truckstops, grinding the box, flowing of black smoke, flaming horses, overloads, speed traps and smokes ... capable of rich symbolism and mythology, at times almost giving the road a life of its own' (Sulzinger, 1979, p13). Many rock bands include versions of truck songs in their repertoire or create their own versions. Early Little Feat songs - such as *Willing*:

> '... smuggled some smokes and folks from Mexico ... give me weed, whites and wine/and I'll be willing (George, 1970; Warner Bros. Music)

bridge the cultural and ethical gap between rock and trucking that angered the Byrds in *Drug Store Truck Driving Man* (1969). The similarities of life pattern between the touring rock band and truck driving that makes for the obvious similarities, and 'The Tour', from Transit van and motorway cafe to private jet and five-star hotels, is another environmental sub-genre of rock lyrics. The Grateful Dead's *Trucking* encapsulates this,

> Chicago, New York and Detroit/they're all on the same street/ a typical city involved in a typical daydream/hang it up, see what tomorrow brings/Dallas, got a soft machine/Houston too close to New Orleans/New York, got the ways and the means/they just won't let you be...

but, unlike the moral majority of the trucking song, the air of outlaw threat is always present:

> Sitting and staring out of the hotel window/wondering if they're going to kick the door in again/but if you got a warrant I guess you're going to come in (Hunter, Carcia, Wier, Lesh, 1971; Ice Nine Publishing).

The travelling life, without ties or possessions, is another recurrent theme. In many songs it is celebrated as a skill, an ability to survive on the edge of place, like Roger Miller's *King of the Road*: 'I know every handout, in every town/every lock that ain't locked when no-one's around' (Miller, 1964; Tree Publishing). This ability to move on, to stay disengaged was summed up by Commander Cody and his Lost Planet Airmen in *Home in my Hand*:

> I'm a travelling man/well I can move pretty quick I just keep my home in my hand/... I don't know what makes me ramble/I guess I really don't care/but you can always find me on the corner of any downtown street/toking a weed/just minding my own (R. Self, 1971; Cable Rock Music BMI).

But not all these songs of the road and its freedom are celebratory. Little Feat's *Strawberry Flats* is the obverse of this myth, with the singer the victim of isolation, rejection and freezing cold, not to mention hippie paranoia:

> Ripped off/run out of town/had my guitar burned while I was fooling/ haven't slept in a bed for a week.../knocked at my friend's house in Moody, Texas/asked if he had a place for me/his hair was cut off and he was wearing a suit/he said/not in my house/felt like part of some conspiracy ... now I'm six hours out on Strawberry

Flats/trying to get to Wacko before it freezes over' (Payne, George, 1970; MCPS).

There's Nothing Else in this Crazy World Except Cars and Girls

Though the Dictators' song *Cars and Girls* may be a mock heroic pastiche, to judge from their poses and attitudes on the album *The Dictators Go Girl Crazy* , they are tapping on a hedonistic *View From the Road* that characterised youth culture. In one of the few academic discussions of the teenage social institution of 'cruising', Theodore Goldberg (1959, p163) observed:

'an initial outlay of $200 for an old Chevrolet or Ford is the best investment a drag-orientated teenager can make. In a single package he obtains mobility, social opportunity, independence, privacy and entertainment; for an additional $200-$300 invested in appearance he can add status and social acceptance to that list'.

Throughout the 1950s and 1960s many songs and whole albums were devoted to drag racing and crusing. They celebrated cars and girls, but entwined in many of them are heartbreak - as in Chuck Berry's *Mabelline*:

As I was motorvating over the hill/saw Mabelline in a Coupe de Ville/a Cadillac a rolling on the open road/nothing could outrun my V8 Ford/the Cadillac doing about ninety-five/she's bumper to bumper/rolling side by side/oh, Mabelline, why can't you be true? (Berry, 1955; Jewel Music)

or sudden death, as in Jan and Dean's *Deadman's Curve*:

I was cruising my Stingray late one night/when an XKE pulled up on my right/he rolled down the window of shiny blue Jag/and challenged me there ... you don't come back from Dead Man's Curve (Berry, Christian, Kornfield, Wilson, 1964; Screen Gems/EMI),

but mostly just *Fun, Fun, Fun*:

Well she got her daddy's car/and she'll cruise to the hamburger

> stand now/she forgot all about the library just like she told her old man now/with radio blasting she goes cruising just as fast as she can now/and she'll have Fun, Fun, Fun/till her daddy takes her T-bird away (Wilson, Love, 1964; Elmwin Music).

Yet now these are so many golden oldies, a part of the sub-culture of images to be recycled occasionally for nostalgia, to be incanted as one of rock's golden formulae. Again, Bruce Springsteen offers an elegiac interpretation. *Racing in the Street* has all the right phrases:

> I got a sixty-nine Chevy/with three ninety-six fuel heads/... tonight, tonight the strips just right/wanna blow em off in my first heat/'cos the summer's here and the time is right for racing in the street ,

but the tempo is slow, accompanied only by a piano, the tone wistful, tinged with heartache and regret,

> I met her on the strip 3 years ago/in a Camero with some dude from LA/I blew that Camero off my back/ and blew that little girl away/ but now there's wrinkles round my baby's eyes/and she cries herself to sleep at night .

There are memories that only one last ride will erase:

> For all the shut down strangers and hot rod angels rumbling across this promised land/tonight my baby and me are gonna ride to the sea and wash those sins off our hands (Springsteen, 1978; Intersong).

In several tracks on Springsteen's next album, driving has become even a more haunting nightmare such as *Wreck on the Highway* or an escape, stolen dreams in a *Stolen Car*:

> I'm driving a stolen car/down on Elridge Avenue/each night I wait to get caught/but I never do ... on a pitch black night/and I'm telling myself I'm going to be alright/but I ride by night and I travel in fear/that in this darkness I will disappear' (Springsteen, 1979; Intersong).

Promised Lands

Though there is a rural escapist line of promised lands (which runs somewhere through Woodstock/build me a cabin up in Utah/down on the farm/getting it together in a country cottage), rock music's promised lands are generally urban and often specially Californian. This is a powerful and alluring cultural dream which:

> 'retains its power in spite of proneness to logical disproof. It is the dream that appears in Le Corbusier's equation: *un reve* x 1,000,000 = chaos. Unfortunately for Le Corbusier's rhetorical mathematics, the chaos was in his mind, and not in Los Angeles, where seven million adepts at California Dreaming can find their way around without confusion' (Banham, 1971, pp239-240).

Rayner Banham includes Ray Bradbury, Nathanael West and Raymond Chandler as fictional guides to the Los Angeles landscape. Griel Marcus (1975, pp119-120) also cites West and Chandler in his placing of Randy Newman in this ambivalent landscape, where there is 'an aggressive and in many ways positive denial of the need for roots, a perception that everything that is old must be covered in neon and sandstone before anyone can be really free'.

In Chuck Berry's *Promised Land* the dream still ensnares. After a series of transport failures and changes it is enough for the proverbial 'poor boy' to arrive:

> Left my home in Norfolk, Virginia/California on my mind ... Los Angeles give me Norfolk, Virginia/try Waterford ten 0-nine/tell the folks back home this is the promised land calling/and the poor boy's on the line (Berry, 1964; Tristan Music).

Twenty years later, in The Runaways' *Hollywood*, it is still alive:

> Each night I dream/I'm a rebel I'm a teenage queen/... Hollywood/feels so good ... Each day at home I scheme/for the fame and fortune dream/Each time the radio plays it tells of the golden days/... Hollywood feels so good

even if, as in Ry Cooder's *Down in Hollywood* (1979) it may be better to dream than to experience, and take his advice:

better hope you don't run out of gas/down Hollywood they drag you right out your car and kick your arse/they're standing on the corner just waiting for a sucker like you/if you want to stay healthy just keep moving right on through' (Drummond, Cooder, 1979; Warner Bros. Music).

Disappointment and disillusionment have frequently been the norm. Otis Redding's *Dock of the Bay* (1968) is a black, soul view from the underside of California's golden days:

I left my home in Georgia/headed for the Frisco Bay/I had nothing to live for/looks like nothing's gonna come my way/so I'm just sitting on the Dock of the Bay ...' (Redding, Cropper, 1968; East Memphis Music, Thine Music, Redwall Music).

The dreams captivate to the point where in The Eagles' *Hotel California* (1976) the state becomes the locale for a deceptive hedonistic lifestyle where:

we are all prisoners here/of our own device/you can check out anytime you like/but you can never leave' (Fedler, Henley, Frey, 1976; Long Run Music, Fingers Music, WB Music).

In an environment where the desert canyon retreat declines into suburbs, this landscape of roads and neon signs is another version of the disappearing frontier wilderness described by Fiedler as a 'world without a West' (Fiedler, 1972). This is *The Last Resort* where: 'call some place paradise/kiss it goodbye' (Fedler, Henley, Frey, 1976; Long Run Music, Fingers Music, WB Music).

In Bruce Springsteen's songs the deceptions and hypocrisies of the notion of a promised land are at the same time deeper, more anguished, but less precise. The person rather than the place is destroyed. It is a world of contradictions: 'Working all day in my daddy's garage/driving all night chasing some mirage', in which belief in a *Promised Land* leads nowhere and in which:

I get up each morning I just wanna explode/explode and tear this whole town apart/take a knife and tear this pain from my heart ... the lies that leave nothing but lost and broken hearted (Springsteen, 1978; Intersong Music).

The Truth is only known by Guttersnipes

Only a microcosmic personal version of the promised land seems to reliably offer a safe and private place. There are two versions of this retreat which recur regularly. The Drifters' rooftop hideaway, *Up on the Roof*, is a concrete enough place:

> When this old world starts getting me down/and people are just too much for me to face/I climb right up to the top of the stairs/and all my cares just drift right into space .

By contrast, the beach rendezvous seems slightly hallucinatory. Martha and the Muffins' *Echoe Beach* is a recent example:

> 9 to 5 I have to spend my time at work/my job is very boring I'm an office clerk/the only thing that helps me pass the time away/is knowing I'll be back on Echoe Beach one day .

The lyrics almost give away its imaginary location: 'Echoe Beach, far away in time'.

I wanna get lost in your Rock and Roll and drift away

The real promised land of rock music is the music itself, and there are many songs that testify to the music's power to save, transform and transcend the pressures of urban life and environment. Tom Wolfe in *The Noonday Underground* (Wolfe, 1968b) described a setting in the heart of swinging London, 'a secret place he goes to at lunchtime ... a kinetic trance, just letting the music grab them and mess up their minds ... and then back to the office as if nothing had happened at all'. Or again:

> Janey said when she was five years old/my parents they gonna be the death of us all/2 TV sets and 2 Cadillac cars/they ain't gonna help at all (not one tiny bit)/then one morning she puts on a New York station/you know she don't believe what she heard at all/then she started dancing to that fine, fine music/her life was saved by rock and roll (Velvet Underground, 1970; Copyright Control).

Chuck Berry's *Schooldays* (1957) contrasts the dull routine of school with the juke-joint heaven around the corner:

> Soon three o'clock rolls around/you finally lay your burden down/out of the classroom and into the street/... drop that coin right into the slot/you gotta hear something really hot/... all day long you've been wanting to dance (Berry, 1957; Jewel Music).

Just as in the Loving Spoonful's *Summer in the City*, the humid oppressive street of the day is transformed by night time and dance: 'But at night it's a different world/go out and find a girl/C'mon, C'mon and dance all night/despite the heat it'll be alright' (J. Sebastian, M. Sebastian, Boone, 1966; Robbins). The same message occurs in Kim Wilde's *Kids in America* where, even in small towns with nothing to offer, some brief unity of youth and music provides a source of belonging: 'We're the kids in America/everyone lives for the music go round', even if beyond such night-long alliances and romances: 'outside a new day's dawning/outside suburbia's crawling'.

Kids in America alludes to another classic pattern of unity through rock music and dance, containing a nationwide list of place names. This theme has run from *Sweet Little Sixteen* onwards through Martha and the Vandellas' *Dancing in the Street*, with its 'invitation across the nation/chance for folks to meet' (Stevenson, Gaye, Hunter, 1964; Jobete Music). Some commentators could see revolutionary or at least subversive undertones in such lyrics. Nevertheless, in the MC5's *Shaking Street* (despite the band's earlier promotional poses, with their claimed allegiance to the White Panthers), the subversion is only that of gathering together to show social and cultural unity:

> Little orphan Annie/Sweet Sue too/they been coming around/because there's something to do... Skylight Sam decided to make the trip/all the way from New Jersey/on his girl friend's trick ... Shaking Street/where the kids meet/got that sound/gotta get down/to Shaking Street (MC5, 1968; Motor City/Cottilion).

Yet these 'cities on flame with rock and roll', these pleasure centres of escape, are only a thin line from the real deserts, the emptiness of a town without music. For example, The Specials' *Ghost Town* depicts a town where, a result of the sub-culture's own exuberance:

> all the clubs have been closed down/... bands won't play no more/... too much fighting on the dance floor/do you remember

> the good old days before/the ghost town ... this town becoming like a ghost town (Dammers, 1981; Plangent Visions Music).

I Miss the City Streets and the Neon Lights

The Velvet Underground's *Train coming round the Bend* seemed curiously out of time when it appeared in 1970 when the new Age of Aquarius was dawning out in the desert communes and the rock festivals, but its rejection of the rural myth:

> been in the country far too long/trying to be a farmer/nothing I planted ever seemed to grow (Velvet Underground, 1970; Copyright Control).

and its driving desire for the city life was simply a part of a longer-standing tradition of rock music as an urban-made music, with an imagery and excitement that belong to the city. As Griel Marcus (1975, p73) concluded in his discussion of The Band, then in retreat in rural Woodstock,

> the pastoral traps of Woodstock had already taken too much of the soul out of (The Band) ... as much as any of us can give. But if America is dangerous, its little utopias, asking nothing, promising safety, are usually worse ... "This country life is killing me, I gotta find my way back to the city, and get some corruption in my lungs.

Just as rock music absorbed and re-orientated many rural blues and folk music forms and traditions, many of its lyrics chart the fatal, destroying fascination of the city. *Me, I'm just a country boy in the great big freaky city* is a Sir Douglas Quintet song, but the most anguished inventory of this downhill slide lies in the songs of Gram Parsons. In *Sin City*, he records:

> This whole town's filled with sin/it'll swallow you in/if you got the money to burn/take it home right away/you got three years to pay.

where however protected and sealed the corruption may be

> we got our recruits/and our green mohair suits/please show your

> ID in the door/on the thirsty first floor/a gold plated door/won't keep out the Lord's burning rain (Parsons, Hillman, 1969; Irving Music BMI).

In *Las Vegas*, the white gospel edge of damnation is ever present, personified in:

> Ooh Las Vegas/ain't no place for a poor boy like me/everytime I hit you crystal city/you know you'll make a wreck out of me (Parsons, Gretch, 1974; Rondor Music).

Characteristically, the attractions of the city are personal rather than topographical. Jefferson Starship celebrate women in *Big City*:

> Now you know the big city women/they know how to give you the blues/early in the morning/when the big city loving begins (Barbata, Hill, Ethridge, 1976; Chappel Morris Ltd.).

and The Human League describe the relationship between the individual and *The Sound of the Crowd*:

> Get around town/where the people look good/where the music is loud/you need to stand proud/add your voice to the sound of the crowd.

while Lou Reed describes *A Walk on the Wild Side*, where the city is a lure for what is clandestine, illegal and forbidden; cities whose victims

> hitch-hiked across the USA/plucked her eyebrows on the way/shaved her legs/and then he was a she ... little Joe never once gave it away/everyone had to pay and pay/a hustle here, a hustle there/New York City is the place where ... (Lou Reed, 1972; Sunbury Music/Oakfield Avenue Music).

The life of the city in rock lyrics is that of a street life, a street corner society which finds itself in a glamourised, synthetised hanging out. Roxy Music's *Street Life* stresses a gossipy uncertainty: 'C'mon with me cruising down the street/who knows what you see/who you might meet'. Yet this is a stylist's view, part of The Roxy Dream (Weiner, 1975), fragments of conversation, broken hearts in an emporium of styles (Raban, 1973). It is 'only window shopping/and strictly no sale'.

The Crusaders' *Street Life* offers a more tragic edge, a brilliant mirror that turns to a trap:

> I play the street life/because there's no place I can go/... there's a thousand parts to play/till you play your life away/you let the people see just who you want to be/every night just like a superstar/that's how life is played/a ten cent masquerade (Sample, Jennings, 1979; Rondor Music, Leeds Music).

while Selecters' *Out in the Street* stresses a restless search for excitement, for the action:

> Out in the streets again/looking for something/just don't matter now/I don't want to care/I want to have some fun/make a connection/feel like a roller coaster/I don't want to stop (Davies, 1980; Selecter Copyright, Rak Publishing).

Once again, Bruce Springsteen's songs offer a more detailed, more vivid and more peopled description, where tension, glamour and action overlay a realistic drab landscape of backstairs, small bars and amusement halls. His song *The East Street Shuffle* describes a world of flashlight phantoms and riot squads through which characters like the 'Boy Prophet' and 'Spanish Johnny' drift:

> The teenage tramps/dressed in skin tight pants/doing the E-street dance/well the kids down there either dancing or hooked up in a scuffle/sharkskin suits packed with Detroit muscle/doing the E-street dance (Springsteen, 1973; Intersong Music).

In later songs such as *Jungleland*, however, these moments of glory are seen as brief and false and poetry impossible:

> There's an opera out on the turnpike/there's a ballet being fought out in the alley... the streets are alive and secret debts are paid ... outside the street's on fire/in a real death waltz/between what's flesh and what's fantasy/and the poets down here/don't write nothing at all ... try to make an honest stand but they wind up wounded/not even dead (Springsteen, 1975; Laurel Canyon Music ASCAP).

The urban landscape of rock are not those of any formal grandeur, the great works of civic design, but the trivial, the ugly and the ephemeral; the kind of places that writers like Robert Venturi or J.B. Jackson have tried to identify and analyse in a sympathetic way. There is little irony in rock's classic, naive, commercial and traditional celebration of this landscape of consumption and neglect; indeed, it was just that absence that was one of the reasons Griel Marcus (1977, p22) so admired Chuck Berry's *Back in the USA*: 'looking hard for a drive in/searching for a corner cafe/where the hamburger frizzles on an open grill all day' (Berry, 1959; Tristan Music). It seems that few elements have been missed: bars and dance halls, amusement halls, movies and drive-ins, boardwalks and hamburger stands line the great vinyl highway in the mind. Today such innocence is lost: twenty years on from Chuck Berry, can Funkapolitan's *Fast Food Rap* (1981) really be without irony? All that lighthearted youthful, unquestioning consumption has a darker side. Its emergence might be placed somewhere around the mid-1960s, and can certainly be illustrated in Bob Dylan's *Highway 61*, perhaps, given Dylan's reworkings of rock's traditions (Grey, 1973, chapter 4), an obverse of *Route 66*. *Highway 61* contains obsessive and systematic descriptions of such low rent losers at Georgia Sam and Howard who 'just pointed with his gun/and said that way/out on Highway 61', or Mac the Finger and Louis the King with their useless and unwanted goods:

> forty red white and blue shoestrings/and a thousand telephones that don't ring/tell me where I can get rid of these things (Dylan, 1965; Blossom Music).

or most sinister of all, the Frozen Gambler looking for a promoter for his Third World War.

Such a reversal, with a fascination with the underside of the city grows to menace in John Fox's *Underpass* (1980) or fetish in The Normal's *Warm Leatherette* with its last-minute fervid car crash embrace, reminiscent of J.G. Ballard's *Crash* in its perversity:

> See the breaking glass/in the underpass/... see your reflection in the luminescent dash/the fear of petrol in your eyes/the handbrake penetrates your thigh/quick let's make love/before we die/on warm leatherette (Miller, 1979; Blue Mountain Music).

The city becomes strange and filled with hostile strangers where music is the only refuge. The Doors' songs *People are strange* and *Soul Kitchen*, from the mid-1960s, convey such messages:

> people are strange/when you're a stranger/streets are uneven when you're down.

> Cars draw past all stuffed with eyes/the street lights show what I don't know/your brain seems bruised in numb surprise/but there's still one place to go/let me stay all night/in your soul kitchen (Doors, 1968/1967; Paradox Music).

Much the same message appears in The Jam's *Strange Town*, a song of fifteen years later, portraying an environment ultimately alienating and destroying any sense of identity:

> they say don't know, don't care, I gotta go mate/gotta move in a straight line/walk it, talk in one more time/can't be weird in a strange town/be betrayed by your accent and manners ... I feel so close where the music's loud/cos' I don't see a face in the single crowd/there's no-one there/I look in the mirror/but I can't be seen/just a thin clean layer/over this machine/looking back at me (Weller, 1979; And Son Music).

Though there are vague and glamorised views of 'the City', a more convincing view is that of a socially-segregated city, even if its early examples are 'a sentimentalized glimpse of poverty ... like someone watching Harlem from the window of a passing commuter train' (Goldstein, 1969, p27), as in the Crystals' *Uptown*;

> Downtown he's just one of a million groups/... but when he comes uptown/each evening to my tenement/uptown where folks don't pay much rent/... he don't crawl/he's a king (Weil, Mann, 1962; Screen Gems).

or *On Broadway*

> but when you're walking down that street and you ain't had enough to eat/the glitter rubs right off ... (Mann, Weil, Lieber, Stoller, 1963; Screen Gems).

The pattern of a divided, rich and poor city seems deeply embedded. Of course, it can always be crossed, usually by love, from *Down in the Boondocks*:

> every night I watch the light/of the house up on the hill ... one fine day/I'll find a way to move from this old shack ... till that day I'll work and slave and nights she'll have to steal away/get together/making love/down in the boondocks (South, nd, Warner Bros. Music).

and by clandestine assignation at *The Dark End of the Street*;

> if you take a walk down town/find some time to look around/if you should see me and I'll walk on by/oh, darling, please don't cry/tonight we'll meet/at the dark end of the street (Spooner, Oldham, Dann Penn, nd, London Tree Music).

Yet even strange and hostile parts of the city may have their comforts, whether it is drugs, as in the Velvet Underground's *Waiting for my man*:

> Up to Lexington, one two five/feel sick and dirty more dead than alive/hey white boy, what you doing uptown?/hey white boy, you chasing our women around?/oh pardon me sir, it was the furthest thing from my mind/I look for a dear friend of mine/... up to a brownstone/up three flights of stairs (Lou Reed, 1969; Copyright Control).

or just another place, a dark side that offers a shadowy refuge in which to hide or to escape. When all values are lost, women and money gone, there is always *The Darkness at the Edge of Town*: 'where no-one asks any questions/or looks for too long in your face' (Springsteen, 1978; Copyright Control).

Don't stop/give it all you've got

> Ring ring seven a.m./move yourself to go again/...just get up and learn these rules.../looking for rise to better my station/buy my baby some sophistication...clocks go slow in the place of

> work/minutes drag and the hours jerk (Clash, 1980; Hineden Ltd., MCPS, BIEM).

The Clash's *Magnificent Seven*, rapped against the chorus 'don't stop/give it all you've got', is one line from lyrics which spell out disillusionment with all the traps and trappings of consumer society. The Rolling Stones' *Satisfaction* predates most overt politicising of rock:

> I'm watching my TV/and a man comes on and tells me/how white my shirts can be/but he can't be a man cos' he doesn't smoke/the same cigarettes as me (Jagger, Richards, 1964; Essex Music, BMI).

but is part of a tradition that is completely at odds with the pattern in Country and Western music (Sulzinger, 1979), which glorifies the safe home comforts of suburbia and a place to settle down. Typical of the attitudes expressed in rock lyrics is Roxy Music's *In Every Dream Home*, where in a de luxe landscape of mail order perfection: 'from bell push to faucet/in small town apartment ... penthouse perfection/but what goes on there', where the only comfort is synthetic, inflatable dolls: 'plain wrapper baby/disposable darling/I blew up your body/and you blew my mind'. XTC spit out their contempt for the *New Town Animal* (1978) in its furnished cage: 'I borrowed all my life and nothing's mine/it's gone eleven and the bar is shut/... there's nothing decent on the TV page'.

The Clash offer a more realistic still life of a *City of the Dead*. Over the baldness of south London municipal housing in the illustrated lyric, they proclaim: 'while all the windows stare ahead/and the streets are filled with dread' (Strummer, Jones, 1977; Nineden, Riva Music). Their *Lost in the Supermarket* portrays an atmosphere of pervasive desperate boredom, where hedges and gardens are a fading memory:

> I came in here for that special offer/guaranteed personality/I save coupons from packets of tea/I got my giant discotheque album/I empty a bottle and I feel a bit free (Strummer, Jones, 1979; Riva Music, Nineden).

In the lyric sheet for London's *Burning with Boredom Now* (Simenon and Jones, 1978, pp24-25) the tower blocks are collaged one over the other in sub-Heartfeld style, suggesting the political edge to those lyrics of desperation:

> Black or white, turn it on, face the new religion/everybody's sitting round watching television ... now I'm in the subway looking for the flat/... the wind howls through the empty blocks looking for a home ...

The Jam have also pictured these desolate places; in *Down in the Tube Station at Midnight* meaningless violence flares, out of echoes and thrown away papers, voices and jostling drunks. Against the flattened refrain of 'That's entertainment', The Jam's song of the same name lists areas of collapse and disorder:

> a smash of glass and the rumble of boots/an electric train and a ripped up phone booth/paint splattered walls and the cry of a tom cat/lights going out and a kick in the balls (Weller, 1980; And Son Music).

No hope is offered at all.

Rock lyrics offer several routes beyond this crisis. Many advocate a return to music, where dance stance is all, but there are more constructive routes from different backgrounds. Black music, drawing on an established literature, poetry and action of revolt, resistance and self-awareness, is often assertive. James Brown's *I don't need nobody to give me nuthin'* is typical: 'we got talents we can use/for our side of town/let's get ahead together/and build up from the ground'/ Griel Marcus (1975, pp91-95) pinpointed an *annus mirabilis* in black music around 1972-3, when, almost as an answer to the despair of Sly Stone's *Riot* album ('enough to make all solutions seem invalid and alternatives false, in personal life, politics or music') a wave of affirmation seemed to grip the music. Several of these songs took environmental form. After an extended life history running through rural and urban black poverty, violence and despair, given extra musical dimension by voice-overs and sound effects of arrests and beatings in its middle section, Stevie Wonder's *Living for the City* concludes quietly:

> I hope you hear inside my voice a sorrow/and that gives you to think about tomorrow/the price is cruel/if we don't change/this world will soon be over.

and against the final chorus of: 'living for the city/living just enough' a voice says: 'stop giving' (Stevie Wonder, 1973; Jobete Music). Curtis Mayfield's *Futureshock* similarly lists a world of soup lines, broken men, futile escapism in dance, men imprisoned, drug dealing and unemployment, choruses:

> we all got to stop the man/from messing up the world/this is our last and only chance/(everybody) it's futureshock (Mayfield, 1973; Curtom Publishing).

White rock has none of this cultural tradition to draw on. In the words of an X-Ray Spex song *Warriors in Woolworths*,

> roots are in today/don't know no history/he threw his past away/he's a rebel in the underground/she's a rebel in the modern town (Styrene, 1978; Mobjack).

The constant flirting with radical philosophies often extends no further than the back page advertisements for Brigade Rosse T-Shirts in New Musical Express, but the lyrics occasionally do point out violence and injustice, like The Clash's *Guns of Brixton* (1980):

> when they kick in your front door/how you gonna come?/with your hands on your head/or on the trigger of a gun (Simenon, 1980; Nineden Ltd., Riva Music).

Such lyrics ask questions of the listener rather than advocate solutions - a mix of ideology and style, posing for the revolution. Style and its significance are vitally important, as Hebdige (1979) has pointed out in his analysis of youth subcultures, while interviews with The Clash and their manager-cum-mentor Bernie Rhodes, frequently referred to the ironies and ambiguities of their rebel stance. Nevertheless, action seems to retreat into music: 'Where were we during the riots? ... Where was Karl Marx in 1917? We were playing a residency at Bon's in New York' (Joe Strummer of The Clash, quoted in Rambali, 1981).

The underlying stance here seems to have changed little in the ten years between the Rolling Stones' *Street Fighting Man* and *Clash City Rockers*. Griel Marcus (1969) pointed out the tension in ambiguity of the dominant words and their associations - revolution, fighting in the street, the sound of marching, charging people - the exhilarating rhythms against the chorus of despondency and self-deprecation: 'what else can a poor boy do/'cept play in a rock and roll band' (Jagger, Richard, 1968; Mirage Music). *Clash City Rockers* (1978), however, is tougher, less rhetorical, more reflective, advocating a more critical stance against urban pressure. Contrasting the rich going to Privilege, 'the chicest of chic Paris nightclubs', with tramps in the alleyway opposite, Joe Strummer remarked 'see those guys out there down the alley, see the angle they see all this from, I saw it from that angle, I was 18 or 19, and I couldn't be fucked to ... to play the game. I saw it from their angle, literally. In this city too. And that's what politicised me more than anything' (Rambali, 1981).

> You see the rate they come down the escalator/now listen to the tube train accelerator/then you realise that you got to have a purpose/or this place is gonna knock you out sooner or later .

Traditional grandiose claims of revolution are realised to be dreams, half imaginings,

> I wanna liquefy everybody gone dry .../burn down the suburbs with a half closed eye.

and the chorus emphasises the strength of the group, the subcultural coherence to withstand the pressures of urban life:

> I wanna move the town to Clash City Rockers/ya need a little jump of electrical shockers/ya better leave town if you only wanna knock us/nothing stands the pressure of Clash City Rockers (Strummer, Jones, 1979; Riva Music, Nineden Ltd.).

Conclusions: *What else can a poor boy do?*

Critical and analytical interpretation of rock music and culture is rapidly developing and this selective account has been personal and subjective by comparison. Any full account would need to place lyrics in the context of their writers and composers, of the music industry and the use and consumption not only of the music itself but the universe of specialist newspapers, advertising and promotion, videos and record sleeves to give a complete picture of the environmental imagery of rock. Critical works, such as Frith's *Sociology of Rock*

(1978), Denisoff and Peterson's *Sounds of Social Change* (1972), and Hebdige's *Subculture* (1979) provide specific insights into rock music as a medium, while Horton (1957) and Carey (1969a, 1969b) have indicated the dual role that lyrics may play in reflecting and shaping ideas of personal identity and interpersonal relationships. Recent analysis of other mass media suggested their social role; Berman (1981, pp103-108) has identified a 'fictitious community' created in adverts where cultural psychodramas play a surrogate role of the friendly advisers of the idealised small town community. Snow (1983, pp237-242) has applied a symbolic interactionist perspective to mass media to develop the idea of 'media culture', where the media play an equivalent role to social and interpersonal relationships in the establishment of an individual's identity.

In specifically developing an environmentally-orientated analysis of rock music and culture, several sets of questions might be tackled. First, what are the effects of the conventions, stylisations and hypocrisies of rock music as it is produced, performed, distributed and consumed, as a business on the environmental imagery? Does rock's apparent self-obsession and isolation affect the accuracy and honesty of its imagery? Secondly, to what extent do marketing stereotypes and fleeting conventions ('this year everyone's doing environment songs - tower blocks an' that') affect the imagery that is current at any one time or in any one style of music? (Fig. 5.2). Thirdly, does it matter how far the image is removed from reality? Making and presenting such images may be important in itself, in turn influencing perception and understanding of the environment.

> In various bedrooms of suburban London, while Little Richard found God, Elvis obeyed Uncle Sam and Chuck Berry was in jail, Mick (Jagger) and Keith (Richards) conspired to re-invent the USA, a giant topographical fantasy hardly less enveloping than Brecht and Weil's imaginary America in the pop-opera *Mahoganny*. It's become such a part of our mental furniture that at least we recognise it as a parallel universe. Naive in the extreme, often exotic as a Japanese Western, it's still funkier than the one we've got (Dalton, 1981).

Finally, is environmental determinism alive and well and playing in a rock and roll band? Is there some causal relationship between environment and the nature of the music produced there, or are various identifiable place-sounds just marketing classifications,

Fig 5.2

reflections of particular entrepreneurial, imitative associations? Ralph Gleason described the origins of 'The San Francisco Sound' in this way - 'none of this would have happened if the San Francisco - Berkeley Bay area was not a very special place' (Gleason, 1959, p25). The determinist view is given by David Thomas of Pere Ubu:

> 'There's this relationship between machines and flesh in Cleveland that is very strange ... Cleveland is a giant blown-out factory town ... the feeling that there's no future for somebody here and all the musicians seem to be in love with that fact ... All I can say is whatever you feel from the music is what it feels like to be here (Thomas, 1978).

In this context, what is the effect of a dominant cultural imagery derived from the USA? Paul Weller of The Jam has claimed:

> It's like a line from one of your songs "The USA got the sea/British kids have got the streets" ... most American songs are about walking round stoned and that or picking up some chicks in a Cadillac, which don't go on in Britain cause it's usually raining and you ain't got no money and you gotta sit in some poxy caff, drinking cold tea. I think British music's a bit harder (Weller, 1981).

The problem of an authentic English Rhythm and Blues is discussed by Wilko Johnson: 'In songs the imagery should have some kind of reality, not just be exotic sounding - all those awful songs where people talk of jumping on freight trains, it just doesn't go down on

British Rail. There's plenty of other things' (Johnson, 1981). Wilko Johnson's recent LP was called *Ice on the Motorway*.

Against the notion of monolithic cultural and commercial patterns must be the accessibility of making rock music with the spread of small record labels and specialist distributors, and the fragmentation of a singular rock music into a range of cults, styles and fashions that are so well known that even popular women's magazines can illustrate them for anxious mothers. Does this make for a more diverse, easily produced imagery of social and environmental concern?

Ultimately, rock music poses a dilemma for the environmentalist. On the one hand is the danger of reading too much into entertainment: Hebdige comments on the suggestions that punk is 'the sound of the Westway' or pogo 'the high rise leap', warning that the rhetoric of style in subculture 'may say what it means but it may not mean what it says' (Hebdige, 1979, p115). Set against such critical caution are the feelings expressed in a letter to *New Musical Express* which raises all the questions and the traps involved in asking them:

> *They* have created an inner city situation so horrific and inhuman ... so that when Jimmy Pursey or Joe Strummer or anybody who knows what it's like gets up on stage and turns it into (a) the best rock and roll in the world; (b) a bloody great bomb to throw back at *them*; (c) someone telling you the real truth about life as you know it to be, of course it explodes in their faces (Copland, 1979).

NOTES

1. These figures from Frith, 1978 and figures published by Media Expenditure Analysis Ltd. and Mintel

2. Lyrics are cited by recording artist in the text and by composer, date and publisher in parenthesis wherever this has been traceable. Many are quoted from transcriptions of recording, rather than published lyric sheets, so a measure of misunderstanding and richness of possible meaning is possible, which, according to Meltzer, is one of the music's aesthetic joys.

CHAPTER 6: FROM 'METROPOLIS' TO 'THE CITY': FILM VISIONS OF THE FUTURE CITY, 1919-39

John R. Gold

'We must invent and rebuild the Futurist city', proclaimed the Italian writer Emilio Marinetti in 1914, 'it must be like an immense, tumultuous, lively, noble work site, dynamic in all its parts' (quoted in Conrads, 1970, p36). In these words and the accompanying sketches of the *Città Nuova* (New City) by Antonio Sant'Elia, one can identify the first comprehensive statement of an imagery that has dominated much twentieth-century debate about the future city. The design of the *Città Nuova* drew heavily upon the ideas of nineteenth century structural engineers and science fiction writers, especially H.G. Wells, but it also gave expression to values that the Futurists felt would characterise the new machine age - speed, novelty, dynamism, modernity and scale. In Sant'Elia's drawings, one sees a bold new urban landscape of colossal, geometrical slabs and towers rising above the 'tumultuous abyss' of restless traffic arteries; a multi-level and modern city that applied new technologies, materials and secondary sources of energy (especially electricity), to meet the changed needs of society.

The ideas of the Italian Futurists were soon to be swept away in the chaos of the First World War and fell into a 40-year obscurity (Banham, 1955) but their work accurately presaged many of the lines of *avant-garde* thinking about the future city in the period after 1918. During the inter-war years, literally hundreds of manifestoes, drawings and lengthy treatises about new urban forms were published in the progressive architecture and design press, especially those publications associated with the so-called Modern Movement in architecture. The terms used in these paper visions of the future city varied, as did the underlying political stances of their authors, but there was considerable consensus in the imagery presented (Gold, 1984c). Again and again one sees iconoclasm for the forms and symbols of the existing city, itself closely identified with the same established order that had so recently led the world into the cataclysm of war. In place of the existing city would rise bold new visions which took full advantage of advanced constructural techniques and liberated the potential of electricity and the new building materials of steel, reinforced concrete and glass. The city of the future would be rationally and comprehensively planned, often on the basis of geometrically harmonious schemata, and would incorporate strict land-use zoning. The challenge of traffic would be met by efficient and sophisticated systems of mass transportation, both conventional and novel, and frequently with lavish provision for aviation. Where housing conditions were shown, the vogue was for flatted blocks on custom-built estates, affording prospects of easy movement to and from the workplace. Yet the defining characteristic was usually the depiction of the central city as consisting of huge buildings towering above the vast chasms of the traffic arteries - a veritable anthill of human activity. It is this emphasis on scale and on the vertical dimension that makes Auguste Perret's felicitous phrase 'the city of towers' an apt description of such visions of the future city (Booker, 1980).

Within architectural circles this imagery remained the preserve of a small, if vociferous, minority during the inter-war years, even if it was to receive far greater attention post-1945. Yet elsewhere the basic notions of 'the city of towers' had taken firm root well before 1939. In part this may be attributed to that influential science-fiction tradition initiated by Wells and others to which we have already referred, but it would also seem that a new pattern of expectation had been initiated. Quite apart from science fiction, other types of novel, comic strips, leisure magazines and consumer advertising frequently turned to 'the city of towers' as a new, exciting and *appropriate* imagery by which to portray the future city (Sheckley, 1978; Gold, 1985). So too did a popular medium that grew to maturity in the inter-war years and which forms the focus of this essay - cinematographic film.

The aim of this paper is to explore the urban imagination of producers, directors, set-designers and others involved in the creation of film during the period 1919-39. A representative sample of feature and documentary, short and full-length films was taken in order to throw light on three broad questions: namely, what was the character of the imagery of the future city that was put forward, how was it created and what did it signify and, finally, what links can be found between the visual imagery of the cinema and kindred ideas in the literature of architecture and the arts? Before turning to these questions, however, three broad points should be noted.

First, there is no attempt here to trace lines of direct influence in the process of communication or, put another way, to see what effects the showing of a particular film had on its audience in terms of attitudinal or behavioural change. Desirable though it might seem to the casual observer to seek such cause-and-effect, the experience of more than 60 years of mass communication research demonstrates the futility of pursuing cause-and-effect relationships outside of the broad matrix of social communication, of which mass communication is but part (see Chapter 1). Indeed, for the purpose of analysis, there is no assumption here that film need be more than a medium of mass transmission (Briggs, 1960, p29). I have simply employed film as an index of the creative imagination at particular times and to trace the relationship between *avant-garde* and popular culture. Both are legitimate uses of media content, dealing as they do with the communicator-communication relationship rather than the far more problematic issue of the links between communication and audience (McQuail, 1983, pp123-46).

Secondly, the treatment of the future city needs to be seen in the light of the cinema's treatment of the city in general. Throughout its history, the cinema has shared that intellectual bias against the city that has marked contemporary literature and the arts. Urban sets and location work are taken to give plausibility to a film's story-line by tapping the widely-held view that large cities are alienating and hostile places, in which there are enormous contrasts in wealth and living conditions and in which there is a seamy underlife all too ready to rise to the surface. Few crime or gangster movies, for instance, lack any reference to an urban setting, and the squalor of the inner-city slum all too often is taken to symbolise the metropolitan housing condition. There are, of course, films that depict the opposite view of cities as warm, neighbourly and stimulating places, but these films are very much the exception to the rule (Gold, 1984a).

Finally, a word should be said about the scope of the survey used here. Even in a period as temporally restricted as the one considered in this paper, an enormous number of films may be taken to have 'urban content' (Sutcliffe, 1984). These range from fleeting location shots as a backdrop to the film's action to detailed film essays on particular cities, which, for example, in the period under consideration would include such classics of the silent screen as Alberto Cavalcanti's *Rien que les heures* (1926), Walter Ruttmann's *Berlin: symphony of a great city* (1927) and King Vidor's *The crowd* (1928). To be considered here, a film had to deal consciously and specifically with the future city; constructing sets to give plausibility to futurist fiction or highlighting existing schemes that gave hope for, or conveyed nightmares about, the urban future. Films that did not meet this strict criterion were excluded.[1]

Feature Films

The natural starting point for this study was Friedrich ('Fritz') Lang's film *Metropolis* (1926). Made at Ufa Studios in Berlin, *Metropolis* is critically acclaimed as a masterpiece of the German silent cinema and as a profound influence upon the Western film industry's portrayal of the future city.

Having said this, it is important to recognise the extent to which *Metropolis* incorporated broader currents of urban thought. Raymond Williams (1973, p274), for instance, indicated the debt the film owed to nineteenth-century literature:

> The sombre vision of man divided into brute labour and trivial consumption, and then of the city shaped physically to embody these worlds is expressed again and again. Once of its most remarkable successors is Lang's film *Metropolis*, in the nineteen twenties.

More directly, the film was indebted to the Expressionist movement, which still flourished in mid-1920s Berlin, to the cinematographic traditions of France and Germany, and, in particular, to Oswald Spengler's book *The Decline of the West* (1918). With its blend of late German romanticism and agrarian mysticism, Spengler's book effectively combined a deep fascination with the city with a horror of the inhumanity of urban life. As Rhode (1966, p87) has noted:

> (The book's) style is turgid, often silly, its content remote from reality and sometimes potentially vicious ... But Spengler's romanticism is powerful staff, and one can see why Lang was stimulated by it ... above all, he is fascinated by the idea of the city.

Yet while these various influences can be discerned, *Metropolis* is far more than a simple fusion of existing traditions, for it broke new ground in its technical achievement, in the power of its visual imagery, and in its striking portrayal of the future city.

Lang described the film as a 'horror tale of the future', presumably set in the year 2000 AD - the date given in Thea von Harbou's book (1972) of the screenplay. A story of oppression, revolt and reconciliation in a tyrannic society, the film's action occurred against the backdrop of a giant multi-level city. For convenience, the depiction of that city may be discussed in terms of its two component parts - above and below ground.

The upper city was the opulent city of commerce and trade, in which were to be found the luxurious homes and pleasure palaces of the ruling classes (Fig. 6.1). Created by using a technique invented by the film's special effects director Eugen Schüfftan - in which miniatures were reflected in mirrors to give the illusion of gargantuan scale (Barsacq, 1976, p33) - the footage showing the upper city appears at several key moments of the film. With the towering buildings of (seemingly) reinforced concrete and glass, the segregated pedestrian and vehicle systems, the espousal of technology and modernity, it is tempting to link the design of this set to the thinking of the Modern Movement in architecture. Lang, after all, had received some basic training in architecure in his native Vienna and modern architecture had recently been depicted in the French *avant-garde* cinema, for example, in the sets designed by the architect Robert Mallet-Stevens for Marcel l'Herbier's *l'Inhumaine* (1923). Yet while some writers have tried to draw such a conclusion (e.g. Tulloch, 1976, pp48-9), Lang made it clear that the real source of his inspiration was New York and, in particular, Lower Manhattan. In an interview, Lang described how he conceived the basic idea for *Metropolis* while in New York for the premiere of his film *Die Nibelungen* (1924). Falling foul of a law that still classified him as an 'enemy alien', even though the war had been over for more than five years, Lang was forced to remain overnight on his ship, the S.S. *Deutschland.* Seeing the city from the ship's deck, Lang commented on what he saw:

> a street lit as if in full daylight by neon lights and topping them oversized luminous advertisements moving, turning, flashing on and off, spiralling ... something which was completely new and fairy-tale-like for a European in those days and this impression gave me the first thought of an idea for a town of the future (quoted in Ott, 1979, p27).

After being given permission to land, Lang proceeded to explore the city. He gained the impression that:

Fig. 6.1

> 'it was the crossroads of multiple and confused human forces (irresistably driven) to exploit each other and thus living in perpetual anxiety ... The buildings seemed to be a vertical veil, shimmering, almost weightless, a luxurious cloth hung from the dark sky to dazzle, distract and hypnotize. At night the city did not give the impression of being alive; it lived as illusions live. I knew then that I had to make a film about all of these sensations' (quoted in Ott, 1979, p27).

The vivid imagery of the overground city was juxtaposed with that of the underground city - a brutal, dehumanising environment in which were to be found the housing of the workers and the machines and powerhouse that serve Metropolis. The daily lives of the workers were set against the starkness of their living conditions and the severity of their working environment. With lives dominated by the call of the factory whistle, the workers were depicted in several scenes returning to their homes in identical, monotonous, tenement structures that represented nothing more than minimal shelters for a workforce that was an extension of the machines which it served. The scene was again produced by means of special effects, using a dual lens camera technique.[3]

After portraying these very different worlds, the plot seemed to bring about a rapprochement between the two major elements of the social order, between labour and capital, and implicitly between the two worlds to which they belong. The audience is left in no doubt that the future metropolis would be a nightmare city. Yet despite the clarity of the message, the moral of the story was quickly overlooked in favour of the strength of the imagery of the upper city. As Eisner (1976, p86) commented: 'Lang's vision of skyscrapers, an exaggerated dream of New York's skyline, multiplied a thousandfold and divested of all reality ... (had) become truly the town of the future'.

The power of the imagery can be witnessed in its impact on two films that appeared shortly afterwards. The first was Maurice Elvey's *High Treason*, made for Gaumont in 1929. A film with a strongly pacifist message, *High Treason* was set in 1940 and contained scenes of aerial bombardment in London and New York. The relevant sets were produced by means of somewhat crude models and bore a strong resemblance to the upper city of *Metropolis*, with the high-rise buildings of a similarly Gothic appearance. The deficiencies of the special effects, combined with the film's naive and 'politically artless forecast of 1940' and its poor sound quality ('actors in need of throat pastilles') meant that *High Treason* soon passed into obscurity (Low, 1971, pp 174, 205).

Much the same may be said for the second film, David Butler's science-fiction musical *Just Imagine*, made for Fox Films in 1930. The plot was a lavish extravaganza involving space-travel and featured a notable set of New York in 1980 (Fig. 6.2). Inspired directly by Lang's film, the set was produced by means of models and was designed by the collaborative efforts of the art director Stephen Goosson, who had worked for some years as an architect in Detroit, and the film's mechanical effects director Ralph Hammeras. The New York of 1980 was clearly a city that had undergone major structural change since 1930. As seen in Figure 6.2, it was envisaged as a city of 200-storey skyscrapers, with vast urban motorways, bridges spanning huge chasms, and skies dotted with aircraft. The use of light to give the set a luminous, almost ethereal, quality is again reminiscent of Lang. In itself *Just Imagine* was a box-office disaster, but some of its losses were to be recouped by re-using the footage of the futuristic city on several occasions during the 1930s, the most notable instance being the Universal serial *Buck Rogers* (1939).

The next significant pointer to the film-maker's vision of the future city came in 1936 with the release of the British film *Things to Come* (London Film Productions). *Things to Come* was based on the novel by H.G. Wells (1933) entitled *The Shape of Things to Come* , and was the result of a collaboration between the film's producer, Alexander Korda, and Wells, then in his declining years. Wells had long wanted to use the cinema as a vehicle for his ideas and *Things to Come* was the first of two such films with Korda (the other being *The Man who could Work Miracles*, 1937).

Things to Come, however, was not an easy collaboration. While those concerned were deferential to Wells' enormous reputation, Wells himself was not experienced in cinematic writing and required three complete drafts before producing an adequate screenplay. Moreover, various allegorical sub-plots were built into the film's scenario, some of which remained incompletely developed in the final version (e.g. see Stover, 1982), and which served to obscure the underlying message of the film. Yet whatever the failings of the screenplay, as with *Metropolis* there is no doubt about the power of the visual imagery of the future city.

The action takes place against sets depicting 'Everytown' at three stages in its future (1940, 1970 and 2036 AD). The first two sets were

Fig. 6.2

based on the contemporary London. Everytown in 1940 resembled a scaled-down version of Piccadilly Circus and surrounding areas; Everytown in 1970 was the same area in ruins (created by artistically destroying the previous set). The 30 years of war that had led to this devastation had led to a vacuum in which society had regressed into a medieval tribalism. From this point an international freemasonry of scientists took over (a familiar Wellsian theme), dedicated to promoting peace and prosperity through progress. They set about the task of rebuilding Everytown.

It is here that the vision of the future city is seen. At this point too, convergence between the elite and popular media's views of the future city almost took place. Korda, himself of Hungarian extraction, employed the Hungarian emigré Laszlo Moholy-Nagy to design the set for the 2036 AD Everytown. One of the major figures associated with the Bauhaus, where he had taught from 1922-8, Moholy-Nagy was a formative influence on modernist approaches to the visual arts (e.g. Moholy-Nagy, 1939) as well as being a skilled artist, photographer, and stage and film-set designer. Models were built for the film and some footage was shot, with sequences emphasising the interplay of geometric shapes and light, but in the event only two short snatches were used in the final version (Banham, 1979, p26) Seemingly the design was regarded as too abstract for the cinema-going audience. New sets were therefore designed by a triumvirate of the film's French cinematographer, Georges Périnal, its American director, William Cameron Menzies, and Korda's younger brother, Vincent. Both Korda and Menzies had extensive experience in set-design, with Menzies being described by Barsacq (1976, p228) as 'possibly the greatest visual talent to work in films'. The results of their collaboration were some of the most durable and exciting images to emerge from the cinema during the inter-war years.

The city portrayed is based again on high-rise structures and rapid, segregated movement systems, but the design is recognisably a decade later in conception than *Metropolis*. Figure 6.3, for example, contains echoes of the new, almost sculptural, forms that were then being deployed on luxury blocks of flats. The effects were again produced by means of photographic illusion, in this case achieved by means of a hanging foreground miniature combined with a stage set on which the actors appear. In later scenes, views are shown of a city of Cartesian unity, with high buildings situated in park-like open space. In addition, room interiors are seen to be decorated in an aggressively futuristic manner, sparingly filled with high-tech

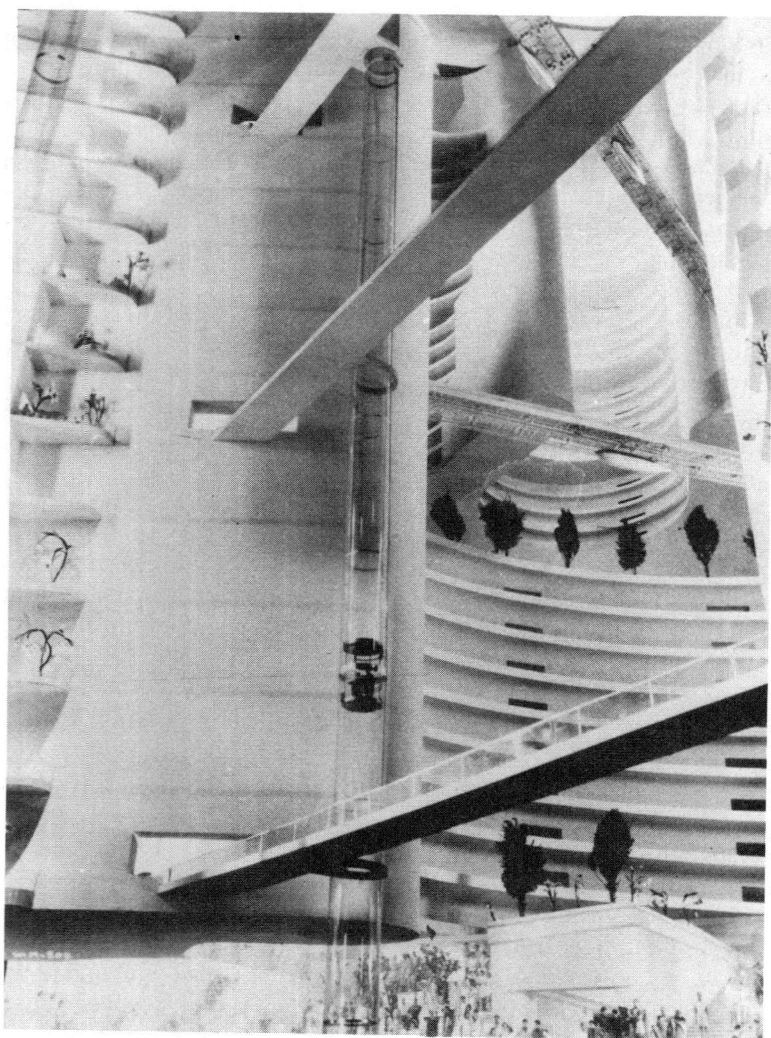

Fig. 6.3

functional furniture and video or televisual equipment.

On the surface, *Things to Come* presents a very different picture of the future city than Lang's *Metropolis*. Naturally both Korda and Wells knew about that film, but had quite different attitudes towards it. Korda admired *Metropolis* and was happy to refer to his own film as an 'elaborated *Metropolis*'. By contrast, Wells grudgingly admired the visual innovations of the film, but described it as 'quite the silliest film' (Kulik, 1975, pp146-7). Certainly there are things about Everytown in 2036 that are very different from Metropolis in 2000 AD. In particular, Everytown is an underground city. It symbolically represents a break with the past; the ruins of the old city above ground are removed and the area is landscaped, allowing the bucolic rural scene to return. The old architecture is implicitly related to the failed social order of the pre-war world, the modern architecture with the new Utopia. This clearly contrasts with Lang's underground city of oppression and deprivation, yet enough ambivalence is injected into the dialogue to cast doubt on whether this was Utopia at all. The note of questioning is a *caveat* rather than a moral, but it still provides a point at which parallels can be made between the two films. So too does the fact that the future cities depicted remain indissolubly linked to the times at which the films were made, despite the best endeavours of their creators. This is a point to which we will return later.

Documentaries and Films of Persuasion

So far the discussion has centred upon full-length feature films that tried to portray the long-term future, but this by no means exhausts the available source material. Changes in film technology in the late 1920s, with the introduction of safety film and smaller formats, meant that it was possible for commercial, governmental and voluntary organisations to make their own films for public showing. The 1930s therefore saw a massive growth in film production outside of the main feature studios, with the widespread use of film for commercial, educational and propaganda purposes and, in particular, the rise of the documentary movement.

The growth of the documentary movement in large measure reflected the concern of individuals on both sides of the Atlantic that social problems were being ignored in the commercial cinema. The feature studios and large distributors virtually turned their backs on the everyday realities of poor housing and unemployment, serving up a diet of fantasy and escape. Censorship also played its part. As Pronay (1981, p125) points out, film encouraged people to regard their economic and social condition as a personal and not a political problem, something that was achieved not through overt propaganda but:

> through the exclusion of any alternative viewpoint from the medium which they regarded as their escape into a world of dreams. Dreams are powerful stuff and so are visions: visions of our country, of other lands and of the future. Censorship ensured that dreams were not turned into nightmares of doubt and distrust and that there were no alluring visions of alternative new orders .

In turning to look at social problems, the documentary movement effectively ensured that its films would rarely be seen in the commercial cinema, tending to be shown at film societies and similar venues to small and committed audiences (Aldgate, 1981, p102). This, however, in no way obviates the value of such films as an alternative source of insight into the film-maker's view of the future city for, while not usually concerned with the city of the far future, documentary films were frequently forward-looking and gave specific indications as to those elements of the emerging urban scene that film-makers felt gave hope for the future.[4]

This was particularly the case in Great Britain, with the long series of documentary films primarily concerned with housing conditions. Perhaps the most significant film in this respect, and the precursor of many similar films, was Arthur Elton and Edgar Anstey's *Housing Problems* (1935). Although the film followed in the broad traditions created by John Grierson and others in the British documentary movement and was directly influenced by the style of the American documentary series *The March of Time* (Fielding, 1978), *Housing Problems* contained two important innovations. First, it was sponsored by an industrial organisation, the British Commercial Gas Association, about an issue of social importance in which there was no *direct* promotion of its own product. Secondly, it used interviews. People living in a slum clearance area in Stepney, London, appeared before the camera and gave their story of the housing in which they lived. They reappeared later to wax lyrical about the new housing they had been allocated. Although filming actually involved sound and camera gear sufficient to fill a large lorry, the seeming 'spontaneity and honesty' of the interview technique left a deep mark on documentary film-making (Sussex, 1975).

From our point of view, the manner and presentation of information in the film is of considerable interest. After sketching out the nature of the housing problem, face-to-camera interviews were held with four people 'who have to live in the slums'. The story told by Mrs Hill was typical:

> This house is getting on my nerves. We're shored up in every room. There's a staircase which you can't walk up ... one leg you want longer than the other. And the upstairs is coming downstairs where it's sinking. We've been to see the new houses and they're lovely. But here it gets on your nerves with everything filthy. Dirty, filthy walls and the vermin in the walls is wicked. But I'll tell you we're fed up.

She then provided the audience with a tour of the house commenting on the stage of the walls, the semi-collapsing staircase, the crumbling plaster and vermin.

After the first set of interviews, the film then moved on to show what can be done. Cutting to a picture of a medium-rise slab block of flats (Fig. 6.4), the Chairman of the Stepney Housing Committee stated that:

> The more enlightened public authorities have been applying

Fig 6.4

themselves to the task of slum clearance with energy. Public authorities have now the power to pull down slums and put up in their place new and fine houses.'

The audience was left in no doubt that flats were deemed an appropriate form for rehousing the working-class population who would be displaced by slum clearance schemes. On showing a model of an appropriate block of flats, the narrator supplied the following pedagogic note on flats and their construction:

> A great deal of thought from architects, engineers and other experts has gone into the design of buildings for rehousing. Here is a model of a block of flats prepared by the British Steelwork Association and based on recommendations by the Council for the Research on Housing Construction. The building has a steel frame which takes the whole weight. The walls do not have to support the weight of the building or the roof. They are made of light standard units which are fitted into position after the framework has been put up. All the parts of the building are standard. They can be brought complete from the factory and put into position at once.'

This sequence was then followed by a lengthy tour of two of the most adventurous schemes for municipal flats of the 1930s, namely Quarry Hill in Leeds and Kensal House in London. Their positive and modern features were elaborated at length (with some mention of the extensive use made of gas as a source of energy in such schemes). By contrast, schemes for cottage estates and individual houses-and-gardens then received a mere 20 seconds, dismissively qualified with the words that they '*could* be built' where land and resources permitted. Finally, the film showed the original interviewees, now tenants in the new flatted estate, and conveyed fulsomely their satisfaction with the new way of life.

There is, of course, nothing accidental about the manner or order in which visual material or commentary were presented. Despite the traditional prejudice against flats in Great Britain due to their association with tenements, a section of opinion amongst architects and social reformers had come round to regarding flats as 'an accepted form of dwelling for normal and respectable families' (Ravetz, 1974, p125) and as offering greater hope for the future than traditional 'overspill' housing estates. The sympathetic treatment that flats received in the film, the 'appeals to authority' made on their behalf (the approval of 'experts', 'more enlightened public authorities'), and the celebrated, but atypical, examples of estates depicted all helped to present the best possible image of flats. Other films were to continue the same themes.

Perhaps the most direct successor was *The Great Crusade: the Story of a Million Homes* (1936). Made by Pathé Films, which ensured it a wide audience in the commercial cinema, *The Great Crusade* was commissioned by the Ministry of Health. In essence it was an officially-approved version of *Housing Problems*, placing a cheerful and optimistic face on the National Government's scheme to eradicate slums in Britain by 1938. It was based on a scenario on which J.B. Priestley assisted, with the architect Alister Macdonald employed as technical assistant.

The format of the film followed *Housing Problems* closely. The audience was introduced to the slum problem through the experience of a family in south London. The two rooms which they occupied were shown to be infested by rats and damp, with peeling walls and rotting woodwork. A rapid survey of nine British cities was then taken (with an itinerary not dissimilar to that of Priestly's (1934) book *English Journey*), demonstrating that each had slums. The pivotal point in the film consisted of a close-up of the Minister of Health, Sir Kingsley Wood, sitting at his desk. He argued that the slums were a national disgrace and that something most be done about them. The story of the demolition of slums and rehousing their occupants was then told, with examples from each of the cities. Finally the original family were shown in their new flat in Wandsworth, with the obligatory statement from the *materfamilias*: 'it's like another world, sir'.

The rehousing schemes shown included both semi-detached, low density cottage estates and blocks of flats, but it is the latter upon which the camera lingered and which gained the truly appreciative comments. Interestingly *The Great Crusade* again followed *Housing Problems* in its advocacy of mass production and factory-building methods for housing. The audience was constantly assured that to abolish slums, greater scale of operations would be required. This would then make it possible for mechanisation to be introduced, which would in turn yield important economies of scale and thus permit improvements to be made in living conditions.

John Grierson's film *The Smoke Menace* (1937), which was again sponsored by the gas industry, gave a new twist to the now familiar story-line. The film was based around the theme that pollution is damaging to health and that its impact could be drastically reduced if people used the secondary fuels of gas and electricity rather than directly burning coal. After some 'science-explained-to-the-common-man' sequences with J.B.S. Haldane, the audience was left in no doubt where the better future was held to lie. The statement 'Gradually Britain is learning to house her people better' was juxtaposed with a visual image of a ten-storey block of flats; a comment about 'far-seeing authorities' did so against pictures of a six-storey balcony access block. Throughout one sees the close identification between blocks of flats and urban progress.

The same formula, with variations, was to be repeated in two more films sponsored by the gas industry. In Paul Rotha's *New Worlds for Old* (1938), a film which has a flippancy that has not stood the test of time, the 'grand tour' approach was again used - a broad survey of different schemes showing the progress being made in rehousing and giving considerable prominence to flats. Frank Sainsbury's *Kensal House* (1937) focused on one specific scheme in Kensal Green, west London, which had been built on the site of a demolished gasworks. Besides the usual presentation of the advantages of secondary fuels, the film was noteworthy for the insight it gives into the considerable innovations of this scheme, both in its design and management. Designed by the celebrated modern architect, Maxwell Fry, and managed by a notable proponent of flatted housing, Elizabeth Denby, Kensal House offered a wide range of social and communal facilities besides simply providing housing for the working class. The estate incorporated a community centre, kindergarten, créche, communal laundry and canteen facilities. Residents were also represented on committees and other bodies involved in the scheme's management. Overall, the scheme was presented as offering a progressive and comprehensive approach to planning, and a modest prototype for modern living. Certainly *Kensal House* was the nearest that the Modern Movement in British architecture came to getting their ideas presented in film during the inter-war years.

Not all the imagery, however, pointed in the same direction and an important, if isolated, exception that must be noted here is Ralph Steiner and Willard van Dyke's *The City* (1939). Unlike its British counterpart, the American documentary movement had produced little on urban subjects before 1939, being primarily noted for such films on rural or agrarian topics as King Vidor's *Our Daily Bread* (1934) and Pare Lorentz's films *The Plow that broke the Plains* (1936) and *The River* (1937). Yet although breaking new ground in its subject material and toning down the strong radical element in American documentary films of the period (Campbell, 1982), *The City* remained in the broad traditions of that movement in its concern with social problems and in its underlying attitude towards the metropolitan city. In addition, its joint directors had both worked with Lorentz and others in the non-profit film company Frontier Films before leaving in 1938 over a disagreement about the political direction of the company. *The City* was their first subsequent film.

The City was commissioned by the American Institute of Planners with the aid of a $50,000 grant from the Carnegie Corporation and was designed to be given its premiere at the 1939 New York World's Fair. It was based on Lewis Mumford's (1938) monograph *The Culture of Cities*, with Mumford himself providing the screenplay. Broadly speaking, the film followed the basic themes of the book in analysing the historical phases and social consequences of metropolitan life, and mirrored the book in that it was itself strongly influenced by the biological approach to urban development pioneered by Patrick Geddes (e.g. 1915). The film is divided into five segments, tracing the evolution of the small town into the great metropolis, highlighting the desire to escape from the city, and suggesting an alternative 'green city' which re-established society's harmony with its living environment.

After starting with scenes of a tranquil small town in New England, with its warm social relations and unhurried pace of life, the film cut dramatically from the blacksmith's forge to the furnaces of a steel-making industrial city. Images were presented of squalor and dirt, of children with nowhere to play except the dangerous streets and railroad tracks, and of smoke belching from chimneys and machinery. The film then moved on to the metropolis, in reality New York. To an accompaniment of the dramatic crescendoes of Aaron Copland's musical score and a scathing commentary, images were presented of noise and pollution, of buildings of inhuman scale, and of repeated symbols of soulless mechanisation. After then showing scenes of people trying to escape, with highways jammed with Sunday motorists en route for the coast, the film finished with an evocation of something better - the planned urban community (or perhaps, more accurately, suburban community). Stressing the continuity between the 'green city' and the small New England town of the opening sequences, the component elements of this harmonious settlement were outlined. Low density and cherishing open space yet clearly comprehensively planned for living and working, the 'green city' was held up as a readily attainable alternative. As the narrator noted: 'You take your choice, each one is real, each one is possible ... You and your children, the choice is yours'.

As it happened, the ideal community shown in the film did not actually exist. The town shown in the film was a composite of pictures from five different locations - Greenbelt (Maryland), Greendale (Wisconsin), Greenhills (Ohio), Los Angeles and Long Beach (California), all 'put together to make a synthetic community' (Levin, 1971, p189). The finished result appeared idyllic to some onlookers and antiseptic, even dangerously misleading, to others - Campbell (1982, p189), for example, complaining that the ending was:

> 'saturated with naive American optimism ... its major emphasis is on the transformation of living conditions prevalent in the contemporary industrial society in the utopian community to come'.

Realisable or not, naive or not, *The City* was nevertheless the most complete exposition of Garden City ideas for the urban future to be found in the cinema during this period.

Conclusion

In drawing this paper to a close, one may again return to the surprising degree of consensus to be found in film portrayals of the future city during the inter-war years. With the major, if important, exception of *The City*, the films examined showed the extent to which that broad vision, earlier termed 'the city of towers', had captured the film-maker's imagination.

Science fiction and fantasy films depicting the far future commonly showed cities of huge scale, dominated by high buildings and roadways. There were, of course, technical and artistic reasons why film-makers should find such imagery attractive. The 'city of towers' could be easily simulated in the studio by means of models and special effects and, in doing so, gave full reign to the creative powers of set-designers. In the process, they were to produce some of the most exciting and durable images to be found in films of this period - a fact demonstrated by the extent to which films such as *Metropolis* and *Things to Come* are still shown in the present day.

Nevertheless, such images would not have been used had film-makers not considered that audiences would find them appropriate and plausible settings for the film's action - at least as conceived at that time. That does not mean, of course, that there were no flaws in the imagery or in the logic that underpinned it. With the aid of hindsight, for example, it is easy to see how much the future cities depicted were tied to the technological knowledge of the period. *Metropolis* was less a prediction of the world of 2000 AD than it was a model of the 1920s scaled up to nightmare proportions and overlain with a pastiche of the latest that New York could offer. Equally, Wells's vision of Everytown now appears similarly timebound, with the portrayal of a twenty-first-century urban society that looked suspiciously like that of the 1930s. However, it would take many years before the gap between the sociological and technological imagination with respect to the 'city of towers' became fully apparent (Gold, 1984b); for the meantime what was presented seemed sufficiently plausible to lend credibility to the action.

It is this same element of credibility that also appealed to documentary film-makers. Concerned with the more immediate future, the documentary movement depicted those elements of the emerging urban scene that they felt gave hope for the future. In Britain particularly, this was often expressed in the form of advocacy of flats as an alternative for the rehousing of working-class communities displaced by slum clearance. In some cases, the advocacy was straightforward, as in the case of *Kensal House*; in other cases, it was more indirect, as when films were so constructed that it was the blocks of flats and other tall buildings that caught the eye and earned the praise from residents and narrators. Yet regardless of how the case was presented, the underlying message clearly emerged.

When taking the films of the period as a whole, it is tempting to suggest strong links between the *avant-garde* in architecture and the arts, links which fundamentally affected the cinema's portrayal of the urban future. While there are those to whom such unitary and tidy views of the world appeal, in reality the links were relatively tenuous - Lang's youthful architectural training, the occasional employment of an architect as technical consultant, and the like. What these films really show is that there was a broad climate of intellectual opinion, at least among an influential minority, that favoured change and was interested in new ideas for the future city. For them, the 'city of towers' held considerable promise, with alternative and more traditional viewpoints of those such as Lewis Mumford in *The City* appearing as merely an isolated cry. The exact significance of this imagery in influencing urban theory and practice in the world after 1945 is a matter on which, at this stage, one can only speculate. What does seem clear is that whichever way one looks at film in the period considered here, a particular pattern of expectation was being fuelled.

NOTES

1. It can be argued that many films could be taken as having a parenthetic relevance to this paper on the grounds that their depiction of the luxurious life-style of low-density American suburbia could be interpreted as an indication of aspirations for the future as, for example, with the output of the MGM studios while under the Art Directorship of Cedric Gibbons. While there is some truth in this point, even if the setting was often little more than stylistic convention, the dictates of time and expense made it essential to focus on those portrayals of the future city that were conscious and specific.

2. *Metropolis* is a difficult film to interpret. Its dialectic plot contains too many ambiguities to be easily summarised; ambiguities which were accentuated by the film's mauling at the hands of the distributors, who cut it down from over three hours to a bare 90 minutes. Indeed, certain elements of the scenario, particularly Lang's metaphysical concerns with the battle between modern science and occultism, were to disappear almost without trace in the process (Petley, 1973).

3. Described in Ott (1979, p125) as using one lens to photograph the miniature set while the other photographed the actors. The image, often monumental in appearance, was thereby achieved without recourse to double exposure.

4. I have left aside here the whole question of 'realism' in the documentary, an area of debate which has recently exercised film critics and historians. For more information, see Williams (1980).

FILMS

Butler, David *Just Imagine* (Fox, 1930)
Cavalcanti, Alberto *Rien que les heures* (1926)
Elton, Arthur and Anstey, Edgar *Housing Problems* (British Commercial Gas Association, 1935)
Elvey, Maurice *High Treason* (British-Gaumont, 1929)
Grierson, John *The Smoke Menace* (Realist Film Unit, for British Commercial Gas Association, 1937)
Korda, Alexander *Things to Come* (London Films, 1936)
Korda, Alexander *The Man who could work Miracles* (London Films, 1937)

Lang, Fritz *Die Nibelungen* (Ufa, 1924)
Lang, Fritz *Metropolis* (Ufa, 1926)
l'Herbier, Marcel *l'Inhumaine* (1923)
Lorentz, Pare *The Plow that broke the Plains* (US Government Resettlement Administration, 1936)
Lorentz, Pare *The River* (Farm Security Administration, 1937)
Pathé Films *The Great Crusade* (Pathé Films for the Ministry of Health, 1936)
Rotha, Paul *New Worlds for Old* (Realist Film Unit for Gas Industry/Paul Rotha Films, 1938)
Ruttmann, Walter *Berlin: Symphony of a Great City* (1927)
Sainsbury, Frank *Kensal House* (Gas, Light and Coke Company, 1938)
Van Dyke, Willard and Steiner, Ralph *The City* (Civic Films for the American Institute of Planners, 1939)
Vidor, King *The Crowd* (MGM, 1928)
Vidor, King *Our Daily Bread* (Viking Productions/United Artists, 1934)

ACKNOWLEDGEMENT

I would like to record my thanks to Martyn Youngs for his invaluable assistance on an early version of this paper.

CHAPTER 7: THE ENGLISH TELEVISION LANDSCAPE DOCUMENTARY: A LOOK AT GRANADA

Martyn J. Youngs

> Every decision to communicate something is, at the same time, a decision to suppress everything else (Gerbner, 1969, p205).

Studies of the feelings that the English have for their landscape and its representation in culture have been a strong tradition within British geography, particularly since the publication of H.C. Darby's (1948) study of Thomas Hardy's Wessex. More recently the tradition has continued with Lowenthal and Prince's studies of 'The English Landscape' (1964) and 'English Landscape Tastes' (1965), which are outstanding attempts to define and understand what is peculiar about the English and the landscapes they value. Other writers have followed Darby's example in circumscribing their topics more closely, concentrating on the works of individual authors, for example, Patterson (1965) on Walter Scott, Spolton (1970) on D.H. Lawrence, Jay (1975) on Francis Brett Young's Black Country, Cosgrove (1979) on Ruskin and Prince (1981) on George Crabbe's Suffolk. These together with Pocock's (1981) *Humanistic Geography and Literature* and Gold and Burgess's (1982) *Valued Environments* constitute a considerable body of knowledge concerned with the portrayal of landscape and places.

Nevertheless the dominant orientation has been towards 'higher culture' - mainly literature and art - to the neglect of studies that concern themselves with what the mass of the population read and view - popular culture. Certainly it is hard to find examples of geographic studies of popular culture. Amongst a meagre literature are papers by Sulzinger (1979) and Jarvis (this volume) on the landscape imagery in contemporary music; Solomon (1975), Clark and Allen (1977) and Gold (this volume) on the relationship between film and the urban environment; and by Burgess (1982b) on her involvement with the BBC programme 'The Fens'.

A much larger volume of relevant research on landscape tastes, however, is to be found in the literature of cognate disciplines. A useful start is found in Giddings's (1978) analysis of the BBC television serialisation of R.F. Delderfield's *A Horseman Riding By*, a series that had an audience of 7.5 - 8.0 million viewers (Paulu, 1981, p357). Giddings (1978, p588) suggested that the appeal of the series lay in the fact that the British have always 'stubbornly and proudly regarded themselves as a rural people, despite all the evidence to the contrary'. 'A Horseman Riding By', along with similar programmes, and advertisements for 'Country Thick Vegetable Soup', 'Country Life Margarine' and 'Farmhouse Cheese', appeal to a rural nostalgia - the idyllic country life is a backdrop to many TV commercials. In *A Horseman Riding By*, the setting is an arcadian myth which Delderfield described as 'the last Summer of the Old World' (quoted in Giddings, 1978, p588). It is an explicit rejection of urban industrial values and a cry for a return to supposedly older rural virtues Giddings (1978, pp588-9) concluded that:

> Not only is the myth very strong, it is almost totally inaccurate... There is something wholesome about agricultural work in the open air - even if we only watch it on our colour TV. Surely it is nearer to the lifestyle that God Almighty had in mind for us British? 'A Horseman Riding By' is one example of a substitute art which protects us from seeing the realities. That long Edwardian summer is a little pocket of idyllic ruralism to comfort and protect us.

Is all of this perfectly harmless? Raymond Williams (1973, p96) believed that it is 'difficult to over estimate the importance of this (myth) in modern social thought'. The theme of the rural idyll seems central to English culture, indeed Newby (1977, 1980a) contended that these mythical beliefs have greatly damaged chances of the improvement of wages and conditions of agricultural workers. They effectively represent a refusal to recognise such rural problems, for example, as poverty, poor communications, youth unemployment and declining social services. How could these problems exist 'in the midst of this splendidly bucolic existence?' (Newby, 1977, p12). The belief that work on the land has some intrinsic value or moral worth had led urban improvement campaigners to overlook these rural workers, 'for the agriculural worker more metaphysical rewards have been deemed to be adequate compensation for his labour' (Newby, 1977, pp14-15).

In a review article of the ten best-selling British non-fiction books, Newby (1980b, p324) addressed the problem of the origins of such images, contending that this list indicates the 'continuing potency of rustic iconography in British culture'. British readers had placed *The Country Diary of an Edwardian Lady* top of the list, followed by *The Sunday Times Book of the Countryside*, *James Herriot's Yorkshire* and *The AA Book of British Villages.* These were 'handsomely packaged guides to a rural Britain which appears more timeless than the public sector borrowing requirement'. Within these guides, a working, food-producing environment has become transformed into a purely visual form, to be visited and admired but never explained: the problems are never mentioned. Indeed this point is readily conceded in the foreword to *The Sunday Times Book of the Countryside* by John Fowles (1980, np):

> I suspect the book's very excellence and attractiveness requires a warning to the unwary. The greatest threat to our countryside is less the physical harm we do them than our detachment from their reality. For two centuries now we have become increasingly an urban culture, increasingly in exile from what exists outside our cities. A major danger of such exile is that one can fall in love with pictures of things.

Perhaps even more significant is the role of television in this respect. Television increasingly fills many lives; viewing has risen from 13.5 hours per person per week in 1960 to 18.5 hours in 1978 (Paulu, 1981, p353) - the major use of time for most people after work and sleep. As argued elsewhere (Jenkins and Youngs, 1983; Youngs and Jenkins 1984), perhaps what makes television so pervasive is that because it looks like reality, people assume that it is reality. Barthes (1979, p11) has called this the 'falsely obvious', for television is the product of many forces, such as a company structure, available technology, advertisers and, of course, many people and their ideas. Yet what images are conveyed and what are the values that underpin them? In attempting to investigate these questions, I have examined the content of landscape documentaries - television programmes and series that deliberately set out to portray the English landscape. In doing so I have taken the documentary maker's own intentions as the defining characteristics rather than impose any terms of my own. Particular use is made here of a case study of a series entitled *This England: The Pennines, A Writer's Notebook* that was made by Granada Television, a major British commercial television company.

At the outset, however, it is important to say something about the historical antecedents of the series at Granada.

The Landscape Documentary at Granada

Writing about Denis Mitchell's programme *Never and Always* (1977), David Wheeler (1977, p825) launched an attack on the television landscape documentary and its portrayal of the English countryside:

> In the English countryside, as every hardened documentary watcher will testify, the sun always shines. Apple boughs cast dappled patterns on old brick walls, the furrows left by the plough are deep and rich and even, lambs frolic, bees buzz, it is *f*11 or better and old men wipe their brows to recall the times when they were a lad ... Most rural documentaries omit some of the other realities of rural living.

Never and Always was part of a wider project entitled *This England*. This project began in 1965 and was to be a wide-ranging series covering many aspects of life in Britain between 1965 and 1968. Around the executive producers, Denis Mitchell and Norman Swallow, were gathered what Granada called 'some of the best young directors in television' (GIP). The series was an attempt to foster what Swallow (1966) has called 'personal documentaries'. The style had its roots at the BBC, particularly the *Monitor* series with which John Schlesinger, Ken Russell and Mitchell himself were all connected: Swallow (1966, p176) defined as personal documentary 'a programme ... which, through its imaginative handling of reality expresses his own attitude not only to the programme's immediate subject matter but to the whole of the world in which he lives'. The 'film school' associated with the *This England* project was seen, certainly by Swallow, to have its roots in the 1930s British documentary movement (see Gold, this volume). In a sense the television documentary was to take over the role the 1930s movement had taken on. '(It) was left for us to pick up the pieces, to assume the social responsibility ... (The films were to be) both personal and true, and ... the individual work of a creative mind' (Swallow, 1966, p219). Denis Mitchell (personal communication, 1981) has said that his idea was, and still is, to transfer what Hazlitt had undertaken in the literary essay into the form of the television film. The methodology and philosophy which informs the personal documentary style had enormous implications for the landscape documentary.

The Personal Documentary

The personal documentary is intended neither for the individual with simply technical expertise nor for someone who desires only to reflect 'reality'; it is a form which enables those with something to say the freedom to do so. In Mitchell's (1966, p178) words, the director who uses this form has the task to 'imply his own view of life, he can never openly state it by editorialising, without distorting the truth that is the lives of the people he has chosen'. It is this form which perhaps is closest to raising the documentary to an 'art', since the director is using the images and sounds of people, places and events as symbols. Mitchell (1981, p108) later described his purpose thus: 'I don't believe you can do serious work unless you have something serious to say, and I find that I can best express my vision in television films about people'. He continued that he wanted to comment on the 'essence of the human situation'. There is no pretence at objectivity, indeed almost a rejoicing at the subjectivity involved. Peter Morley, originally part of the *This England* team, asked 'how can you get at the pure, uncontaminated truth when right at the beginning there is a subjective selection, not only of the scene being filmed, but also of the composition of the shot, let alone the final selection and juxtaposition of material in the cutting room?' (Morley, 1966, p187).

The method of the personal documentarist requires considerable skill. For example, it could involve the juxtaposition of sound and visual material to invest meaning; the counterpointing of sound on visuals, or the use of music to build an emotional content which was not previously present; or the use of wild-track and voice-over [1] to accomplish a similar objective. The film *Chicago* (BBC, 1961), made by Mitchell, was not intended to be an objective portrayal of place, but rather a personal essay on the violence and pathos of urban society. As such, it is a superb example of the personal documentary style, in which Mitchell manipulates images and sounds so that something may be said which is more powerful than the sum of the individual elements.

The camera shows the floor numbers changing in a rising lift whilst the sound track is composed of a man saying:

> I'd like my children to live in a world where if I had shortcomings and I couldn't keep up, the world would come and take me by the hand and say 'Alright, you're going to slow us up a little bit but you've got to come along too; you're a human being, you're a human being'.

Swallow (1966, p188) argued that the use of that particular sound over that particular image sums up not necessarily Chicago *per se*, but what Mitchell felt about the manner in which modern cities treat their citizens. Following on from this there is a temptation simply to apply auteur theory[2], but these films are not the work of 'a single creative genius'.

These film-makers would probably have languished in obscurity if a business structure had not felt that there was a marketable commodity and supplied the funding. Michael Grigsby who worked at Granada during this period felt that it was no coincidence that he, and others like him, were brought to Granada. He concluded that it was 'enlightened management ... very intelligent people. Denis Forman is a very perceptive man' (Grigsby, 1981, p103). Denis Forman, who commissioned many of these documentaries, was asked if he thought that his influence was decisive in enabling this type of documentary to be made. He replied: 'Partly yes, I mean if there had been someone else there who wasn't interested in this sort of thing there wouldn't have been so many made' (Forman, 1981, p102).

Apparently, there was a positive policy at Granada to seek out and allow the production of low-budget personal documentaries, perhaps as part of Granada's company image of being non-aligned with the Establishment. However, it may have been also due to the IBA rules[3] on 'balance' in programming. Furthermore, one should not forget the effect of technology; 'each technique demands its own precise technical resources' (Swallow, 1966, p192). Surprisingly for a visual medium, it was the development of the portable quarter-inch audio tape recorder which enabled advances to be made. Previously, a film needed large and cumbersome optical sound equipment to obtain synchronised sound. With the new recorder, spontaneous speech could be captured and then placed with silent film during editing. Hence, it was the combination of sound cut to vision that contained the subtle emotion of the form, a combination imposed by technical limits, and perhaps an example of the mode of production's influence on culture. The large 35mm film equipment and its attendant crew also presented problems, for it is difficult to remain unobtrusive with such equipment. The ability to catch people going about their everyday business unawares had to await the introduction of the high quality 16mm camera. Whilst one problem was overcome with its use, the problem of sound still remained since the camera became very unwieldy when it was 'blimped' (silenced). The situation was finally alleviated by the introduction of the light and quiet 'Eclair' camera. This allowed directors and cameramen to move discreetly and unobtrusively around the location, while maintaining the quality that was demanded. The final significant development was the ability to edit videotape with as much precision as film. Granada initially developed this themselves. The use of video technology allowed longer periods of 'filming' without the need for reloading, with again the emphasis upon being inconspicuous.

The landscape documentaries produced by Granada were therefore heavily dependent on a technology, a company, a management ethos and the ideas of a small group of creative personnel. It is worth repeating that the films were not supposed to be objective portrayals of reality, and must be approached from an awareness of that position. They wanted to communicate ideas to the audience, which they undertook by utilising two sound and vision technologies and putting them together to say something more than that which the individual parts could ever do.

From *This England* to *Gosling's Travels*

Granada's landscape documentaries were generally based around central characters. To take an example, while including the usual visually picturesque parts of Yorkshire (the Calder Valley), *The Gamekeeper* (1968) was essentially concerned with a gamekeeper, Joe Pye. Nevertheless, there were exceptions. For instance, *Elegy* (1967) seems more concerned with a place (Hebden Bridge) and was a 'portrait of decline' (GIP). The programme and the visual material presented fall into the tradition of a stark image of industrial despoliation set in the North of England. *Living for a Change* (1967) was also concerned with what two men are doing to change Oldham's reputation of being 'the oldest, dirtiest town in the North of England' (GIP). Both *Elegy* and *Living for a Change* belong to a fairly traditional treatment of industrial places - traditional, certainly, within the context of romantic imagery. In another film, *A Hill, Some Sheep and a Living* (1966), the backdrop is provided by the 'bleak hills in one of England's northern counties' (GIP). It relates the story of farmers battling in a hostile environment and is a heroic portrayal of man's struggle against the elements to scratch a living. Like much of the output from Granada, it was a story related with warmth for the people presented, with the landscape standing as a symbol for the harshness of the environment.

The *This England* project appears to have been curtailed in 1967 and only reappeared in the late 1970s with a new series, opening with a rather predictable portrayal of Blackpool. The programme entitled *Home from Home* (1977) rejoiced in stating that Blackpool is a 'brash, boisterous - some would say vulgar - seaside resort' (GIP). All of these qualities are exploited to the full by the human interest element - the Wynter family - but Blackpool is as much a character in the show as Grandma Wynter. However, *This England* returned to its earlier tradition in a later film *The Wanderer* (1978) which looks at 'the modern industrial landscape' (GIP) through the eyes of the Czechoslovakian artist Jirc Borsky. It is concerned to show his sense of Britain as a place and his mixed feelings for the landscape as an immigrant. 'I like the place I am staying at very much. I like the countryside. But the churches I seek, the walls, they were not built by my forefathers' (GIP). This theme continues as we are shown Borsky's pictures and their depiction of industrial landscapes. The film traces the sources of these renderings of place, 'in the houses, the factories, the people and the way they spend their leisure hours in modern British towns' (GIP). Whilst *The Wanderer* seems concerned with place it also exemplifies another aspect of television landscape documentaries, namely, the concern to find the off-beat element and the 'character' (a theme to which we will encounter again presently).

In *Millom, Just a Name* (1979), there is a return to the idea of northern England's industrial decline by the portrayal of the closure of Hodbarrow iron ore mine and associated works. The film examines this decline through the eyes of the former employees and their families and is concerned with the people, their place and the landscape of decline. *Millom* is also familiar in its nostalgic reflections on our industrial past, a character in the film recalls the 'whistles and clanking . . and at night the sky would be red with the glow of furnaces' (GIP). In its search for human interest, we meet Hodbarrow's oldest surviving miner, then 95 years of age, who recounts a story or two. The emphasis is upon the strength of people 'against the odds' (a familiar theme), against redundancy, against unemployment, against the destruction of their lives. The camerawork appears to be good in its evoking of the atmosphere of the place, revealing its 'down-to-earth' nature. People being portrayed in their place seems the strength of the *This England* series.

Ray Gosling's Travels

Gosling's Travels began as a series for regional use by Granada in 1968, with the first two films being on Barrow-in-Furness and Bournemouth. According to the Granada publicity, all the films are 'about places' but they remain also personal reflections on the places that Ray Gosling visited and the people he met, or contrived to meet.

Alan Coren (1975, p14) placed Gosling alongside such other British documentary presenters as Fyfe Robertson, Slim Hewitt, Monty Modlyn, Johnny Morris and Alan Whicker. All are 'characters' in their own right and are needed by television 'to ginger up documentary with personality'. Furthermore, Gosling seeks out the quirky and eccentric kind of person for his programmes. He is portrayed as a 'working-class lad', with deep 'working-class roots'. It is an image that brings with it a supposed naivety, innocence and non-conformity; qualities that he brings to bear on the places and people that he descends upon. The publicity material aids this image, revelling in the fact that he has brought controversy to many of the 'posher places' that he has visited. 'Posher places' is a term used with purpose. It exemplifies his image as a 'working-class lad' looking at what the 'nobs' are getting up to. This tone is always just beneath the surface.

The programme *Bath* (1975) exemplifies Gosling's quirky style of presenting places. He states that the programmes are about the 'small talk of our country. The detail, the feel of a place' (GMP, 1975). In other publicity material Gosling has written that:

> The films are portraits of places ... They don't pretend to be comprehensive portraits, but I do aim to give an accurate flavour of the place ... the tiny but significant ingredients that give each particular place in Britain its own special character (GMP, 1975.

This particular programme centres on Bath's past, particularly the city's Roman and Regency associations. Gosling also considers the effect of the Department of Health and Social Security's withdrawal of funding from the spa waters and he also claims that 'Bath has been savagely attacked and sacked by economic forces ... Bureaucracy, property developers, planners have tried to reshape it' (GMP, 1975). Yet the first example of seriousness is lightened by Gosling considering the implications of bottling the water for sale, like that of 'Vichy'. 'May I have two bottles of Bath water, please?', Gosling muses. In another sequence, Gosling hardly had time to stand up from sucking a buttercup in a meadow than the viewer was 'plunged among freaks and quirks' (Coren, 1975, p14). Gosling meets a lady with a tame blackbird, people doing the 'Hokey-cokey' dance in the Roman baths, and a transcendental meditator. To Coren the film indulged Gosling, arguing that perhaps the film might not be about Bath or its people, rather it is concerned with the media personality Ray Gosling. The impression is reinforced by the fact that Gosling himself is rather quirky and the Granada publicity makes much of the eccentric people that he meets - 'a man who's a wizard on Druids and magic lines, with a clipped privet toad in his garden'. The man is also 'a pamphleteer and propagator of the legend of Kind Bladnd, ancient king of Britain' (GMP, 1975). The old accusations against television of trivialisation and sensationalism can be evoked.

A Village for Christmas was produced in 1975 as a Christmas Special. The village is described by the publicity material as a 'dream village', going on to say that 'Ray was looking for a working village, yet as pretty as the picture on a traditional Christmas card and settled for Hook Norton in Oxfordshire' (GMP, 1975). In the publicity material, and one suspects the film, there is an apparent ambivalence. On the one hand the emphasis is placed upon an entertaining portrait of a picturesque Cotswold village. On the other there is an awareness that change is occurring in rural areas, with traditional crafts and industries being transformed if not actually disappearing. 'The hedges are traditional but the man who lays them turns out to be a night-shift worker at a car factory' (GMP, 1975). Granada seem to have wanted to make a traditional travel documentary, showing the Christmas viewer a slice of 'olde England', but they seem to have been in difficulties finding material to fulfil their prejudices. There remains the question of why there was the desire to do a programme about a 'Christmas Card' village. Commonsense informs us that it would have been light, pleasant Christmas television fayre. In a more general sense it is indicative of television adhering to tried and trusted formats which are known to deliver an audience to advertisers.

Mitchell's *'Never and Always'*

> *Never and Always* is the story of one year in the life of the country village in Norfolk (Great Massingham) where Denis Mitchell lives. It is the story of the changing seasons, the cycle of life and death, seed time and harvest, generation succeeding generation as cornfields ripen, lambs grow old, children are born and old men die (GIP, 1977, parentheses added).

If my intention was simply to wage a polemic bewailing television documentaries reinforcing a romantic, idyllic and picturesque image of the English countryside, then *Never and Always* would have been the case study to labour that point. Christopher Dunkley (1977) wrote that: 'Mitchell showed us the conventional images of the pastoral idyll - pink roses and blue skies, a white wedding in a country church, those indefatigable seagulls following the plough'. Furthermore, it was all 'soft focus pastoral scenes in high summer; slow dissolves: intense close ups ... the picture remained that all the countryside was idyllic' (Trewin, 1977, p15). Denis Potter (1977, p35) stated that '*Never and Always* paced out the seasons of the year with all the traditional lyricism of country portraiture'. Finally, Bernard Davis (1977, p16) recalled that the image presented was attractive on one level - the 'picture postcard level ... (for it) showed us both in intimate close-up and in panoramic view the beauties of the traditional Norfolk countryside'. It is as if Mitchell had intended to parody the traditional landscape documentary. All the ingredients are present; sun light (smeared and diffused), hedge-hopping helicopter-borne cameras, and those ever-present 'country characters'. Mitchell seeks out the latter with a vengeance; 'he interviewed the crusty old characters so beloved of the traditional TV documentary' (Dunkley, 1977, p13).

This film fulfilled Howard Newby's thesis of the media propounding an image that the countryside is where English traditional values lie and that our urban-based society is in decline. Mitchell used the imagery to convey his sense of depression about contemporary society, as such it lies within the personal documentary sub-genre; but it remains a deeply reactionary film. An elderly woman says, "I wouldn't want to be born now. I'm glad I was born when I was". This film, notes Wheeler (1977, p825), has none of the 'realities of rural living (where) the doctor will not come unless you are dying, and the last bus went half an hour ago ... and where rheumatism is a way of life ... The visual evidence was that the countryside is still a good place to live in, better still if you are not on a countryman's wages.' As Raymond Williams (1973) has suggested, a romantic attachment is only usually felt for the land by those who do not toil upon it. In Mitchell's countryside the sun always shines and the wind does not cut. This is not the Norfolk landscape, but the melancholy result of a very troubled man. It is a reaction against those who would seem to have most to gain from the things that Mitchell bewails.

Maryport (1979)

In this programme, Ray Gosling once again played the role of 'the visitor' - the naive innocent at large. Gosling leans over backwards to convey the idea that people are special to him and are all really the same. Maryport is described as a 'one class town', but the interviews with the fisherman and the Lord Mayor's agent tend to seriously undermine this thesis. Commenting on the programme Mitchell is cited in one review as stating that Maryport was 'not offensively pretty, but pretty enough' (Lane, 1979, p3) and in another that it 'was pretty enough for all normal purposes' (North, 1979, p15). This does beg the questions of what 'pretty enough' and 'normal purposes' actually mean. The answer is presumably to convey the message of nostalgia and despair. There is an atmosphere, a sense of Maryport as a decaying seaside town. The poignancy of this film's portrayal of a town in decline in the Solway Firth cannot be escaped.

A Writer's Notebook

Nostalgia for an idyllic past age pervades the documentary films mentioned above. Leo Marx (1973), Lowenthal (1975, 1982), Raymond Williams (1975), John Barrell (1980) and Fraser Harrison (1983) are among many who have noted that successive generations have mused upon a supposedly happier time, which is usually just before their own birth. As Lowenthal (1982, p74) put it:

> Much of the pleasure taken in relic strewn or reminiscent landscapes derives from their apparent contrast with the scenes that surround us. The belief that things were better back then is

> widespread, especially among the elderly, whose preferred landscapes often antedate their own arrival on the scene (Lowenthal, 1982, p74).

Within *This England: The Pennines, A Writer's Notebook* people profess their belief that there was an arcadian age superior to today and images of activities and landscapes reinforce these notions. At times this is explicit, for example, as when Gosling talks of a 'Montague Burton' shop with eyes misty for a bygone tailoring age, and other times implicit, such as when we are shown images of people and landscapes which presumably are meant to evoke that Elysian past. For the purposes of this discussion I have reduced the images to two categories; namely those relating to people, and those relating to places and landscapes, although the difference within any one scene is largely a matter of emphasis.

People

Near to the end of the first programme there is a section of about six minutes in length which seems to stand apart from the rest of the film. It has a number of informal interviews interspersed with landscape shots, and the impression given is totally nostalgic. Past times and activities are discussed, whilst pipe music echoes plaintively in the background. The section opens with an elderly man overlooking Swaledale. With his weather-beaten face and accent he certainly qualifies as a 'local character'. We then go to 'Bill-up-steps' and a conversation ensues:

> DAVID WRIGHT[4]: "Seen a few changes then?"
>
> BILL: "Oh aye, by gum aye. Dale was full o' folk, good folk. We're getting a lot of incomers now. Some of 'ems alright and some of 'ems now't; Foreigners."

Immediately after 'foreigners' the image cuts to hikers, these presumably are the 'now't'. The question invited Bill to be nostalgic, and nostalgic he was as he stands at the top of his steps in an ancient collarless shirt and braces. From here we travel to men building a dry-stone wall. The pipe-lament comes up and one of them says "It's the old fashioned way, isn't it?" The emphasis is clearly on bygone skills.

We return to Swaledale, the old man talks of the hay crop and we cut to people racking hay. A tractor appears, but this quickly goes out of our view as a close-up begins of an elderly woman hay-making. On then to a churchyard, where another elderly man, replete with cloth cap, is shown scything. Wright immediately places the emphasis of the conversation on the past by enquiring where he learnt to scythe, but he only replies that he was taught as a boy. Undaunted, Wright has another try:

> WRIGHT: "What was the first job you had on the farm when you left school, then?"

> MAN: "Well mostly shepherding, shepherding and this sort of work ... but it wasn't bailing in those days ... it was all cut by hand, all round the dale was cut by hand."

As the man says this the pictures are of the dale - of old buildings, fields and moorland. Presumably they are intended to evoke that boyhood landscape.

In this section of the programme the emphasis is on people, this is a dominant theme in the series, as we might expect. Earlier Wright had questioned Gosling:

> WRIGHT: "This book you are going to write about England, what's it going to be about?"

> GOSLING: "Well I don't know yet, that's the point of the notebooks, but I tell you one thing that strikes me; everywhere we go we meet people of strength and quality and yet you read the papers and it's gloom, Britain in decline and all that."

The nostalgic element in this concerns Gosling's philosophy, which was expressed in programme three as a belief that 'people will overcome all obstacles, all themes, all concepts'. His philosophy is an optimistic belief in people, which from the evidence may be taken to mean older people and their values, but the nostalgia resides in the belief that in earlier periods people had less obstacles to overcome. He believes in people, but not the society and institutions that some of those people have created. This is essentially the idea that Rousseau popularised - the chains of contemporary society replacing the supposed freedom of an arcadian past. In programme three Gosling says that a Mr Leet, the owner of an old water-mill, "has a problem". He wants people to come and look around the mill, but he also wants donations, for if he was to charge an entrance fee this would cause the problem. "If he did charge", states Gosling, "he'd have all the bureaucrats, all the inspectors of health and safety, he'd have VAT, he'd have all the troubles upon him and he doesn't want that". Gosling clearly desires a supposedly simpler age, when all men were free to do as they wanted, in itself as naive and blinkered an approach as ever nostalgia produced. Further, he seems disagreeably disposed to many of the facets of contemporary society - even the humour. After looking at illustrations by George Cruikshank he commented to Wright, "I liked those because they were for everybody, they weren't clever like so much of satire is today". Gosling and his people are common, everyday folk who talk of a simpler past, as they sit eating their fish and chips from newspaper.

Landscapes and Places

Many of the landscape shots serve to reinforce the soundtrack. The man with the scythe talking of past haymaking in Swaledale has already been mentioned. When he was talking we were presented with pictures of empty moorland and old stone buildings set starkly against a brooding sky. However, there remains the deeper question of what constitutes a nostalgic landscape. In this series they are images of a slow moving, little changed, and largely upland agriculture; a picture of streams and hills, lanes and farmyards and picturesque stone walled buildings. It is not suggested that these do not exist, but the televisual montage conveys the impression that all is quiet, blissful and static. Where are the corrugated-iron dutch barns, fertiliser bags, limestone quarries and ordinary people who don't wear caps or look as if they have just walked off the film set of *All Creatures Great and Small* (the BBC television series set in the Pennines of the 1930s)? Boyd (1981) has noted the phenomenon of places seeming like stage-sets in relation to both Manhattan and Oxford, whilst Lowenthal (1977) has written on the creation of 'bicentenial landscapes'. Men walk with sheepdogs (where are the poodles?), down quiet lanes and through sleepy villages.

Gosling and Wright might travel past old barns and farms, through nucleated and street villages and hamlets, and look at isolated farmsteads. These appear ageless, yet are there no new houses? Does the ubiquitous semi-detached house and bungalow not exist in this arcadian landscape? We want to be shown where Grandad lived, a place where perhaps all proper Englishmen should really live. It remains true that this is the country viewed from the city, an idealisation of cold, damp, rheumatism-giving landscapes, draughty cottages which have the quaint trait of an outside privy and no running water and a working environment of long hours, low pay and poor conditions.

Not all the landscapes are portrayed through a filter of nostalgic romance, for the landscape is also spectacle. Helicopter-borne cameras show a bird's eye view of the Pennines, swooping over Malham Cove and the Settle-Carlisle railway line, whilst the major use of the aerial shot is to show the landscapes that Gosling's car is passing through. Perhaps from a height even mundane landscapes become sublime. These travel shots essentially link one location to the next, but they are the same as the other landscapes presented: the Pennines idealised and prettified.

In true travelogue style, places are described by the use of voice-overs. This fits well into the style of the programme, for we are supposed to be hearing what Gosling is typing into his notebook, in many cases the sound of a typewriter is audible. Gosling is clearly attempting to impose his personal sense of place:

> Skipton is a sturdy country market town, where tea-time is taken seriously and three-tiered cake stands overflow with hot buttered muffins and pink fancies. The local paper puts adverts on its front page like *The Times* used to, and uses an old press which printed the news of the relief of Mafeking. But, the issue inside today is, "when will the by-pass be finished?"

The last point is emphasised by the roar of heavy traffic noise. The visual image alternates between a tea-shop, complete with cake-stand, and Gosling sitting at a typewriter in a hotel garden. The description continues:

> Skipton means 'sheep town', 'gateway to the Dales'. Where the pasture land ends and the hills begin, staunchly Yorkshire. A market town with a grammar school, sensibly going about its business. Dominated by a castle which boasts the first water closet in the north of England. Skipton is rooted without unnecessary frills, older than the Norman conquest and still going strong.

The style of the description is individual, yet it seems a forced idiosyncratic point of view. The emphasis is nostalgia once again; for tea-times and newspapers like they used to be, for grammar schools, water closets and roots in the Anglo-Saxon past. The imagery and projection of a supposed lost world hangs like a pall over this series. Descriptions of other places are similar: 'Alston's purpose has been industrial since the Kings of England got their silver from here. It's an intriguing, unique and pleasant place'. It is hardly surprising that the only large-scale industry we are shown is disused. Apparently, industry becomes interesting only when it becomes industrial archaeology. Temporal as well as spatial distance can make the heart grow fonder. The people who decry contemporary despoliation seem to view the same process, when it is historically distant, with no similar feelings of displeasure. As we might expect, contemporary industry is displayed but it is of the cottage variety, including a potter, an illustrator, a glass-engraver and a woman who owns a castle and makes four-poster beds - scarcely the stuff of everyday life.

Alston is further described as 'altogether a curious place. The highest market town in England, perched on the raw, weathered roof-top of the Pennines'. Perhaps they can make places into characters rather like they did with people, the desire to make the ordinary strange. The description of wild, romantic, perched Alston seems strained in its search for the correct adjective. However, even though much of the description is flushed with stereotyped phraseology, there remains a vigorous attempt to capture a sense of these places. The description of the Yorkshire village of Hawes is a fine example:

> Hawes is a tiny market town, more a village. Surrounded by grand scenery, green and buttercup yellow in Summer at the head of Wensleydale. They live on one main street straggling 'higgle-de-piggledy' behind the river Ure in Yorkshire. There are lots of shops that sell postcards and bed and breakfast, and in every pub you're having to clamber over mountains of rucksacks. At hay time it all smells marvellous. As 'Pinky' Blades the grocer said - "the Arabs would give you a pound a sniff for this".

When considering the work of Mitchell and Gosling, one is aware of an important ambiguity, in that despite being aware of their skill in visual and prose evocation of a place, there remains an ideologically commonsense vision of the countryside. These skills could be used to overthrow stereotyped images, but instead only reinforce them. Only in the description of Hexham, in Northumberland, does Gosling convey anything other than the quiet, quaintness of country villages and towns - 'Hexham is a racy kind of place'. Yet the visual images appear to contradict this, and it is only when we visit a discotheque that 'racy' becomes an apt word. It almost appears that the words are tacked on to the available visual material. If Hexham, for example, had been about local craftsmen, then the town would have been described as 'folksy' or 'sleepy'. Since all places are complex, the selectivity involved in regarding one place as 'sleepy' and another as 'racy' remains an entirely selective process controlled by film-makers like Mitchell, Gosling and Wright.

Conclusion

The process of making a landscape documentary at Granada may be complex but its result is the reinforcement within popular culture of a nostalgic, pastoral, arcadian vision of the English landscape. That landscape in reality is essentially a commercial, professionally-managed, food-producing environment, but is presented in a manner that effectively strips it of any of the conflict that lies at the bedrock of relations within rural areas, and relations between the city and the country. As Harrison (1982, p21) has noted: 'Rural industries are not less a part of contemporary capitalism than motor-car manufacturing or microchip computerisation.' Furthermore, whilst the majority of agricultural holdings are becoming increasingly mechanised, fertilised and subsidised, these landscape documentaries are showing us images of quaint, olde England. Such documentaries completely ignore the economic pressures that exist within rural England, pressures which have been created, for example, by successive Agricultural Ministries and more recently the EEC Common Agricultural Policy. These policies have encouraged the change from pasture-land to arable farming in areas such as the Pennines, and have encouraged the use of larger machinery at the loss of agricultural jobs. Moreover, as Body (1982, p49) notes, it has also led to an increase in farm size:

> Many of the farmers who have ploughed up their pasture to take advantage of ... higher prices have had incomes of over £50,000 a year. By investing in new and more powerful tractors and combine harvesters they have been able, quite legitimately, to avoid much

> of the income tax they would otherwise have had to pay. However, they have also been using twice the amount of fuel that the older ones used to need ... In mechanising our farms we have replaced manpower with oil.

This, of course, lies hidden behind rustic images of old men in cloth caps, quaint hill-farms and limited or non-mechanised agricultural practices. It is the country from the city, urbanised nostalgia - the longing of an essentially urban culture for a rural existence which is, and always was, a fantasy. It is probable that the pervasiveness of these notions is due in large part to the alienation of a population from the reality of its existence. Why else would we turn and create for ourselves pictures of a golden age which lies just over the next rolling hill, or around the bend of a country lane? It perhaps gives us comfort, and the spurious reality of tourist 'honey-pots' serve to increase the estrangement from the real socio-economic life of the contemporary English landscape. Yet as Harrison noted (1982, p20):

> not only are such fantasies expressions of reaction, but they have a reactionary impact too. They lend ideological strength to those in the country whose interests lie in resisting change, while disguising from those who have most to gain in the process of change which is in fact underway.

More simply, we could add that it is an agent of the reproduction of hegemonic cultural values and ideas. Earlier I indicated that problems do indeed lie within the landscape of England, for example, those of low pay, depopulation, declining services and youth unemployment. Furthermore, the myth does have a real social and economic impact; the *terra incognita* of the mind has influenced *terra firma*. Agricultural workers are amongst the lowest of the low-paid, with basic wages currently (1983) at around £75.00 per week. Furthermore, the government, via the Department of Health and Social Security, considers that a two-child family with an income less than £74.00 per week is poor enough to get Family Income Supplement. The average for full-time manual workers in this category in April 1980 was 8 per cent; that for agricultural workers was a staggering 35.5 per cent (Body, 1982, p26). This endorses Newby's case that the agriculural workers seem to have been forgotten in the pay round. By contrast the farmer has become the most heavily subsidised business man in the country, with every farmer on average receiving £13,000 in 1981 from the taxpayer (Body, 1982, p27). In the tax year 1980/81 the taxpayers' support, as a percentage of a farmer's net income, was 166 per cent (Body, 1982, p9). In the period 1979-1981 expenditure on housing was down 13.6 per cent, on education 3.5 per cent, but the budget of the Ministry of Agriculture was up 13.9 per cent (Hansard, 12 Nov. 1981, Col. 164).

The farming lobby has successfuly diverted to itself the sum of £3,350 million per annum (1981), slightly more than the total assets of the four main clearing banks (£3,346 million). In part its success has been based on the mythology that surrounds farming. The image of the small gentleman farmer, the steward of our unchanging heritage, is light years away from the agri-business that now dominates. Nor are the effects of the myth limited to the countryside, for they reverberate through the economy as a whole:

> The diversion of capital this year (to agriculture) equals the capital of thirteen companies the size of Courtaulds. Whether it has the effect of closing down thirteen companies the size of Courtaulds is arguable; certainly it has deprived some efficient industries of the capital they need for their growth and development. The consequent loss of jobs caused by this diversion of over £3,000 millions is incaculable: one million, two million, or is it more? The TUC has claimed that a reflation of £5,000 million would end the problem of unemployment, and the CBI seems not to have dissented from that view. (Body, 1982, p125).

Perhaps it is no accident that the oil company Shell has over the years developed an advertising campaign that encourages the pastoral idyll (Bommes and Wright, 1982; Youngs and Jenkins, 1984), since they, along with Fisons, ICI, BP, Ford and Boots Chemicals have been the major beneficiaries of all this investment and subsidy. Body (1982, p20) calculated that the total diversion of capital to agriculture from other industries since 1945 has been £40,000 million (at the 1982 level of the £ sterling).

Only a nation which believes it it still populated by yeoman farmers could allow this state of affairs to continue. Popular culture generally, and in the instance cited here, the landscape documentary, encourages and propagates a belief in an aspatial and ahistorical landscape. In 1980 Newby asked how could the problems of the countryside be made clear and known when the myth was so pervasive. He went on to ask if he was being a 'kill-joy' to question the myth. I believe that he was not, and that there remains a myth which must be exploded.

NOTES

1. 'Wild track' and 'voice over' refers to the phenomenon when the soundtrack of the film is not the sound which would have been actually recorded along with the visual images on the screen. In particular, 'wild track' could be any sound including speech, whilst 'voice over' is usually a commentary.

2. 'Auteur theory' or 'author theory' is a particular way of analysing a film. It sees one person, usually the director, as being of paramount importance in the making of the film product.

3. The IBA or Independent Broadcasting Authority is the governing body of the British commercial television network. Their rules on balance state that 'balance', usually meaning 'political balance', may be within one programme or spread over a series of programmes. The British Broadcasting Corporation's ('non-commercial') rules officially stipulate that balance must be within any one programme.

4. David Wright started out as a researcher on this series of programmes. However, Gosling appears to have become disenchanted, and increasingly Wright came to the fore as virtually a co-presenter.

CHAPTER 8: RACISM, NATIONALISM AND THE CREATION OF A REGIONAL MYTH: THE SOUTHERN STATES AFTER THE AMERICAN CIVIL WAR

Catherine P. Silk and John A. Silk

This paper represents a Marxist approach towards evaluating the role played by certain elements of the mass media in shaping people's images of the American South in the period from the end of the Civil War in 1865 to the turn of the century. The items of popular or mass culture considered are novels and magazine articles, with one novel, *The Choir Invisible* by James Lane Allen (1897), selected for more detailed textual analysis. Of particular interest to geographers is the prolific use that was made of 'local colour' themes to portray the defeated Confederacy in sympathetic terms while also confirming the victory of the North. The notion of local colour was important with respect to all parts of the nation, but was particularly important to the South due to the need for reconciliation. A closely associated theme was that of 'unity in diversity', stressing the contribution of all parts of the United States to the reality of national unity and to an awakening sense of nationalism. Local colour can be regarded as an ideological and literary device employed, consciously and unconsciously, to put forward other ideological notions useful to the ruling class - one of the key themes being racism. *The Choir Invisible* provides an excellent example of a popular novel that illustrates these themes.

The approach adopted means that the 'messages' contained in such literature cannot be properly understood or evaluated without reference to the economic, social and political context in which they were produced and to whose characteristics they also contribute. To do the matter justice requires that four elements are discussed here: first, elaboration of a theory which accounts for the role played by culture in a society like that of the United States after 1865, within which industrial capital and then industrial and finance capital (imperialism) dominated; secondly, more specific analysis of the role played by the institutions responsible for producing and disseminating popular novels and magazine articles about the American South; thirdly, a means for analysing the texts themselves which serves to link the works produced by writers with those accepted and published by the media institutions; finally, the need to understand, act upon and transform their experiences so as to provide explicit or implicit support for the interests of the dominant class.

Marxist Cultural Theory

Marxist cultural theory has taken various forms, including base-superstructure relations (Marx and Engels, 1974), mass culture (Horkheimer and Adorno, 1972), culturalism (Williams, 1958; Thompson, 1963), and structuralism (Althusser, 1971; Eagleton, 1976; see also J. Silk, 1983). Common to most of them is the concept of 'ideology', used here to refer to ideas, images, 'mental maps' and theories which serve to promote the interests of a particular class or of a coalition of strata drawn from a number of classes in a society. We also extend the term to describe the way in which people come to understand their daily lives and experiences so as to bolster the interests of a particular class. More specifically, 'dominant ideology' has been used as a term to convey the contention that 'the ideas of the ruling class are in every epoch the ruling ideas: i.e. the class which is the ruling *material* force is, at the same time, its ruling intellectual force (Marx and Engels, 1974, p64). In capitalist societies, therefore, the dominant ideology would bolster the power of various fractions of the bourgeoisie, and in slave-based societies, that of the slave-owners or slavocracy.

The ideas of Antonio Gramsci (1971, pp5-23, 123-205) are particularly relevant here, because of the emphasis he placed on ideology and culture (in the broadest sense of the term), when analysing the balance of class forces in advanced capitalist society and because of his attempt to analyse the relative importance to the ruling classes of either employing coercion or mobilising consent. Gramsci, like Marx, argued that the *dominance* of a ruling class in any society was founded upon its economic power. This could be in the form of ownership of the means of production (but not of the labourers themselves), as under industrial capitalism in the American North both before and after 1865, or alternatively could be in the form of ownership of both the means of production and the labourers, as under chattel slavery in the American South before 1865. Gramsci further argued that the dominance of the ruling class depended upon the use of a system of *coercion* - constituted by the legal system of courts, police and armed forces in most advanced capitalist democracies - to punish or even wipe out its opponents. However, the dominant class must also be able to exercise leadership, both in economic and in moral and intellectual terms, and Gramsci used the term *hegemony* to describe this role. Such leadership may be based on various compromises that emerge after a period of conflict and negotiation, but it is important that the essential economic interests of the ruling class should remain untouched.

The hegemony, and hence the dominance, of a ruling class is more firmly established if the relationships between the ruling classes and other classes and groups in society can be represented as transcending the interests of any particular class or group, and as embodying a force for universal expansion and development. It may well be that the state is seen as being in the hands of a particular class or as serving their interests, but the progress and prosperity of that class is also seen as the key to prosperity for most or all subordinate groups. This typically occurs when appeals are made for 'national unity' - as in the case of industrial capitalists and their supporters in the American North - or to 'States' rights' or to the guardianship over blacks exercised by the 'Anglo-Saxon race' - as in the case of the slavocracy in the American South. The case that is established for hegemony thus must be primarily ideological.

A further important implication of Gramsci's work is that ideologies exist which counter the dominant ideology, so that struggles are also conducted at the level of meaning (Volosinov, 1973; Hall, 1982). Just as dominance is rarely achieved without some form of armed struggle, so hegemony cannot be achieved without ideological conflict. Even when hegemony is achieved conflict continues, even if it is more readily contained.

It must be emphasised that the dominance of a specific class may be established and maintained on the basis of both coercion and consent. However, such dominance depends upon continuous negotiation and compromise, for Gramsci argued that any class society or 'historic bloc' consists of inherently contradictory and discordant relationships. Any equilibrium that is established can only be relative, in particular because splits may occur between two or more key groupings within the ruling class. In the case of the United States the conflict of interest between the industrial capitalists, located in and identified with the Northern States (the 'North'), and the slaveowners or slavocracy, identified with the Southern States (the 'South'), sharpened until an inevitable Civil War established which was to dominate. The North was militarily victorious and her economic dominance was thereby assured, but within the South the problem remained as to the precise economic and political roles that the various classes and class fractions (white proletariat, black proletariat, white petit-bourgeoisie, white ex-slaveowners and so on) should play. It is argued that a period of 'hegemonic crisis' occurred in the South for up to 30 years after the Civil War, assuming its most acute form between 1865 and 1877, in which these roles were so uncertain that the North continued to rule in the South largely by force alone. Although, from the point of view of the ruling class, coercion in various forms was essential for the maintenance of relative stability in the South, the justification for the social and economic relations that were established depended heavily upon an ideological offensive conducted through the mass media of newspapers, magazines, and best-selling novels. Of particular interest here is the way that both factual and fictional accounts, which rely heavily on a sense of place and locale and upon promoting 'image geographies' (Watson, 1970/71; Watson and O'Riordan, 1976), worked (and still work) to justify a particularly vicious system of exploitation and oppression.

Gramsci, and also Althusser (1971), provided clues as to the way in which the key ideological mechanisms and institutions in society need to operate if they are to be effective. When hegemony reigns, the systematic theories and philosophies of the world developed and propagated by elites must link up in some way with the unsystematic philosophies of the mass of the populace. Such linkages are established through language, commonsense and folklore, making use of stories, practices and experiences already well-known and used by people. Before the industrial revolution and the rise of industrial capitalism, the Church and, to some extent, the (private) schools were the most important 'ideological apparatuses'. Together with the family, these were the agencies most responsible for establishing 'what made sense'. By contrast, public education systems and the mass media have become steadily more important in the nineteenth and twentieth centuries. As will be seen, the mass media in the form of magazines and novels played a significant role during the period which we are analysing in the United States.

When it comes to an analysis of the texts themselves we shall show that consideration of economic and political forces is essential if the impact of such texts upon their readerships is to be understood. In fact, we should say immediately that the very wording of the previous sentence gives a false impression of the way in which texts convey their 'messages', as such messages are just as much a function of what the reader brings to the reading process as it is of how writers shape their work (Bennett, 1979). It is our contention that what a reader brings to the reading of a text is a set of presuppositions and understandings which allow her or him to make sense of that text: presuppositions and understandings which may be more or less perfectly shared with those brought to bear by the writer. As Althusser and Balibar (1970) argued, these are often unstated or 'taken-for-granted', so that 'absences' and 'silences' are just as important as what is present. As a result, they recommended a 'symptomatic reading' of texts in order to reveal such presuppositions (see also Macherey, 1978). In our view, this can be achieved only if the constraints imposed on both reader and writer by critics, editors, publishers and, ultimately, various fractions of the ruling class, can be identified. In turn, this requires a wide-ranging analysis of the economic, social and political forces operating at any given time and, where practicable, distinctions between readers on the basis of class, race, gender and region. Having said this, it is unfortunate that we cannot deal with significant sections of the population, especially blacks, who were illiterate, but who came to understand their position in society in terms of oral histories and other expressions of folklore.

Before analysing our selected text, we must therefore first summarise the main events, trends and relationships of the economic and political history of the United States in the nineteenth century, paying particular attention to the post-bellum period, and also examine the role played by those who owned and controlled publishing houses in the latter period.

Economic and Political Context

From Independence to the Civil War

The Declaration of Independence in 1776 and subsequent Constitution of the United States (1787) formally brought together two societies based on different modes of production - independent farmers and early industrial capitalists dependent upon 'free' labour in the North and a slavocracy, based on the ownership of labourers, in the South. Both the Declaration and the Constitution dealt with blacks and slavery simply by remaining silent about them. The Constitution was therefore based upon a contradiction: independence from Britain had been achieved through war and bourgeois democratic revolution, yet a pre-capitalist form of economy was sanctioned within the Union. Until industrial capitalism got truly under way in the North by the 1820s (Carroll and Noble, 1977, ch 6), the notion that the 'government should rest upon the dominion of property' could be interpreted without undue friction in terms of slaves in the South and industry and commerce in the North (Franklin, 1974, p100). The successful addition of cotton to tobacco as one of the staple crops in the South during the 1790s ensured an even greater demand for slaves as well as land (Franklin, 1974, pp104-105), despite the fact that the importation of slaves was outlawed in 1808. The methods used ensured rapid depletion of the soil and, as the highest profits were to be obtained from virgin soil, this effectively generated a strong westward movement by the slavocracy (Logan, 1970, p7). For some time, at least, the articulation (Amin, 1977) of the capitalist mode of production with slavery worked to the advantage of the ruling classes in both North and South.

A system grew up within which Midwestern farmers provided food for slaves and merchant capitalists in the North helped finance and export cotton to Britain. British manufactured goods were imported in return. These interests provided the basis for a coalition which underpinned the power of the Democratic Party and, through it, the slavocracy; so much so that the federal government and the Supreme Court were under direct control of the slaveowners for most of the time up to 1860 (Camejo, 1976, p20). Such control meant that Northern industrial interests could neither get protective tariffs for their products, nor obtain federal subsidies for transport improvements to reach ever-expanding Midwestern markets. The accelerated growth of manufacturing in the Northeastern states from 1815, the growth of the proletariat, the later railroad expansion and introduction of steam power, meant that manufacturing was no longer an adjunct of merchant capital; investments from the latter being transferred into the former. Another crucial change was the increasing conflict between the free farmers of the Midwest and the slavocracy. The extension of slavery was indispensible if the slavocracy was to survive as the dominant class in the South (and in Washington), but the interests of this class came into ever greater conflict with those of the free farmers. Collectively, these factors led to new political alliances and socio-economic relations of forces. In particular, the growth of the Republican party was based on a coalition of industrial capitalists, Midwest farmers, and some workers, united in their opposition to slavery and its expansion. This counterweight to the political power of the South in Washington was sorely needed by Northern industrialists and bankers. Although the Northern region or 'section' of the nation was becoming the most powerful economically, it found great difficulty in resisting the political initiatives taken by the South. For example, the Missouri Compromise of 1820 that confined slavery south of the 36th parallel was repealed in 1854, and the Dred-Scott decision of 1857 theoretically opened up *all* territories to slavery. Numerous attempts at compromise in the 1850s failed (Franklin, 1974, ch 12), and the seeds of contradiction embodied in the Constitution finally gave rise to the bitterness and terror of the Civil War (1861-1865) and its aftermath.

Although the slaveowners relied almost entirely upon brutal forms of coercion to keep their slaves in line, the ideological struggle between pro- and anti-slavery forces was also being waged in the first part of the nineteenth century. Ideological arguments for the slavocracy were aimed chiefly at those outside the South - in the North, the expanding West and in Europe - who opposed slavery on various grounds. Racist ideology began to be used to justify chattel slavery, doctors coming forward to justify it on ethnological grounds and the church on religious and moral grounds. From the 1820s, 'culture', and in particular literature, in the South was distorted by the necessity for white writers to defend the social system in which they produced their work. It was continually emphasised that the 'higher' culture of whites could only be maintained if there were slaves to carry out the menial work.

The ideological struggle was also waged on behalf of the North. The arguments of white abolitionists, who had been largely ignored or derided, began to attract greater attention. High-sounding moral and humanitarian arguments provided excellent justification for opposition to the slavocracy and, even better, in support of the material interests that we have described. However, racist and white supremacist notions were also very strong in the North. As Frederickson (1971, p323) pointed out, during the pre-Civil War crisis the South wanted both slavery and blacks, but the North wanted neither. Dreams of an all-white America showed themselves in proposals, such as that by Abraham Lincoln, for eventual settlement of all blacks abroad. Southern blacks were a 'problem' for the interests united politically under the Republican banner, but the exigencies of war and the subsequent need to reconstruct the Union meant at least temporarily that influential opinion in the North favoured equal rights, 'principally because their co-operation was essential to the establishment of Northern political, social and ideological hegemony over the South' (Frederickson, 1971, p323).

The Civil War and Radical Reconstruction

Deep controversy remains among American historians as to what precisely happened to the socio-economic relations of forces after the defeat of the white South in 1865. We agree with Camejo (1976, ch 3) that the most important effect of the Civil War was the destruction of the slavocracy as a social formation, with real economic power in the South now shifting from landowning to urban commercial interests. At least in part, the contradiction inherent in the American Constitution had been resolved, and the struggles of the post-bellum period culminated in the full triumph of industrial capital in the United States.

However, the new order took time to be consolidated. Logan (1970, p20) commented that '(r)evolutionary changes in a way of life generate fresh acts of violence which complicate and prolong the period of adjustment'. Moreover, Gramsci (1971, pp275-6), placing the more explicit emphasis on the ideological aspects, although not having the American Civil War specifically in mind, stated:

> if the ruling class has lost its consensus, i.e. it is no longer "leading" but only "dominant", exercising coercive force alone, this means precisely that the great masses have become detached from their traditional ideologies, and no longer believe what they used to believe previously ... The crisis consists precisely in the fact that the old is dying and the new cannot be born; in this interregnum a great variety of morbid symptoms appear.

It would certainly be correct to argue that the picture of the South was exceedingly confused in the post-bellum period and that the great masses of the population, whether black or white, were sufficiently detached from their traditional ideologies so as to make coercion the factor upon which the ruling classes had to rely.

Immediately after the War, Northern industrialists wished to see social stability conducive to investment in the South. Fearing that the revolutionary changes brought about by the War might lead to 'excessive' demands by blacks and poor whites for land, free education and the widespread provision of various social services, the Northern industrialists were relatively lenient with those groups of whites in the South who had previously formed the slavocracy. However, the effect of this policy was to allow legislatures in the Southern States (abetted by Lincoln's successor to the presidency, Andrew Johnson), to fall under the control of unrepentent Southerners. One of the first actions of these bodies was to enact 'Black Codes' which, although formally recognising the end of chattel slavery, established guidelines which would have again made blacks into slaves in all but name. No provision was made for black suffrage. Such legal coercion was backed by organised white patrols, on lines similar to those established under slavery, who carried on a kind of guerilla warfare against blacks and sympathetic whites (Franklin, 1974, pp262-4). The most infamous of these was the Ku Klux Klan, but many other secret societies with a similar role also sprang up, such as the Knights of the White Camelia, White Brotherhood and the Pale Faces. Between 1867 and 1871, 20,000 blacks and sympathetic whites were murdered. Although economically dominant and militarily victorious, the North found that political control was slipping from its grasp, and fears of a counter-revolutionary challenge arose.

The Republican Party, now based on an alliance between black 'freed men', industrial capitalists ('carpetbaggers') and a relatively small number of poor white farmers ('scalawags'), inaugurated the period of 'Radical Reconstruction' (1865-1877). For the Republicans, Radical Reconstruction meant more seats in Congress since no black would ever vote for parties supported by former slaveowners. For the industrial capitalists who supported the party it meant governmental power *and* effective economic exploitation in the South. During the period of Radical Reconstruction, all Southern legislatures were boycotted by the former slaveowners and their supporters. This bitter opposition was heightened because a military governor was installed in 1867 in every confederate state except Tennessee. The governors were backed by a federal army of occupation which, although only present in token numbers (Camejo, 1976, p184), illustrated how seriously the counter-revolutionary challenge was regarded by the North.

The unstable Republican coalition, however, could not last. Blacks and poor whites really believed that 'free and equal treatment' was what those in control of the liberating Northern armies had in mind for them, since in one legislature after another demands arose for free education, for libraries, hospitals and social welfare systems and for industrial infrastructure (e.g. see Nathans, 1968). The threat of counter-revolution was replaced by a demand for reforms that had revolutionary implications. Most white Southerners could not (and would not wish to) afford to pay for such developments, either through taxation or investment, (once stripped of their vast investment in slaves, most former slaveowners had little remaining capital). The North was not prepared to foot the bill, with the exception of a few sectors and regions where profitable major industrial investments could be made or existing enterprises taken over (Carroll and Noble, 1977, pp274-5). Furthermore, the hunger of Southern poor whites and blacks for land was not satisfied, for Northern backing and industrial interests had bought up much of the land cheaply during the Radical Reconstruction period. Finally, for reasons already given, Southern whites could not afford to pay free labour according to the capitalist dictates of supply and demand. Although formally sharing political control in the South, blacks became economically subjugated in a system of share-cropping and peonage. The Radical Reconstruction governments were also charged with widespread corruption and with enormous increases in state debts, but although true such charges camouflaged the real motives behind opposition to these regimes.

Radical Reconstruction gradually came to an end during the 1870s. Only two states had failed to be 'redeemed' by 1877, when a so-called 'compromise' between Democrats (North) and Republicans (South) was reached after the disputed presidential election of 1876. Among other things, any federal troops remaining in the South were now removed (Camejo, 1976, pp175-87). Once Northern industrialists had ensured that the white South could no longer be a threat to their interests in the West, the ruling classes in the South *and* the North saw it as in their interests to subjugate Southern blacks. In part, this was represented by the fact that by 1871 the upper echelons of the Democratic Party were also coming to be dominated by industrial capital (Camejo, 1976, p117), thus constituting an alternative expression of the same class interests as the Republicans. The unlikely coalition of interests in the Republican Party had served its purpose, securing the position of industrial capitalists within the Union. As Camejo (1976, p103) so aptly commented, '(during Radical Reconstruction) the industrial capitalists wanted both government power and effective economic exploitation. The first aim required that the Afro-Americans be raised up, temporarily; the second that they be restrained'.

Redemption or Counter-Revolution

As the 1870s proceeded, therefore, a Conservative and Democratic counter-revolution was born - a new coalition of industrial capitalists and Southern white farmers against black labour. Supporters of this movement gave it the ideologically-charged title, and task, of 'Redemption' from the rule of blacks, carpetbaggers (portrayed as white speculators from the North) and scalawags (portrayed as Southern whites turned traitor to their race). It is clear that the counter-revolutionary groupings were no longer regarded as threatening the interests of the Northern ruling class. The decisions of the United States' Supreme Court showed that, from 1870 to the early twentieth century, this ruling class was only too willing to connive in the use of terrorism to secure its interests. Immediately after the Civil War, the federal government had made some attempt to counter the activities of vigilante and patrol groups like the Ku Klux Klan. However, many of these groups re-emerged in the 1870s, operating openly with tens of thousands of members. These bands were effectively the military wing of the Conservative and Democratic political counter-revolution. In 1875, two sections of the Act providing for federal supervision of elections and enforcement of rights guaranteed by the fourteenth amendment were declared unconstitutional. The (anti) Ku Klux Klan Act was effectively nullified in 1882 by a Supreme Court ruling that the thirteenth, fourteenth and fifteenth amendments to the Constitution did not authorise Congress to protect the civil rights of individuals who suffered violations at the hands of private citizens, i.e. those bands of whites responsible for assaulting and murdering blacks. In 1883 the Supreme Court declared the Civil Rights Act of 1875 unconstitutional. Throughout the 1890s the Supreme Court kept finding legal bases for new anti-black state laws, and in 1896 came the notorious 'separate but equal' ruling which made school segregation constitutional. We must emphasise here that blacks tried to resist such measures by using what democratic rights they had (they were still technically enfranchised in most states until the 1890s), and by uniting with the most exploited and oppressed whites in the Populist movement, but they faced overwhelming odds (Woodward, 1974, pp60-4).

By the time Allen's book *The Choir Invisible* appeared in 1897, any economic or political restraining forces on the conservative redeemers had relaxed to such an extent that not only were blacks thoroughly subjugated economically and oppressed physically, they were also becoming subject to the rigidly enforced segregation statutes or 'Jim Crow' laws being adopted throughout the Southern states (Woodward, 1974, p7). However, the agrarian depression of the 1880s and 1890s provoked a final surge of Populist revolt supported by some independent farmers and by blacks. The reaction to such popular dissent was harsh, the breach between white factions being effectively healed at the expense of the blacks. The fragile Populist movement finally collapsed and most whites united around the theme of 'white supremacy'. Steps were taken to disenfranchise blacks, with the scheme initially adopted by Mississippi in 1890 being copied and adapted throughout the South by 1915 (Woodward, 1971, ch 12). What Woodward (1974, p86) described as 'bloody mob wars against the Negro' were also waged in various Southern states from 1898.

So far, we have concentrated on the various measures employed by the forces of reaction in the South because it was these forces that had triumphed by the early twentieth century. Yet, as both Woodward (1974) and Camejo (1976) illustrated, there was appreciable resistance by various groupings, e.g. the Populist movement, and considerable friction between the various coalitions which effectively governed the South on behalf of the industrial capitalists of the North. Due to our interest in *dominant* classes and *dominant* ideologies, we cannot deal here with the ideologies propounded and taken up by certain groupings among the subordinate classes. From the evidence available, it is tempting to argue that Marx's thesis that the ruling class often dominates economically without governing applies to the American South (Callinicos, 1983, pp100-4). Industrial capitalists in the North had been able to invest in land and industry while members and allies of the Southern ruling class, which had been destroyed as a result of the Civil War, gradually consolidated their new position. They became economic agents of such capitalists and members of a newly-constituted Southern ruling class which governed at the expense particularly of blacks, but also at the expense of many independent white farmers. Southern whites were eventually allowed to pursue many of their old ways and indeed to elaborate considerably upon them in the ultimate interests of a nationally dominant ruling class located in the North.

Imperialism

While never thought of as possessing an 'empire', the United States had, nevertheless, entered an imperialist phase by the 1890s. The enormous increase in industrial production since the Civil War meant that industrial capitalists, together with their financial backers, began to look for new markets and sources of raw materials. Exports of both commodities and capital skyrocketed and, by the end of the Spanish-American War in 1898, the United States was one of the world's great powers. America's 'empire' gave it jurisdiction over many islands in the Pacific and in the Caribbean; financial and political influence 'wrought wonders' in Central and South America (Franklin, 1974, ch 17). Most of those living in such areas were members of so-called 'darker peoples', and great care had to be taken not to grant civil and political liberties in the colonies which would prompt blacks within the United States to fight for such rights. Equally important, the subjugation of blacks within America, and especially in the South, could be used to justify the super-exploitation of non-whites abroad (see also Kirby, 1978, p6).

Ideology and Ideological Themes

Although it is our contention that ideologies are grounded in material interests, the connection between the two spheres is often extremely complex, if only because taking what people say or think about things, including interpretation of their own behaviour and experiences and those of others as *explanations* of such behaviour, is highly suspect. For example, before the Civil War pro-slavery arguments by white Southerners were *justified* by appeal to the biological inferiority of blacks and the benign custodianship exercised by whites, although the true explanation was to be found in the perpetuation of the slavocracy and of white oppression. Anti-slavery arguments were justified on moral grounds, although for the industrial capitalists of the North they formed an integral part of the defence of their interests in the Union as a whole and, in particular, in the West. This is not to say that groups of either industrial capitalists or slaveowners met to decide how an ideological offensive was to be mounted, carefully articulating justifications which concealed their true interests from those whom they were exploiting and oppressing. Rather, members of such ruling classes may not have been truly aware of their own exploitative and oppressive role (although it is hard to believe this in the case of slavocracy). We would argue that in the majority of cases ideas and themes already exist which have become incorporated in the everyday commonsense notions or folklore of large, or key, sections of the population in a society, and which can be adapted to justify and defend the material interests of a dominant class. As already mentioned, those abolitionists in the United States and Europe who had long opposed slavery on moral and humanitarian grounds suddenly found that the time for their ideas had come in the period leading up to the Civil War. Such ideas provided a universal, high-sounding and idealistic (in both senses of the word) justification for the defence of the material interests of industrial capitalists in the North and independent farmers in the West. Similarly, high-sounding and universal forms of justification had to be found by apologists for the South.

By the 1870s and 1880s therefore, a number of problems faced the ruling class in the North if they were also to be recognised as hegemonic. First, reconciliation with the Southern white ruling class had to be justified - not a straightforward task, given the bitterness generated by the Civil War and by the counter-revolutionary activities in the late 1860s. Secondly, the disenfranchisement and economic subjugation of blacks in the South also had to be justified. This was perhaps not so difficult to achieve, but it was still necessary to counter pre-Civil War ideological campaigns against slavery and support for Radical Reconstruction. For both these tasks, the prime 'audience' was the mass of the population in the North and the West. Thirdly, the Southern whites had to be persuaded that the period beginning with 'Redemption' was one in which all white Southerners had the same material interests and in which the white South had indeed snatched victory from the jaws of defeat.

The ideological themes that appeared in magazines, newspapers and books were closely interrelated. An over-arching notion was that of *national reconciliation* or *national unity*. For a considerable period after the Civil War, national unity was more problematic than any other single factor, yet, as we have seen, remained vital to the interests of industrial capitalists. Once the period of generalised reliance on force was over, the task of winning people over to the notion of 'America' and an 'American national interest' had to be undertaken. It can be argued that the concept of the nation state is remote from the day-to-day lives and concerns of the majority of its citizens, so that there is a constant need to relate the former concept to the ideas and practices embodied in the latter. Certain principles and practices which 'make sense' historically, and which are already deeply ingrained in people's lives, can be drawn upon for new purposes - in this case, to cement American nationalism under Northern hegemony.

Stories and novels of the highly popular local colour genre articulated notions of national unity with those of regionalism and localism. Great stress was laid upon differences between regions and upon differences between locales within regions, with scrupulous attention often being given to descriptions of the flora and fauna. At the same time, the 'unity in diversity' of America was emphasised by the complementary nature of the contribution made by each locale to national unity. The notion of the rugged *pioneer* was frequently used here, in conjunction with the most important single theme - *racism*. Despite conflicts, all whites had a common destiny because they were members of the superior Anglo-Saxon race. Blacks are portrayed a docile and inferior, as childlike 'Sambo' figures. However, they are held to be harmless and happy only when kept in their place, otherwise they become ferocious, resorting to murder and rape. A closely related theme is that of *Southern white womanhood.* White women were obviously essential to the propagation of the Anglo-Saxon race, and must be placed on a pedestal and protected. If not treated firmly, blacks would be free to rape, diluting the stock and so attacking the very foundations of white superiority. This threat was dealt with in terms of the notion of *Southern chivalry*, writers constantly harking back to the presumed knightly ancestors of Southern slave-owning aristocrats, and implying that their modern equivalents - lynch mobs and the Ku Klux Klan - engaged in a crusade to protect Southern women.

Local colour novels set in the South justified the 'place' of blacks as in the South, keeping the 'problem' away from the North and under the firm supervision of Southern whites. Some justified the matter subtly, like James Lane Allen, others were less so (e.g. Dixon, 1903, 1905). White Northern readers could take vicarious pleasure in local colour stories and novels based on such themes, while feeling reassured that their Southern counterparts posed no threat to the Union. These novels built up a powerful image of the South as a region in which plantation life, Southern belles and docile black servants were an integral part. The fact that such a society never existed (Youngs, 1980), being an ideological construction, is not to deny its power. For most people it was, and for some it still is, the South.

The above themes were employed time and time again in magazine articles and novels about the South. There is, of course, a gap to be bridged between the works that embodied these ideological themes and the general public. The active role of the publishing houses and their editorial policy, and of the American transport and communication system, is crucial here.

The Role of the Publishing Houses and the Transport System

The appetite of newspaper, magazine and book publishers for 'local colour' stories, whether factual or fictional, was prodigious after the Civil War (Mott, 1957, p113). Although the South potentially had suitable themes and writers in plenty, it had no major publishing centres - Southern writers expounding on Southern themes to Southern audiences failed to find enough patronage to survive in the late 1860s. Acceptability in the North was vital therefore, for it was the home of all the major publishing companies in the United States. Northern magazines pursued a policy of promoting the 'new nationalism' after the Civil War, particularly from 1880 onwards. Editors were looking for nostalgic portraits of the 'Old South' combined with a wholehearted acceptance of reconciliation between North and South. As Buck (1937, ch 8) pointed out, the abolition of slavery and the defeat of the South allowed Southern themes to be treated without this being regarded as a defence of a system which was hostile to Northern interests - 'a culture which in its life was anathema to the North, could in its death be honoured'. *Schribner's Magazine* sent out agents to scour the South for writers who provided 'quaintness of detail and picturesque particularism' (Buck, 1937, p222) in 'local colour' stories set in the South, but with no trace of the old hostility between South and North. Editors and assistant editors sent several letters to writers 'discovered' in the South - James Lane Allen among them - urging 'love for the Union' and 'the broadest patriotism'. Potential contributors were instructed that stories liable to revive sectional differences would not be used, and items that contravened such advice were either rejected, or returned for revision. By 1888, two-thirds of the stories provided to newspapers by syndicates were 'Southern stories' (Buck, 1937, p235). Major writers owing their discovery to magazines were Joel Chandler Harris, George G.W. Cable, Thomas Nelson Page, Mary Noailles Murfree, and James Lane Allen. Different authors were associated with different locales within the South - Murfree with the Tennessee Mountains of the Southern Appalachians, Cable with New Orleans and Creole society, Grace King and Kate Chopin with Louisiana and Creole society, Page with Virginia, Johnston with Middle Georgia, and Allen with the Kentucky blue-grass region.

There is little evidence available on the clearly important matter of how relationships between editorship and ownership influenced decisions on content (Curran, 1977; Murdock, 1982), except for those few cases, e.g. McClure's, in which editor and owner were one and the same person. Available accounts simply stress the powerful managerial role of magazine and book editors (Buck, 1937; Tebbel, 1974, ch 13), and the notion that 'editors make great magazines' was certainly current for a considerable period from the 1870s onward. What is quite clear, however, is that Southern literature of the kind investigated here could not have developed on a large scale unless purveyed to the Northern reading public. This, in turn, required that Southern writers 'surrender(ed) all aspirations for independence' (Buck, 1937, p220).

Publication in magazines was particularly important to writers for two sets of reasons. First, the period after the Civil War has been referred to as the 'Second Golden Age of Magazines' (Tebbel, 1974, ch 13). This boom depended in turn upon major improvements in the country's transport and distribution system, and upon government policy with respect to mailing rates. The transport system, relying chiefly on the railways, had been built up as part of the North's war effort and was rapidly expanded thereafter (Carroll and Noble, 1977, ch 11). Congress realised that magazines, because of their known effect on public opinion, could be used to

> present simultaneously identical facts, uniformly treated, in every locality. Men and women, North, South, East and West, could read and judge the same materials instead of forming their beliefs and reaching their decisions on the basis of varied accounts published in different sections and often distorted by regional prejudice. Such, at least, was the ideal possibility (Wood, 1956, p99).

The Postal Act of 1879 reduced the cost of distributing magazines by mail and a reduction in second-class mailing rates in 1885 contributed directly to a boom in magazine publishing in the following eight years. A free rural delivery service was also introduced in 1897. By the

1880s the prices of magazines dropped because paper and printing costs, as well as those of distribution, had been considerably reduced (Mott, 1957, ch 1). Over the 20-year period from 1885-1905, 7,500 periodicals were founded (although many also folded). A further factor in their success was the income generated by the prodigious growth of national advertising - magazine and newspaper advertising as a whole grew by 80 per cent in the 1880s, by a third in the 1890s and by over half between 1900-1905 (Mott, 1957, pp20-34). Such advertising was directly related to growth of national mass markets for many commodities. The free public library system also expanded enormously during the period 1885-1905, although it is not known whether books alone, or both books and magazines, were provided by them (Mott, 1957, pp142-3). Thus the infrastructure and facilities which laid the basis for the economic dominance of industrial capital could also be used to propagate the ideological messages which would ensure its leading role in the cultural sphere and hence its overall hegemony.

The second important set of factors was closely linked to the above. For American writers at this time, publication in book form depended upon the establishment of a reputation on the basis of short stories accepted for magazines. Otherwise, it was impossible to ensure a profitable volume of sales (Mott, 1957, pp41-2). Southern writers were brought out of isolation by the groups of established Northern authors and critics who were attached to each magazine. Allen, for example, initially wrote 'Kentucky blue-grass' stories for *Century Magazine* before signing a contract with MacMillan's, and based his novel *The Choir Invisible* on a previously published story entitled *John Gray*. Furthermore, the lack of any international copyright agreement before 1891 made it doubly important for a writer to be published in one of the leading magazines, since the latter could and did print extracts without copyright payment from the best English, French and German writers, thus placing American authors at a disadvantage (Mott, 1957, pp41-2; Wood, 1956, pp53, 76). By the 1880s, Southern writers had conquered both the more staid and serious monthlies (e.g. *Schribner's, Harper's*) and the newer popular journals (e.g. *Cosmopolitan, McClure's*). Buck (1937, ch 9) described in detail how the successful formula applied in the pages of magazines was reproduced, amplified and elaborated in novels by Southern, and even by Northern, writers. That such novels were highly popular is shown by the best-seller lists which first appeared in 1897, with Southern themes appearing consistently in the 'Top Ten' until 1916

(Kirby, 1978). Details on the reverse of the title page of *The Choir Invisible* show that after its initial publication in May 1897, it was reprinted no less than seven times in the following five months.

It is not entirely clear who read the monthly and quarterly magazines like *Harper's Monthly, Schribner's Monthly* (later the *Century Magazine*) and *Lippincott's*, although it appears to have been members of the Northern bourgeoisie, together with high-level managers and technocrats. The considerable growth of public school education, at least in the North, together with the rise of an army of supervisory and clerical staff working for the new railroad corporations, industrial companies, in banking and insurance, and for local municipalities, provided the basis for an expanding middle class who were catered for by a variety of new magazines founded between 1870 and 1900 (Wood, 1956, p103).

In brief, editors in Northern publishing houses acted as 'gatekeepers' to the vast system which could be used to disseminate ideas and themes in written form to the mass of the reading public. Some writers on Southern themes fought against the tide. Amongst their number would be included the abolitionist Anne E. Dickson in *What Answer?*, the carpetbagger A.T. Morgan in *Yazoo*, and A.W. Tourgee, who in five novels from 1874 to 1883 dealt with the issues of 'moral reform' and justice for the negro (Buck, 1937, p234). The most liberal of them all, George G.W. Cable, actually explored themes which show how the myths of a chivalrous, picturesque South in a 'Golden Age' before the Civil War were used to assuage guilt over treatment of blacks and to justify slavery and the Ku Klux Klan (C. Silk, 1977). However, the stringent conditions placed on the Southern literary revival by Northern editors so disheartened him that in 1894 he wrote *John March Southerner*, in which blacks are portrayed as happy, childlike and worthy only of protection by whites (Butcher, 1959).

This kind of evidence supports our view that dominant ideologies do not hold complete sway in a given class society, and that one of their roles is constantly to find ways of countering opposition to ruling interests without resorting to coercion.

The Choir Invisible

The Choir Invisible has been chosen for analysis for several reasons. First, it is a typical example of the popular local colour genre that was already well-established by the time that *The Choir Invisible* appeared in 1897. It would have been recognised by potential readers, who would also have had definite expectations as to the kinds of themes, settings and devices they would encounter (although probably not consciously putting it in these terms), including precise and detailed evocation of a region, portrayal of blacks and whites in particular ways, and posing of obstacles to national unity which are heroically surmounted. The second reason, closely associated with the first, is that certain preconceptions could be assumed among the white, educated middle-class readers for whom Allen wrote. Readers brought with them a common and commonsense ideology which, as we have seen, had been created and reinforced by a quarter of a century of ideological struggle. Third, Allen's novels were more subtle than those of his race-baiting contemporaries like Thomas Dixon - author of *The Leopard's Spots: a Romance of the White Man's Burden - 1865-1900* (1902) and *The Clansman: an Historical Romance of the Ku Klux Klan* (1905). *The Choir Invisible* is a genteel tale of chivalrous romance set in the Kentucky blue-grass region, the local colour representing a literary device which provides a far more quietly spoken apologia for a vicious theory of white supremacy. Fourth, Allen's novels - including *The Choir Invisible* - are not only highly specific in their spatial (and temporal) setting, but deal with certain themes in their own specific way. For example, *The Choir Invisible* is set in the late eighteenth century whereas other novelists, like Dixon, often set theirs in the present or the relatively recent past; blacks are conspicuous by their virtual absence, and never speak, whereas other writers use blacks to 'tell the story', often in picturesque strong dialect, in such a way that Southern philosophy of race relations is put into the mouths of black characters; the immediate setting is not a large plantation, but centres on the modest residence of a white woman who can afford only a few slaves. Finally, the white supremacy movement was reaching its height at the time, and the disenfranchisement of Southern blacks and America's interest in 'colonies' were getting under way - all factors of which the reading public would be aware and for which explanations or justifications would be sought.

The overt structure of the novel is that of historical romance, so that it is seen primarily as a love story set in the picturesque scenery of Kentucky in 1795. At that time Kentucky was at the forefront of the movement west; an unstable new state in the new Union, only a short time after the Constitution of the United States had been written. The book tells of the fated love of one John Gray for an older married woman, Mrs Falconer, who initiates him through the gift of the book *Le Morte D'Arthur* into ideals of chivalrous love and perfect manhood. Through coincidences and misunderstandings their love is never fulfilled, but John at least learns the true meaning of chivalry. Thus the novel ends, with the last sentence of a letter given to Mrs Falconer, now an old woman, by John Gray's son, many years after the two principal characters had last met, 'If I have kept unbroken faith with any of mine, thank you and thank God'. It is upon this plot that important ideas of black inferiority, American nationalism and manifest destiny are hung, with even a not so oblique justification of lynching.

There are two important lessons which John Gray learns in the course of the novel; ideas of chivalrous love of a very particular kind, and the fundamental importance of the nation state and of the necessity for a union of interests between North and South. The readers are meant to experience and identify with the education of the main character in the novel into some of the most fundamental ideological notions of the American ruling class.

Before looking at what John Gray learns, it is necessary to look briefly at the ideology of chivalry, love and idealised white womanhood which Allen was using. A retreat to a Utopian chivalrous past of idealised plantation existence in a mythical Golden Age, characterised much Southern literature by the 1830s (C. Silk, 1977). Of the ante-bellum Southern writer, Hubbell (1954, p714) wrote: 'He must either undertake to defend the *status quo* or else take refuge in historical romance that dealt with the past'. Such devices were used by many writers after the Civil War, in order to present an idyllic picture of life under slavery, and to romanticise the 'Lost Cause' - that of the slavocracy. The idealisation of the Southern white woman, and her identification with the white South and its ideology, was an integral part of the mythology and used to good effect by writers like Allen. Vigilante groups, past and present, were romanticised as knights whose function was to protect white women and, in turn, the white South, from the ravages, or potential ravages, of blacks. The logic of this is drawn out by racist writers, one of whom (Cash, 1941, pp115-116) wrote:

> To get at the ultimate secret of the Southern rape complex, we need to turn back and recall the central status that Southern women had long ago taken up in Southern emotion - her

> identification with the very notion of the South itself. For, with this in view, it is obvious that the assault on the South would be felt as, in some true sense, an assault on her also, and that the South would inevitably translate its whole battle into terms of her defense ... this Southern woman's place in the Southern mind proceeded primarily from the natural tendency of the great basic pattern of pride in superiority of race to centre upon her as the perpetuator of that superiority in legitimate line and attached itself precisely, and before everything else, to her enormous remoteness from the males of the inferior group, to the absolute taboo on any sexual approach to her from the Negro.

Idealisation of white women is therefore an essential part of the justification of white supremacy in which the lynching of blacks became the ultimate in chivalry. For instance, the full name of the Ku Klux Klan was the *Chivalrous Knights* of the Ku Klux Klan. In the novel, this conclusion is never spelt out. It does not need to be because it is implicit in the depiction of the relationship between Gray and Mrs Falconer, and in the lessons he learns about what it means to be an Anglo-Saxon man.

Mrs Falconer is portrayed throughout the book as the ideal Southern white women, ancestor of those women who, 100 years later, needed to be protected at any cost from freed blacks. Thinking of her early in the novel, John Gray muses:

> A sunbonnet for the tiara of asprey plumes; a dress spun and woven by her own hand out of her own flax, instead of the stiff brocade; log hut for manor house; one negro boy instead of troops of servants; to have possessed all that, to have been brought down to all this, and not to have been ruined by it, never to have lost distinction or been coarsened by coarseness, never to have parted with grace of manner or grace of spirit, or been bent or broken or overclouded in character and ideals - it was all this that made her in his eyes a great women, a great lady (pp26-7).

Towards the end of the novel, this white slave-holder is portrayed as an earthly saint - 'It was about this time also that there fell upon her hair the earliest rays of light which is the dawn of the Eternal Morning' (p346).

It is she who educates John Gray into the ideal of chivalrous love, an ideal closely related to a notion of manhood based on the superiority of the Anglo-Saxon race and its ideology, as embodied in Sir Thomas Malory's *Le Morte D'Arthur*: 'it was the first time that the ideals of chivalry had ever flashed their glorious light upon him; for the first time the models of Christian manhood, on which Western Europe nourished itself for centuries displayed themselves to his imagination with the charm of story' (*The Choir Invisible*, p244). The love story at the centre of the book is therefore explicitly related to ideas of white supremacy.

The second important lesson which he learns is that the sacredness of the Union is also related to ideas about Anglo-Saxon superiority. Unlike Dixon, Allen chose, by setting his novel in Kentucky in 1795, to apparently distance it from the problems of America in the 1890s. Yet he used this temporal distancing, and precise historical detail, to universalise notions of Anglo-Saxon superiority. He shows that the problems facing John Gray and Mrs Falconer are fundamentally the same as those facing white Southerners in the 1890s. The exception is the role of blacks. They pose no problem in 1795 because they are so completely subjugated. The implication is that they would be no problem in the 1890s if the white South is given a free hand to disenfranchise, segregate and lynch them. In the early 1790s Kentucky was, for a while, unhappy about her role in the new nation and there was talk of secession. What Gray learns is what white Southerners must also learn in the post-bellum period, namely that ultimately the interests of the superior race, North and South, are the same, and they have a common history and future as a nation state, at the expense of all inferior races, both internally and externally. The episode during which he meets the President (George Washington) on behalf of troubled parties in Kentucky can be structuraly juxtaposed to the scene in which he received Malory's book from Mrs Falconer. Centuries of Christian Anglo-Saxon tradition and superiority in Europe must be perpetuated in a New World setting. Convinced after his meeting that Kentucky must remain in the Union, Gray writes

> 'I think I can quote his (the President's) very words when he spoke of the foolish jealousies and heartburnings, due to misrepresentations, that have influenced Kentucky against the East as a section and against the Government as favouring it: "The West derives from the East supplies requisite to its growth and comfort; and what is perhaps of still greater consequence, it must of necessity, owe the secure enjoyment of indispensable outlets for

its own productions to the weight, influence and the future maritime strength of the Atlantic side of the Union, directed by an indissoluble community of interests, as *One Nation.*" (pp326-7).

Both lessons are related to the ideological concept of the Anglo-Saxon race. It is not simply an ethnological label, but carries with it connotations of superiority, a rich and specific history, and common destiny. The very title of the book, which serves to bind together the various themes, is a reference to the invisible ranks of the white ancestors of those middle-class readers, North and South, who are presumed to be reading the book. Much of the early material in the book also stresses that it was 'a few tired, rugged backwoodsmen of the Anglo-Saxon race' (p12) that fearlessly probed westward, opening up the Kentucky wilderness.

It is typical of Allen's work that the specificity of historical events in 1795 is used, in classic bourgeois fashion, to universalise his themes, attempting to make certain attitudes and values true for all places and times. Anglo-Saxon superiority is a 'fact of life', based on qualities which earlier allowed them to conquer the West and keep the blacks in their place, and which now (in the 1890s) justify continued black subjugation at home, and the conquest of 'the darker peoples' coming under American imperial rule overseas.

The explicit use that Allen makes of blacks in the text is very different. They are rarely present or mentioned. Unlike the whites, they have no history, and simply form part of the background. This use of blacks is especially effective in such writings. Because they are controlled by whites, they are of no more significance and by extension no more of a threat than the scenery of which they are quite simply portrayed as one element. Thus, John Gray imagines Mrs Falconer's past: 'Her childhood gone, then, he followed her as she glided along the shining creeks from plantation to plantation in a canoe manned by singing black oarsmen; or road abroad followed by her greyhound' (p196). Such descriptions serve to dehumanise blacks and to rob them of thought - they are precisely an harmonious element in a picturesque scene, no more important than the greyhound. They provide the local colour which emphasises the distinctiveness of the region, while their happiness under white Southern control (note their singing), emphasises their docility. Such blacks would never rebel. The happy and childlike condition of blacks under white control, together with the benign tolerance with which their stupidity and idleness are countered by genial whites, is graphically portrayed in such passages as 'She (Mrs Falconer) turned to the negro: "Go to the spring-house and bring some water". The lad moved away, smiling to himself and shaking his head. "He has broken all my pitchers", she added. "Today I had to send my last roll of line to town by Amy to buy more queen's ware. The grass will grow on the bucket before he gets back" (p34).

The scant references to blacks, and the type of reference, serves to take for granted the notion of white supremacy. A picture is built up in which blacks have their picturesque and silent place. No black ever speaks throughout the book; they are uncomplaining yet happy. Indeed, they have no need to complain. So charitable is the childless Mrs Falconer, that 'On Christmas Eve many a child's sock or stocking was hung - no-one knew when or by whom - around the shadowy chimney-seat of her room; and every Christmas morning the little negroes from the cabins knew to whom each of these belonged' (p344).

The impact of such novels, and the mass of other 'local colour' items to which we have referred, has been described as that of producing a popular attitude of complacency to images of a South in which blacks were lynched and white under-educated (Buck, 1937, p235), and of permitting liberals and moderates, while expressing some concern for Southern blacks, to acquiesce in Southern policies of segregation and disenfranchisement in terms of 'a benevolent internal colonialism' (Frederickson, 1971, p325).

Conclusion

We have shown how the literary device of 'local colour' had a complex ideological function which served both to bolster the new concept of the American nation-state and to build up a specific 'image region' of the South in which racism and national unity were articulated. Moreover, we have shown that the material base for equality - even in bourgeois terms - did not exist after the Civil War. The ideological struggle we have described contributed to the victory of the industrial capitalists of the North and later could be used to justify American imperialism. An important element of this economic triumph was the resolution of the ideological struggle in such a way as to ultimately serve the Northern interests while allowing Southern whites to believe that they had achieved a victory in ideological terms. This struggle in turn depended upon Northern dominance in spheres whose operation is crucial to the successful transmission of ideas, themes and images via the mass media - publishing, markets, distributive systems and readership. The successful achievement of hegemony is illustrated by the fact that the racist Southern historian Buck (1937, pp208-9) was not embarrassed to write:

> 'In every case the plantation "lived once mo', ... an' de ole times done come back ag'in". "Uncles", "Mammies", "Colonels", gracious ladies, fair maidens, and brave cadets crossed the pages with smiling faces and courteous manners; and "songs floated out upon the summer air, laden with the perfume of rose and honeysuckle and peach blossom". Even the "moonlight seemed richer and mellower before the War". What if the tradition omitted much that was true and exaggerated the attractive features of the departed life? It rested upon a bedrock of fact, and distorted the actuality no more violently than had the abolitionist attack whose unfriendly picture it was now fortunately correcting. The tradition itself became a fact, giving to Southern youth a conception of courage, energy, and strength upon which could be erected the foundations of a new life, and to Northerners an insight into the Southern heart which made it easier to understand why erstwhile foes had been inspired to "live and die for Dixie".'

and to state later:

> Once a people admits the fact that a major problem is basically insoluble they have taken the first step in learning to live with it. The conflicting elements of the race problem had dropped into a working adjustment which was accepted and rationalised as a settlement - Imperfect as it was, it permitted a degree of peace between North and South hitherto unknown, gave to the South the stability of race relations necessary to reconcile her to the re-united nation, and gave to the Negro the chance to live and to take the first steps of progress (Buck, 1937, p297).

What we have shown is that the ideological struggle was a refraction of an intense economic and political struggle which Camejo (1976) referred to as America's second revolutionary upheaval, and we have analysed the interaction between these kinds of struggle and evaluated the relative importance of coercion and consent in each case. Struggles against the dominant ideology require fuller investigation, as do the relationships with those centred directly on the capital-labour contradiction and the women's movement (Davis, 1982). Changing images of the South, and of other parts of the United States, in terms of the role played by newer forms of mass media - the cinema and television, in particular - should be investigated in relation to shifts in the balance of economic and political forces which have occurred in the twentieth century, particularly for the period after the Second World War when the relatively stable equilibrium was severely jolted by internal campaigns for Civil Rights and external struggles by blacks for liberation from colonialism in Sub-Saharan Africa.

CHAPTER 9: NEWS FROM NOWHERE: THE PRESS, THE RIOTS AND THE MYTH OF THE INNER CITY

Jacquelin A. Burgess

> Every myth can have its history and its geography; each is in fact the sign of the other: a myth ripens because it spreads. I have not been able to carry out any real study of the social geography of myths. But it is perfectly possible to draw ... the lines which limit the social region where it is spoken. As this region is shifting, it would be better to speak of the waves of implantation of the myth ... Some myths hesitate: will they pass into tabloids, the home of the suburbanite of private means, the hairdresser's salon, the tube? The social geography of myths will remain difficult to trace as long as we lack an analytical sociology of the press. But we can say that its place already exists (Barthes, 1972, pp149-150).

Events take place but often the geography of the news remains an unquestioned backcloth to those events. A few film shots establish location; a few sentences in a newspaper report place and occasionally explain the news. Nevertheless these references are important since the majority pass into our taken-for-granted understanding of the world.

Research concerned with the content and genesis of urban and regional imagery has already begun to consider media representations of places (Burgess, 1981, 1982; Goodey, 1983). In this chapter, I take this process further by exploring the ideological role played by news media in which the meaning of places is implicated in class and culture-based explanations of urban life. Through the selection, reproduction and interpretation of 'news', the media construct preferred readings which give meaning to events. People-in-place, the subjects of the news, are presented in the context of preferred readings. In analysing this material, particular use is made of insights derived from semiology. Semiology has contributed much to an understanding of the social production of meanings through its focus on the language within which events are encoded and the social forces which influence the ways in which messages are produced and 'read'. The concept of myth as developed by Roland Barthes (1972) provides a valuable analytical tool for empirical studies of place imagery, having greater explanatory power than the largely ahistorical conceptualisations of stereotypes as used in social psychology.

In this chapter I examine the ways in which the British national daily papers interpreted the 'riots' of the spring and summer of 1981. We shall encounter many struggles over the appropriation of meaning in this paper and here is the first. Words do not have fixed internal meanings. 'Riot' was the signification used by the news media. What the word means and whether the street disturbances were 'riots' or not is open to debate. How did the media make sense of what happened in the three major conurbations of London, Liverpool and Manchester? For most people, the drama of the events of that year were caught and committed to memory in the form expressed by the mass media. Banner headlines, dramatic, confrontational photographs, and extended coverage signalled the riots as profoundly significant social events. Not only were these violent and dramatic happenings very clearly located but the press were anxious to find some causal link between the riotous behaviour and the conditions of life in the inner cities. Hamnett is not correct in his assertion that 'little or no attempt was made by the media to systematically relate the timing and areas of occurrence of the riots to the underlying social and economic conditions of the areas concerned' (1983, p7). The newspapers in particular were much exercised not only by the social and economic circumstances but also the environmental conditions in the inner cities.

Most research about the events of 1981 and their aftermath has concentrated on racial and policing issues, with much attention being given to Lord Scarman's report (1981) and recommendations after the Brixton riot (Cowell *et al*, 1982; Deakin, 1982; Field and Southgate, 1982; Kettle and Hodges, 1982; Keith and Peach, 1983; Benyon, 1984). The role of the television news media in stimulating 'copy cat' disturbances has also been discussed (Tumber, 1982). The context of the disturbances are liable to be forgotten as the names of Brixton, Toxteth and Moss Side become part of the half-remembered folklore about the period. I discuss the meanings given to the concept of the inner city in the press reports of the disturbances, and argue that the newspapers fulfil an ideological role in which a myth is being perpetuated of *The Inner City* as an alien place, separate and isolated, located outside white, middle-class values and environments. The first section of the paper addresses the question of news and the means through which its selection, production and impacts might best be analysed. The second section turns attention back to the events of 1981 and explores the myth of the inner city by drawing on reports in the national daily and Sunday papers for the period April-September 1981.

Making the News

North American and European approaches to mass media studies contrast sharply in their approaches to the organisation and production of news, the analysis of media content and the assessment of the effects of content on attitudes and behaviour (Curran *et al*, 1977; McQuail, 1983). On the one hand, traditional American approaches have been mechanistic: modelling communications systems, quantifying messages through content analysis and assessing the impact of content in terms of individual responses. On the other hand, European approaches have gone some way to meeting Barthes' (1972) request for an 'analytical sociology of the press'. Marxist analyses, structural and semiotic studies of meaning and sociological studies of sub.cultures and deviance have all contributed to the development of media studies which regard the media as playing a central role in the shaping of social reality (Westergaard, 1977; Murdoch and Golding, 1978; Gurevitch *et al*, 1982). A major emphasis has been on the question of meaning. Within the behaviourist approaches of American research, meaning has not been an issue. The 'social psychological impulsion tended to obscure the analysis of media messages which was in any case dependent on the impoverished method of content analysis' (Curran *et al*, 1977, p311). Content analysis assumes a 'transparent' text, i.e. that meaning is fixed, universally understood and unproblematic. It is an assumption which has been shattered by more theoretically-informed work. Meaning is not given: it is negotiated between different groups, some of whom have more power than others. Different sub cultures have their own specialised discourses and different groups will 'decode' the meanings of messages in different ways (Hall and Jefferson, 1976; Cohen, 1980).

The mass media play a profoundly significant role in the appropriation and interpretation of the meanings of social reality. They have the capability to shape conceptions of our physical, economic, political and social environments. Despite their relative autonomy from the state, the media serve as an important agency of social control (Cohen and Young, 1981). The mass media have:

> 'progressively *colonised* the cultural and ideological sphere. As social groups and classes live, if not in their productive then in their 'social' relations, increasingly fragmented and sectionally differentiated lives, the mass media are more and more responsible (a) for providing the basis on which groups and classes construct an "image" of the lives, meanings, practices and values of *other* groups and classes; (b) for providing the images, representations and ideas around which the social totality, composed of all these separate and fragmented pieces, can be coherently grasped as a "*whole*". This is the first of the great cultural functions of the modern media: the provision and the selective construction of *social knowledge*, of social imagery, through which we perceive the "worlds", the "lived realities" of others, and imaginarily reconstruct their lives and ours into some intelligible "world-of-the-whole", some "lived totality" (Hall, 1977, pp340-1).

Gathering Fallen Apples: the Selection and Presentation of News

News does not exist; it is created. Questions must be asked about the processes of selection, the means of presentation, and the influence of the organisational demands on the eventual determination of 'news'. The broadcasting news media, for example, have different technological capabilities, not least of which is the ability of television to capture actuality (see the Glasgow Media Group, 1976, 1982). The newspapers are competing both with television and among themselves for a declining readership, a situation which has had a noticeable effect on the commercial and entertainment orientation of the 'popular' press (Burns, 1977; Tunstall, 1982).

Newspapers present a text for analysis which can be read in terms of layout, the relations between headlines, written text and photographs, the placings of items within the paper. Chibnall (1981) accuses media sociologists of a 'dangerously simplistic view' of news production in which news-gatherers find stories for news-producers to abbreviate and fit into pages. 'The reporter does not go out gathering news, picking up stories as if they were fallen apples, he (sic) *creates* news stories by selecting fragments of information from the mass of raw data ... and organising them in a conventional journalistic form' (p76). Three basic criteria are required for an event to be reported; *temporal recency, action* and *newsworthiness* (see

Galtung and Ruge, 1965; Tuchman, 1978).

The selection of news and the construction of stories reflect both organisational demands and journalistic practices. Newspaper production demands certain routines and encourages an emphasis on certain types of events. The 24-hour cycle of production tends to favour immediate events or events which have reached a climax (Molotch and Lester, 1974; Rock, 1981). Events which unfold over a longer time period are less likely to be reported, which leads to an emphasis on their *form* rather than their underlying causes (Murdoch, 1981). News is short-lived and transitory, yielding to the pressures of all the following days. Editors allocate space within newspapers for different types of news. Sport, light entertainment, features, home and foreign news stories are selected so as to fit those space requirements. Only in exceptional circumstances is the balance of news changed.

Events become visible and potentially newsworthy through a chain of organisational and personal contacts. Temporal deadlines encourage journalists to use sources who provide information in a form already suitable for translation into newspaper styles. Reporters experience very few events first-hand. They are dependent on agencies, on 'stringers' from other parts of the country, and especially on the organised voices of the state - politicians, government departments, the police. The dependency on external agencies and processes of exchange link journalist and source together. In the case of crime reporters, for example, the links with the police are most significant because the exchange is relatively exclusive and gives the sense of powerful 'inside' knowledge (Chibnall, 1978; Fishman, 1981). Politicians also exploit the relative dependency of journalists for information. Murphy (1976, 1978) for example, is critical of the dependency of local newspaper reporters on local politicians.

> My research and experience as a reporter leads me to believe that whatever claims the interested participants in the world of newspapers make for themselves as guardians of democracy ... reporters and editors spend most of their time solving immediate organisational problems of news production and little or none on democracy ... the nature of the daily activities of news production, with its pressure on continuous and fast production ... and a legal and political system which values statements from some individuals ... while others are ignored ... leads to conservatism

> and a passive reliance on established contacts and procedures in newspaper reporting (Murphy, 1978, pp187-8).

Tumber (1982) illustrates how establishment figures used the television news to put across their point of view during the riots. The figures highlight questions of unequal access to the media. Between 14 and 16 July 1981, government ministers were given 373 seconds of television news time, senior police had 367 seconds, community leaders had 147 and the rioters themselves had just 52 seconds time in which to put their points of view. Hansen (quoted in Murdoch, 1984) found that national newspapers allocated similar proportions of space to the different groups.

Criteria of 'newsworthiness' are most difficult to define. Journalists fall back on the indefinable sixth sense of their craft, known as *News Values* to account for the selection of one event in preference to another. Hall (1981b, p234) describes news values as 'one of the most opaque structures of meaning in modern society'. In addition to those values which meet the organisational demands of the paper such as frequency, other 'qualities' are needed for an event to become news These include the involvement of elite persons, the consonance of the event with others that have gone before, 'meaningful' qualities in terms of the home culture, unexpectedness, and personalisation (Roshier, 1981; Hartley, 1982). Events should also be relatively unambiguous, open to only a limited number of interpretations. News values connect people to anonymous events and, Hall (1981b) argues, search out 'the "drama", the "human interest" behind impersonal historical forces'.

News values establish a hierarchy of newsworthy events. Different areas of social and cultural life are mapped into different domains which are then organised hierarchically to give front page news (Murdoch, 1974, 1981; Hall, 1978). New, troubling, unexpected or problematic events are assigned to their respective domains before they can be said to 'make sense'. Murdoch (1981), for example, demonstrates how the *Guardian* and the *Daily Mirror* both interpreted the 1973 demonstration in Grosvenor Square from an initial story line which anticipated violent confrontation between peace marchers and the police. This interpretation provided the framework for reports of the actual march, which concentrated exclusively on the small number of violent incidents. Mapping realities in this way perpetuates certain assumptions about society: for example, that social life is basically composed of the actions of individuals whose lives are divided into separate parts - work, home, leisure, children, and so on. These fragmentations are organised hierarchically in terms of their social significance: thus domestic 'private' life is assigned a lower rating than 'public' political or social events. Mapping gives 'meaning' to events while the continual presentation of news within established frameworks recharges familiar knowledge and increases the chance of selection next time. Most important, readers are continually presented with a set of assumptions which reinforce the fundamental framework of social consensus. Hall (1978, p55) sees consensus as the critical assumption behind the mass media, one which operates at 'an extreme ideological level. Because we occupy the same society and belong to roughly the same "culture", it is assumed that there is, basically, only *one* perspective of events; that provided by ... *the* culture'. Thus, dissent of many kinds is mapped as being outside the consensus. It becomes deviant, marginalised behaviour (Hall and Jefferson, 1976; Cohen, 1980).

Within cultural studies, the operation of the drive for consensus meaning is described by the concept of hegemony (Gramsci, 1971; Clarke *et al*, 1976). Hegemony is used to explain the apparent consent given by the subordinate classes to the world view of the dominant class. The concept accounts for the pervasiveness of a particular way of viewing the environment, human nature and social relationships. Hegemony differs from Marx's concept of ideology because it requires the willing acceptance by the subordinate classes and is therefore significant in societies where 'public opinion' is thought important, in societies where 'social practice is seen to depend on consent to certain dominant ideas which in fact express the needs of a dominant class' (Williams, 1976, p145).

There is no crude domination by the ruling class over the media or by the media over the rest of us. The media operate within a relatively free environment and, further, there is always uncertainty that the intended meaning of text and photograph will be decoded 'legitimately' by its readers. Morley (1980) argues that words, sentences and pictures carry many different meanings at the same time; their 'multi-accentuality' makes for doubt that readers will achieve a particular interpretation. 'The meaning(s) of a text will be conducted differently, depending on the discourses (knowledge, prejudices, resistances) *brought to bear on the text by the reader*' (p171). He goes on to argue that the dominant, negotiated and oppositional meaning systems identified by Parkin (1972) are not simply class-based. The taking of meaning depends on a 'repertoire' of decoding strategies which reflect the opportunities and limitations possible in different social positions.

The mass media are profoundly implicated in the maintenance of hegemony. Fiske and Hartley (1978) have described this role as a 'bardic function': 'Both the original bardic order and the modern media constitute distinct and internally coherent social organisations, but they both occupy the very centre of the cultural stage - their position is not that of alienated artist and their "message" is at once the source and the result of pervasive common meanings - "common" sense' (Hartley, 1982, p105). Commonsense is unsystematic and inconsistent, it is an understanding which has no underlying theory. Lawrence (1982), in a study of 'commonsense racism', concluded that newspaper reports of the 1981 riots used racist themes but in a way which appeared to be designed 'to revamp and update commonsense rather than to organise it' (p79). Commonsense has been described as 'a storehouse of knowledges gathered together': the knowledges are appropriate for the practical struggles of everyday life because they represent the assimilation of contradictory views without discomfort (Hall, Lumley and McLennan, 1978). This feature has significance in the winning of consent for the dominant hegemony because it allows for two very different kinds of knowledge and meaning; the generalised and the situated (Hall, Critchner *et al*1978, p155). Situated judgments reflect individual experience and relate directly to the positions that people find themselves in. Generalised knowledge, on the other hand, represents the 'naturalisation' of the existing social order.

In Barthes' (1972) terms, the difference between situated and generalised knowledge is the difference between meaning and myth. Myth transforms meaning into form, history into nature:

> Myth is constituted by the loss of the historical quality of things; in it things lose the memory that they were once made ... (Myth) has turned reality inside out, it has emptied it of history and has filled it with nature, it has removed from things their human meaning so as to make them signify a human insignificance. The function of myth is to empty reality (Barthes, 1972, pp142-3).

In *Myth Today*, Barthes identifies two semiological systems; a linguistic system (the language), and a metalanguage, which is the language of myth. Following Saussure, Barthes distinguishes in each level between the *signifier* (the sound image) and the *signified* (the concept) which combine to form the *sign*. Signifier and signified are related in an arbitrary way, there is no natural connection between them and so a signifier can carry many different meanings in different times and different places. In the first order system, language objects 'speak things'. They are direct and active. Myth operates at the second level, by taking as its signifier the sign of the first system. Myth speaks about things: as such it is ambiguous, being both full of meaning and empty of form. 'The meaning is *already* complete, it postulates a kind of knowledge, a past, a memory ... When it becomes form, the meaning leaves its contingency behind; it empties itself, it becomes impoverished, history evaporates, only the letter remains' (Barthes, 1972, p117). In myth, ideological connotations are obscured by an apparent denotation, by an apparent literalness whose function is to 'naturalise' class propositions.

The illustration Barthes uses to demonstrate this relationship is a photograph of a black soldier saluting a French flag, printed on the cover of *Paris Match*. The meaning at the first level is the situated reality of the soldier but the photograph is being used to signify something greater, the myth of French imperialism. Readers believe the denoted 'truth' of the photograph. The event took place and so the soldier's behaviour and French colonialism are naturalised. The connotation (the reading of the 'meaning' at an ideological level) allows the myth of black people willingly serving the demands of the French colonial system to be innocently consumed.

Barthes (1977) recognises that it is impossible to separate the ideological from the phraseological, the words from the intention. 'Contemporary myth is ... (expressed) in "discourse", at most it is *phraseology*: a corpus of phrases (of stereotype)' (p167). To read myths is to evaluate the degree of phraseological density and the levels of reification in texts. He introduces the notion of 'thick' languages which are full of citations and references to other meanings and circumstances. The main criticisms levelled against Barthes's concept of myth have concerned his primary focus on linguistic processes of signification, whilst neglecting the complex social environments in which texts are produced (Weedon *et al*, 1980, p182). In this section, I have discussed some of the social practices which encourage the production of certain meanings in media texts, but it is language which carries meaning and we need to be alive to the myths: 'the mythical is everywhere sentences are turned, stories told' (Barthes, 1977, p169).

Telling Stories: The street disturbances of 1981

In the previous section, I have discussed the bureaucratic and organisational constraints within which newspapers operate, the power of news values in the way journalists and editors frame their accounts, the unceasing drive for the drama of the ordinary, and the continual personification of news which obscures the causes of social and political activities. When events unfold over a period of time, as the riots did, then newspaper reports share a tendency to group and link events and to put together a 'signification spiral' (Cohen and Young, 1981), through which meaning is given to events. In this section, I shall analyse texts from a range of national newspapers to explore the meanings given to the localities in which rioting took place. The period covered is April to September 1981, and I used six daily papers - *The Guardian, The Times, Daily Telegraph, Daily Mirror, Daily Star, Daily Mail,* and four Sunday papers - *Observer, The Sunday Times, Sunday Telegraph, Sunday People.* This gives a cross section of the 'quality' and 'popular' press, covering the current political spectrum.

The major disturbances occurred in Brixton, south London, Toxteth in Liverpool [1] and Moss Side in Manchester. They were largely confined to a few streets in each locality - Railton Road and Atlantic Road in Brixton; Upper Parliament Street, Lodge Lane and Park Road in Liverpool; Princess Road in Moss Side. The streets gained some notoriety, especially Railton Road which quickly became the symbol of a 'front line'; between blacks, whites and the police. Table 9.1 provides details of selected events associated with the disturbances in 1981.

Newspapers provide both linguistic and visual texts. News itself can be reported in three forms. First, there is the 'factual' reporting of events. Secondly, papers carry special features where, for example, journalists are despatched to places to provide fuller accounts of events. Features also include commissioned articles exploring aspects of the issues (e.g. Beryl Bainbridge on Liverpool 8) [2] and depth analyses which may take a few days to research (e.g. *Daily Star* enquiry into race relations). [3] Thirdly, editorials comment on the news and give voice to the political perspective of the paper. One consequence of this threefold treatment is that particular views are considerably reinforced. Photographs and cartoons provide visual text. Cartoons generally reflect the dominant framework within which news is interpreted. Photographs are designed to be read in

Table 9.1: The 1981 Disturbances - a timetable of selected events

Date	Description of Event
10-12 April	Disturbances in Brixton - between black and white people and the police. Centred on Railton Road, Atlantic Road. 226 casualties; 196 arrests
14 May	Lord Scarman begins preliminary hearing for enquiry
19 May	Police Federation conference delegates demand riot protection gear
2 June	Boycott of Scarman enquiry recommended by Brixton Defence Committee
3 July	SOUTHALL: clashes between Asian youths and skinheads after rock concert. Police involvement
4-6 July	LIVERPOOL 8: disturbances in Upper Parliament Street, Park Road, Lodge Lane. Black and white youths attack police after street arrest. Looting. CS gas used in mainland Britain for first time.
7 July	Wood Green, looting
7-8 July	MOSS SIDE: rioting on Princess Road. Police station beseiged
11-12 July	Street disturbances in 20 different locations, including Liverpool, Hull, Leeds and Leicester
15 July	BRIXTON: police raid properties in Railton Road
21 July	Heseltine in Liverpool
26-28 July	TOXTETH: rioting. First fatality. David Moore run over by police vehicle
28 July	Lady Margaret Simey says she would consider people apathetic if they did not riot, because conditions are so bad in Toxteth
11 August	Funeral of David Moore, fracas with police
15 August	Liverpool, anti-police march
17 August	Hytner enquiry into Moss Side riots opens. Boycotted by local communities and police refuse to give evidence
26 August	Heseltine package for Liverpool announced. Normal mixture of economic incentives
13 October	Hytner report published
15 October	Heseltine plea for the inner cities at Conservative Party Conference
25 November	Scarman report published

association with headline and caption which deeply colours interpretation. The determination of the news values of photographs and their apparent reality are both interesting issues to explore (see Hall, 1981; Barthes, 1982).

In terms of the selection of photographs and the language used to describe events, there was very little difference between the 'quality' and 'popular' press. Photographs concentrated on the police who were shown in confrontation with white and black people, standing behind riot shields, being led away (bloodied) by colleagues. The aftermath of the riots was portrayed in photographs of burnt-out buildings, looted shops and damage to property. Very few photographs shared the rioters' perspective, partly because of danger to cameramen and equipment, partly because the opposite visual perspective also offered potential for different interpretations of what was happening [4] (see Barber, 1982).

Riot discourse was a metaphor of war: **RIOT TORN, RIOT RAVAGED, THE BATTLE OF BRIXTON, BLOODY SATURDAY, WAR ON THE STREETS.** The inner cities were being BLITZED by 'mobs' of young people. Extracting maximum drama from what were already dramatic events, headlines and texts carried extreme emotional tones. Some were blatant, others evoked drama more subtly. Reporters and sub-editors wrote of 'the Toxteth terror, the horror of it all, fear stalking the streets, violence and hate, orgies of looting and violence'. A common description was of the 'anarchic ferocity' of many encounters between police and people. The rioters themselves were supposed 'insane'. The interpretation of the activities of the 'mob' hearkened back to the nineteenth century - 'the rioters were "irrational, insane, running berserk and losing control'.

Journalists fashion accounts in line with the public voice of their paper and its readership. Take, for example, these two first-hand accounts of Toxteth on the night of Monday 6 July:

A NIGHT ON BOTH SIDES OF THE LINE
'I was trapped in a council flat as the battle of Upper Parliament Street reached its insane climax just before midnight. (...)Reporters like myself shambled like tramps, removing ties to avoid being identified by looters and attacked. Suddenly a pink bloom of smoke rose from the other end of Upper Parliament

> Street. One and a half miles of devastation had been cut through the city. When I got there, I saw my car was burned out. I escaped down a side street, my eyes stung with CS gas'. [5]

> **BLOODY BATTLE**: a nightmare on the streets of hatred ... 'It was like a horror picture with a cast of thousands (...) For seven hate-filled hours I ran with the rioters on their rampage of terror. I heard them howling as they drove the police down Upper Parliament Street and saw: (...)
> HORROR ... as the masked men set up a base camp in a tower block and handed out petrol bombs to their frenzied army of teenagers (...)
> HORROR ... as a child hurling bricks stopped me to ask the time and said "I'll have to get home soon. Me mam will kill me if I'm late". (...)
> HORROR ... as the police hit back with CS gas, the only weapon in their meagre armoury capable of halting the mayhem'. [6]

The style of the two pieces is different but the basic constructions are the same. The criminality of the participants, the insanity of the events, the threat to the reporters and the acceptance of CS gas. In the former, its use is reported 'factually' although linked to the car theft; in the latter it is justified in terms of the 'meagre' armoury of the police. Murdoch (1984) has argued recently that public acceptance of a militarised police force will probably be the long-lasting impact of the reporting of the riots, because the press were instrumental in changing what had been seen as an exceptional response by the police into one which is a normal and necessary part of crowd control.

The press divided in the extent to which conditions of life in the inner city areas were thought to be causal factors behind the disturbances. Papers such as the *Daily Mail, Daily Star, Daily* and *Sunday Telegraph* came down firmly on issues of law and order, immigration policies, criminality, lack of parental control and the need to equip the police (Fig. 9.1). These papers were also exercised by the possibilities of a conspiracy. For example, the *Daily Mail* editorial for 9 July 1981 - FIRST CATCH THE RING LEADERS - argued that 'teenage violence is uglier and more destructively anarchic than anything before'. It called for examplary sentences for offenders and advised the police to turn to the Royal Ulster Constabulary - 'the specialists in contemporary urban terror, for practical advice'. The more 'liberal' press, such as the *Guardian, Daily*

Funny, I could have sworn the Home Secretary said we were to have water CANNONS

Fig 9.1

Mirror, Observer and *Sunday Times* were much more concerned with the 'deprivation' thesis and its associations with government policies. The *Daily Mirror*, for example, in a front-page editorial for 7 July entitled: SAVE OUR CITIES, stressed the immediate necessity of removing the mobs from the streets but went on to argue: 'The smoke that hangs over burning communities is also a pall of despair. The spending on the inner cities has been ruthlessly and blindly cut ... The riots, the racial attacks, the tensions and the intolerance have social causes and political solutions'. None, however, supported the actions of the people who took to the streets.

Over the five months, attention given to the conditions of life in the inner areas varied. The first disturbances in Brixton prompted some discussion of the inner city, largely in the context of policing 'black' communities. The policing issues were reinforced by the Terms of Enquiry given to Lord Scarman. During the major disruptions in July, the newspapers devoted more attention to discussion of underlying causes which included unemployment levels, urban deprivation, race and policing issues. The event which brought the inner city to the forefront, however, was the decision to send Michael Heseltine (as Secretary of State for the Environment) to Liverpool, where he was to investigate the economic, social and environmental problems of that city. This political manoeuvre by the Conservative government effectively shifted attention back into the well worn, familiar debate about relative deprivation. For a crucial period, the much more explosive issues of racism and policing practices were marginalised. [7] The presence of Heseltine in Liverpool for three weeks allowed journalists to make the most of their long-standing fascination with the city (see Bedford, 1982) and much good copy was generated by the contrast between the affluence of 'the menswear ad' Minister [8] and the poverty of the local people.

The Myth of the Inner City

Myth hides nothing: it distorts meaning by appropriating and reworking first order signs for its own ideological purposes. The language in press reports is 'thick' in that it is full of reference to commonsense understanding and stereotyped phraseology. Four separate domains contribute to the inner city myth by weaving together the streets, shops and houses, the empty spaces, the different cultural styles, class and racial characteristics, legitimate and 'illegitimate' forms of behaviour. The place which is created is empty of reality. The inner city is alien, outside 'normal' places. It is populated by white and black people who are outside 'normal' society. Both the inner city and its inhabitants threaten the values and standards of 'civilised society'.

I identify four distinct ideological domains which combine in the inner city myth. Each has a history of its own which has been documented elsewhere (see, for example, Eversley, 1973; Swingewood, 1977; Hartmann and Husband, 1978; Lawrence, 1982; Steadman Jones, 1982; Pearson, 1983; Oakley, 1984). Aspects from each domain are used in press reports and together they constitute the inner city. To summarise:

1. **The physical environment** of the locality: through which reports describe the houses and the streets in which events took place. These features are used to explore changing social structures, to provide an explanation of the psychological states of inhabitants; and to make judgments about policy, notably planning and local authority economic and spatial policies.

2. Characteristics of **white working-class culture**, which in the context of the inner areas is a discourse about poverty, family structures

A portrait of Liverpool 8

BEFORE the fury spilled over

THIS is the grim face of Toxteth, Liverpool 8 — the rundown area which became front-page news after a weekend of savage rioting.

These pictures, specially taken for the Daily Mirror in March, show the squalor and desolation and what was once a middle-class suburb.

Unemployment in the area, now virtually a black ghetto, is critically high.

Muggings and housebreakings are commonplace.

Red-light girls thrive in the shambles of tatty terraced streets and modern tenement slums.

But it is the despair of unemployment which probably lies at the heart of Toxteth's festering troubles.

A city councils survey last year put the number of jobless in the area at 37 per cent.

Other estimates paint an even more dismal picture.

A recent Liverpool University report on the Liverpool and district put white unemployment at 43 per cent and black at 47 per cent.

In its 1980 report the Merseyside Community Relations Committee claimed that half the black people in the city were out of work.

Latest unemployment figures for the city show 81,000 people chasing just over 1,000 jobs.

At the careers office, with thousands of school-leavers looking for work, there are just twelve vacancies.

Against this background, the ugly and unacceptable face of Toxteth has little hope.

SEEDY: A broken-down car is left to rot against a background of rundown houses. Picture: MARK RUSHER.

SHABBY: Three men relax outside a boarded-up slum house.

SHARING: Two children enjoy a spot of racial harmony. Picture: MARTIN ARGOS.

Please turn to next page

Fig.9.2 (see page 228 for enlargement of text)

such as large numbers of children, and poor parenting, domestic overcrowding, illicit sex, thieving and hooliganism, poor educational attainment, lack of ambition, and despair about unemployment and the lack of opportunities.

3. Characteristics of race, which in terms of the major disturbances means West Indian or **'black' culture**. The major features are immigrant status, a desire for repatriation, the marked generation gap, a volatile and excitable nature; alienation from white society,

high unemployment, low levels of attainment, and criminality which makes young blacks particularly hostile to the police.

4. The final strand which overlaps with the other three is the meaning given to the street. **Street culture** draws on ideas of illegality and loose moral standards among white, working-class culture as expressed in prostitution, illegal gambling and drinking dens, vandalism and graffiti. From the black culture it draws on the perceived criminality of young black people, using as evidence muggings and other street crimes which have been the subject of considerable media attention in the past (Hall *et al*, 1978; Smith, this volume). Drugs are another significant contribution from the black culture.

The *Daily Mirror* piece about Toxteth before the riots (Fig. 9.2) illustrates the way in which the myth is constructed. Four grainy black and white photographs, one an inset showing a bloodied policeman, the others showing different views of 'derelict' Toxteth. The vandalised, burnt-out car carries reminders of the riot photographs; the men sitting on the ledge of a boarded-up, crumbling mansion convey ideas of what Toxteth once was before the collapse of 'civilised' life; the posed picture with the two little girls is a romanticised comment on 'racial harmony'. The text, in best *Daily Mirror* tradition (see Waterhouse, 1981), is sparse, direct and conveys enough information for its readers to grasp the essential meaning of Toxteth and the inner city.

An editorial in *The Times*[9] in a more complex text creates the same understanding. Entitled **SOUND THE ALARM** the paper expresses great concern for the younger generation who:

> (...) have to live in the decaying inner cities, from where the more able, the more self sufficient, the more ambitious have quit, leaving behind less fortunate and the inadequate. Their housing is often substandard; they live in vandalised tower blocks or soulless estates ... any community life there may have been has broken down'.

The implications of this paragraph are that the inner city is a place to 'escape from', and that the activities of the young people left behind can be explained by a pathology of inadequacy. The tone is relentlessly individualistic: individuals by dint of their own actions can escape from the decay and degeneration. The editorial blames poor educational facilities, bad teachers and the lack of parental control for the production of these inadequate people. It suggests that blacks have additional burdens because of discrimination. In consequence, young people are 'rootless, jobless, alienated from their parents' generation, resentful of the deal they are getting from society'. The editorial concludes that both white and black young people 'find excitement in crime, in violence, in fighting authority first with attitudes, then with stones ...' The newspaper does not connect feelings of alienation and resentment with the street disturbances. It interprets these actions as a desire for 'excitement' rather than as a valid political protest.

'The Derelict Terraces and Rundown Tatty Streets'

The language of the built environment is limited. A few adjectives and stock phrases are used to describe all three localities: rundown, decaying, derelict, delapidated, shabby and sleazy. Railton Road, for example: 'this street of sleazy shops, old terraced houses and derelict sites'; [10] 'a rundown impoverished road without distinguishing features'; [11] 'a mile of cracked windows and peeling paintwork'. [12] Upper Parliament Street was described as 'a desolate shambles of rundown Victorian houses and modern tenement slums; [13] Liverpool 8 as 'a sprawling hatch of rundown houses and shops'; [14] Moss Side as the 'decayed area' of Moss Side. 'Rundown' is ubiquitous and carries two meanings; first, of unsightliness and second of neglect. 'The dilapidated rundown shops are as unsightly as ever'. [15] Rundown as neglect reflects either on the activities of residents or the policies of the local authority. In Toxteth, Heseltine apparently saw 'the self inflicted wounds of people who have vandalised their own housing estates, brought terror and anarchy to their own streets'. [16] Most papers preferred the easier target of local authority policy, which accorded more directly with readers' commonsense understanding. Rundown means planning blight, or the failure to complete schemes because the money ran out. [17]

The press describe only two kinds of houses in the inner areas, Georgian and Victorian mansions and terraces, which have seen better days, and modern public authority estates which are either tenement or high rise. Many of these are 'slums' unless the resident is being interviewed, in which case the property will be 'neat' and 'spotlessly clean'. Both types of property harbour illicit activities. The *Daily Telegraph*[18] comments on the 'irony' of blacks living and rioting in an area where 'the fading Victorian houses' were built by wealthy merchants who had made their money from the slave trade. The houses 'have now been converted into either flats or seedy nightclubs'. *The Times* reporter [19] contrasts the mansions of Toxteth 'some derelict, boarded up and smeared with graffiti ... others restored to something like their former glory'. Note the use of an emotionally loaded word like 'smeared' rather than a more neutral word like covered or marked. The *Daily Telegraph*[20] also reminds its readers that Brixton used to be 'a middle-class suburb of tree-lined avenues and elegant houses' before commenting on the 'gaily painted terrace houses' in which the 'immigrants' live. The decaying mansions ideologically chart the decline of the area from bourgeois suburb to working-class slum and black ghetto.

The press commended evidence of gentrification still to be found in the inner city despite the appalling dereliction. The middle class, in Brixton at least, are engaged in the 'colonisation' [21] of the large mansions. It is an interesting choice of word, suggestive of reclaiming the useful parts of the inner city back into 'civilised' society. However, the new colonists living in the streets off Railton Road in Brixton are not entirely straightforward; 'they are often left wing ... and determined to make a multi-racial community work ... there has rarely been trouble in their own streets with their pleasant gardens and pretty Victorian houses'. The *Daily Telegraph*[22] also commented on the 'varied' nature of the Brixton environment, with 'tree-lined streets of beautiful Regency houses - most protected with burglar alarms'. The threat of black criminality lurks, as ever just beneath the surface of the report. The resurgence of private, single-household, middle-class families in the inner city is signalled as being favourable in press reports by a change in language: pleasant streets, pretty houses and gardens, clean paint, areas 'coming up in the world having fallen for a while on hard times'. [23]

These attitudes contrast with the opprobrium directed towards public housing schemes. Public housing is almost always described as being 'substandard'; tower blocks are always 'vandalised', housing estates are inevitably 'soulless'. The 'popular' press is satisfied to speak simply of 'poor' or 'abysmally inadequate housing', or 'modern tenement slums'. The 'quality' press elaborate, blaming planners and architects for creating such dreadful environments with tower blocks 'placed at random' [24] which even denies the existence of a plan. The *Daily Telegraph*[25] reifies both policy and sociology in allocating responsibility for the environment and, by implication, the riots. 'Policy ... imposed on the poor, hideous public housing in the name of social theory'. The destruction of 'the local community' through redevelopment, compulsory purchase and high rates is attributed directly to the authorities and 'explains' the collapse of the economic and social fabric of the areas. The people 'who are the *natural* source of leadership - homeowners, shopkeepers, landlords and small businessmen' (my italics) have been driven away by these activities.[26] Asking who 'the real vandals' are, Beryl Bainbridge[27] says: 'after all, they only burned down the Rialto, the Racquets Club, a bit of the hospital and most of Lodge Lane. She (Mrs Thatcher) should have asked who knocked down the rest of it'. The designers were even accused of facilitating the riots. In an editorial, *The Times*[28] stresses the dangers of over-simplifying causes but goes on to include housing policies in its list of factors: 'Large tenement blocks were often the refuge of rioters escaping from the police, and a grandstand for audiences looking on from a safe height'.

The built environments of Brixton and Toxteth offered considerable scope for emotive, 'creative' features which relied on the stereotypes of slum life and public housing. Charles Laurence,[29] writing in the *Sunday Telegraph* introduces Toxteth in **A TALE OF TWO CITIES:**

> It is the sort of area where it is hard to tell the riot damage from the urban decay. Rows of grimy back-to-backs, some lived in, others heaps of rubble and charred timber are punctuated by stark modern flats and stretches of waste ground. Many of the shops and pubs were fitted with steel grilles or heavy wooden shutters long before the riots began. There is graffiti everywhere. Old men with swollen faces wander in and out of the bars. Young men kick footballs around derelict lots and prop up street corners. Children, including truants from school run through the alleyways.

(While this relates to Toxteth, it could equally relate to any northern city - see Burgess, 1978, pp78-9.)

When the urban environment simply will not allow for this kind of interpretation, reporters adopt different strategies so as to tie the place back into commonsense understanding of the inner city. Redevelopment is complete in Moss Side, so the few reports which focused in any detail on the physical environment took a different route. *The Times* reporter [30] found 'a black boy sprawling on a lawn in Princess Road. "It's not deprived. Look at those houses". He waved at neat council houses'. The report continues: 'Moss Side has 2500 modern council houses, largely concentrated in three estates. But the favourite haunts are clubs and bars which the planners ignored and left' - which effectively 'relocates' the illegal behaviour back in the seedy old buildings, obviously preferred by the low-living locals. J.B. Weatherby, [31] returning to Moss Side, writes that he has known the 'Moss Side ghetto since childhood' and remembers 'bitter resentment' among blacks. Nothing has really changed. 'New buildings have replaced much of the old property, but the spirit behind the *facade* remains the same' (my italics). Another strategy is to rehearse the components of the 'typical' inner city area before proclaiming difference. In a major review of the summer disturbances, the *Observer*[32]says 'not all the problems of inner city neighbourhoods - poor housing. poor schooling, poor social provision, declining production, a high level of footpad crime, an ugly physical environment ravaged by heavy motor traffic - are equally present. Much of Toxteth's housing is new.' The effect is to reinforce the traditional understanding and reduce the level of contradiction.

The motives of the 'mobs', in so far as papers were willing to concede motive behind the mindless irrationality, were often linked to the physical conditions of the inner city. Journalists and editors interpreted the mental states of residents on the basis of stereotyped assumptions about living in such areas. Environmental determinism 'makes sense'. In the 'popular' press, a few words are sufficient to make the necessary connections: the 'decaying areas are breeding grounds of mob violence'; [33] in every inner city slum ... there is the despair and frustration of the badly housed, unemployed youngsters who are losing hope'.[34] The litany of unemployment, inadequate education, 'poor housing and the collapse of inner city areas create feelings of utter despair'. [35] Articles in the 'quality' press pursued the theme further. Writing about Mr Heseltine's first week in Liverpool, Philip Norman [36] began: 'Last week on a Liverpool housing estate, Michael Heseltine, Secretary of State for the Environment, came face to face with a man whose 'environment' was such that he had twice attempted suicide. Despairing at the conditions in his council flat ... Merseyside young men and women are ageing at a fearful pace from the inside'. The consensus is that 'the decivilising conditions of urban life' in places like Toxteth make 'violence, individual and collective, inevitable'. [37] Like so much else in these reports, the connection is made on the basis of commonsense. It 'stands to reason'. Little evidence is given to support such interpretations. Equally, rioting could be regarded as positive action taken in response to deeply-felt grievances. Despair generates apathy rather than riot. Rioting could also be fun (see Southgate and Fields, 1982; Tumber, 1982; Nally, 1984).

'Nine Children in a Brooding Dockside Tenement'

'Poor' environmental and housing conditions are linked naturally with the existence of poor parenting and a distinctive street culture. The commonsense interpretation is that domestic 'overcrowding' drives young people out on to the streets where - bored, aimless and unemployed - they get into trouble looking for excitement or fall prey to 'left-wing agitators'. Thus, domestic overcrowding combined with unemployment 'does much to explain the increasing crime rate' in Brixton; [38] 'the crammed housing encouraging more youths to head out for the streets' [39] whilst the *Daily Star*[40] found evidence of young black and white people 'left to roam the streets during the day and most of the night. When they did go home, many of their dwellings were substandard and in need of repair'.

Domestic overcrowding is caused not only by 'poor' housing but also by the large number of children in working-class and black families. The *Daily Star*, in a feature called **ANGRY CITY**, [41] interviewed John (white) who lives in a flat 'in a brooding dockside tenement ... which he shares with his wife and 9 children'. Leroy and Linda (black) live in Moss Side in 'a neat 3 bedroomed council flat'. She is 23, expecting her fourth child and 'longs to escape from Moss Side'. [42] (The main photograph accompanying this feature does not show the council flat, however, but a back lane between nineteenth century terraced houses with six children playing in the alley by the rubble of a tumbledown shed.) In Liverpool 8, the family life is even more 'bizarre' and illustrates the 'cosmopolitan' features of the area. 'Family units don't consist of mum and dad and two kids ... more likely, there is a white mother, 3 or 4 children and a variety of West Indian fathers, never seen or long forgotten'. [43] Assumptions like these can be used to account for 'the army of social workers' needed to service the inner city communities and contribute to a concept of working-class family life as pathological.

It was an interpretation by no means confined to the 'popular'

Fig. 9.3

press. In the *Sunday Telegraph* article cited above, Laurence[44] writes: 'everyone agrees that few parents have any control over their children who spend most of their time playing in the street'. *Everyone* is a direct appeal to commonsense, who is 'everyone'? Playing in the street is linked causally with bad parenting, and social disorder. The press were enthusiastic about the 'bad parenting' thesis, giving prominence to the comments of the Home Secretary, who expressed 'sadness' that 'the young hooligans did not stop to think' that their actions would jeopardise Liverpool's chances of attracting jobs; and the demand by the Chief Constable of Merseyside for a return to 'basic civilised discipline'. Parents should make sure 'these kids are in bed at midnight - not throwing bricks and breaking windows' (Figure 9.3 offers a wry comment).

The Sunday Times[45] used the framework of family pathology to discuss inner city policies, suggesting that the inner cities should perhaps be treated like juvenile delinquents. They should be 'taken into care', brought up to national standards of housing and employment and only then handed back 'like rehabilitated children to the parent councils'. It is an interpretation of Urban Development Corporations which explains away a highly contentious political decision that challenges local democracy as well as suggesting that local authorities are inadequate, 'bad parents'.

Lawrence (1982, p50) argues that commonsense ideologies are

most often constructed around the family, which is 'portrayed as the crucial site for the reproduction of those correct social mores, attitudes and behaviours that are thought to be essential in maintaining a civilised society'. An example in *The Times*[46] illustrates the point. The reporter draws on a Home Office report to discuss the problem of 'lax parents'. In a style redolent of the nineteenth century, he writes that laxity 'is not related to any inherent weakness in the working-classes which renders them less likely to watch over their children'. Rather, laxity is closely associated with 'living in poor overcrowded conditions'. The argument developed in the article is that 'permissiveness' is acceptable for the 'educated middle-class' living 'in the leafy suburbs', but is 'counter productive for the families of manual workers living in inner city housing estates'. They have not enough space to indulge their children 'of whom there tend to be more than in middle-class families'. He concludes that housing and other environmental factors, 'apart from the familiar economic ones' are affecting children divisively. 'The poorer ones are *driven* into vandalism and delinquency *for no other reason* than there is not enough space or excitement at home to stay there' (my italics). Whilst 'better off children' have benefited from permissive attitudes, they 'have done poorer children more harm than good'. The evidence for this was shown in the past by 'unprecedented juvenile delinquency' and 'now in rioting'.

The article takes 'class' as its only social division, making no mention of additional social, cultural or ethnic characteristics which might well influence child-rearing practices. Class relations are seen as fixed and immutable with the clear implication that the working classes should not try to change their 'traditional' approach despite the acknowledged benefits of permissive regimes in middle-class families. Middle-class child-rearing habits are seen as natural because more suitable to the conditions of middle-class life. Middle-class parents limit their families to fit the domestic space available and also provide the stimulation which 'growing souls' need. The environment is being used as the means through which to reduce economic and political issues to a more uncontentious biological level, in which 'improvements' in social behaviour can be achieved quite simply by improving the standards of the physical environment. The article also reinforces demands for tougher measures to deal with the rioters. If parents are unwilling or unable to control their children, then the state must reluctantly take over their natural responsibilities. Working-class parents in not exerting more discipline over their children, are guilty by association of delinquency and rioting. Parental guilt-by-association shifts attention away from political issues back on to the rioters themselves. Undoubtedly this was the meaning that government spokesmen were hoping would be taken. It also successfully reduced the seriousness of the disturbances by equating the rioters with 'children', thus rendering their actions 'childish' and unreasonable.

Although white families have problems, by incorporating aspects of the third domain upon which the myth draws, relations between black children and their parents are portrayed as being significantly worse. In black families, according to press reports, parents as first generation immigrants accepted 'menial jobs' with 'gratitude'. By contrast, their British-born offspring are unemployed and alienated, both from their parents' values and British society. The *Daily Telegraph*[47] writing of black young people in Brixton, says in some surprise that many of the rioters were 'second or even third generation Britons'. 'Having rejected the values of hard work, in often menial jobs which brought their parents to Britain, often unqualified and directionless, they are unable to find a job'. Having set their sights higher, so the argument goes, black youths despise their parents, are bored and drawn into crime by the dubious attractions of the street. Scarman was obviously convinced of this interpretation, labelling the young people of Brixton as 'a people of the street' (1981, p11). It is a street culture which 'corrupts many of them and deters others from seeking escape by way of school, the public library and by hard work when jobs are available'. [48] The commonsense understanding is clear - if black youths were to espouse white middle class values of self-improvement through education, they would be able to 'escape' from the inner city 'prison'. Black young people are labelled as being resistant to education (if not unintelligent) and lazy. *The Sunday Times*[49] uses the same definition of generational tension but turns it round by suggesting that the young black people 'often have exam qualifications to buttress their sense of injustice', but even here the use of 'their' distances the paper from any firm stand (see Thomas, 1984, for the views of a Brixton resident).

'Buying what you want on the Streets of the Ghetto'

The 'children' are exposed to a social environment in the inner city which is both corrupt and corrupting. The inner city is the place for prostitution - 'redlight girls thrive in the shambles of tatty terraced streets' (Fig. 9.2). (Sexism as well as racism: when did any woman forced into prostitition by poverty or other circumstances manage to 'thrive'?) Houses in Upper Parliament Street have notices telling kerb crawlers to keep away; a white youth offers a white girl 'a present' in Moss Side. [50]Life in Railton Road, symbolising amongst other things the Front Line between white working-class and black culture, is even more exotic. 'You can buy anything you want on Railton Road, a woman, drugs, anything' (a white man told the *Sunday Telegraph* reporter). [51] Railton Road 'is a centre for a criminal sub culture dealing in drugs and prostitution'; [52] it is the street with clubs where the smell of marijuana was so thick that *Daily Star* reporters 'gasped for breath'. [53] It is where on a Friday night 'in an almost empty street, a worn, coloured whore stood in front of my car, offered me a good time for £20 and a spliff (marijuana joint) thrown in'. [54]

Blacks are pathologised, once by their association with the cultures of deprivation of the decaying inner cities, and again as the bearers of specifically Black cultures (Lawrence, 1982, p56). Railton Road offers a street culture which reflects life in the 'ghetto'. It is the place where 'black youths, not only locals but from many parts, live on the proceeds of social security - and crime'. [55] They are to be found 'hanging aimlessly round its street corners looking for action and excitement'. [56] Such is the 'ghetto mentality' identified by the *Telegraph* and the Conservative Member of Parliament for Lambeth and Norwood. In both the 'popular' and 'quality' papers, the word *ghetto* was used to label all three areas but it was never defined. In much the same way, papers designated 'typical working-class neighbourhoods'. Both phrases carry meanings which grow and feed on knowledge which has become sedimented into commonsense understanding. *Ghetto* is used in reports as if its meaning is unproblematic and uncontested.

The *Daily Star*[57] for example, in more 'authentic' interviews, produced a feature headlined **THE NO GO GHETTO**. Two people are reported: Abel Winstanley ('his black hair dusted with white') who would 'gladly' go back to Trinidad if he could raise the fare), and Big Maxie Fuller ('as white as the spot on a domino'). These characterisations both convey an understanding of the ghetto as a place where black overwhelms white. Other papers used the same construction. *The Sunday Times*[58] for example headlines an article about Brixton as **PROFILE OF A 'GHETTO'**. The apostrophes distance the paper from the label but the text reinforces an understanding which equates concentrations of black people with disorder and tension. The article begins by saying that few people would have been surprised if the clashes in Bristol in 1980 had occurred in Brixton. 'To many whites, the name of Brixton epitomises a black ghetto'. But it continues 'the image is *in some ways* false' (my italics). 'Black faces are plentiful' (the use of 'faces' rather than 'people' turns individuals into objects), 'but population statistics counter the ghetto claim'. Yet, 'Brixton has long been recognised as one of the areas most vulnerable to racial tension'. It is sense and non-sense at the same time. How do readers 'make sense' of being told that the area does not have high concentrations of black people while at the same time, it is known for its potential racial tension? In both kinds of report, the 'ghetto' is used to echo and reinforce the meaning of the inner city as a prison from which to escape (see Wallman, 1982 for the alternative view put by inner city residents in South London). It interprets black people's experiences for them. It also allows newspapers to relate the British experience of rioting with that of North American cities and the riots of the 1960s. Rattray Road in Brixton is placed in this way: 'this unoppressive open street is by no means Harlem'. [59]

The ghetto/prison construction echoes the entrapment of white and black in the inner city. It also connotes meanings to be used in association with the thesis of young black 'criminality'. The *Daily Mail*[60] for example writes that Toxteth 'has become an inner city prison for decent residents. They cage themselves behind protective bars and grilles to foil thieves ... everywhere is an undercurrent of restless violence'. The press have focused consistently on the 'racial' nature of crime in the inner city areas and ignored or neglected other forms of criminality including racist attacks on black people (see Hartmann and Husband, 1978; Joshua *et al*, 1982). The reporting of the riots did nothing to challenge the black criminality thesis, although there was discussion towards the end of July of 'insensitive policing'.

Many newspapers spoke of hatred between blacks and the police. For papers towards the right of the political spectrum this hatred was totally unjustified. The police were forced into inner city areas by the 'exceptionally high' crime rates. For example, 'hatred of the police and police methods has been festering for years in the rundown streets of Brixton where high levels of street crime make their presence inevitable'. [61] Other papers too commented on local distrust of the police which often bordered on hatred. [62] These were more sympathetic to the possibilities of police harassment. The *Guardian*[63] reported complaints by the 'ordinary law abiding folk' of Moss Side who were shocked by police behaviour. 'They were coming to believe that long-standing complaints from the black community of police harassment and racism may have some substance'. The police were anxious to enforce the interpretation of the riots as young people acting against entirely reasonable efforts to enforce law and order on the streets. Tumber (1982, p19) reported a police spokesman who was pleased with media coverage of the riots because 'the media were very quick off the mark to realise that this was not a racial issue but a social one whose principal victims were black'. The issue of racism within the police forces was strongly denied by police spokesmen who received considerable coverage in the press, both through news reports and features involving local policemen. [64]

To give the riots meaning through reference to the criminality of inner city residents was thus a useful device, for it allowed the police to distance themselves from any blame, and it allowed a not unrelated myth of 'our wonderful British policemen' to remain untarnished. The notion of criminal greed also provided a means of 'making sense' of the violence and looting. Black people were violent, attacking the police. White people looted from shops. It was the construction put on the events in Liverpool by the Chief Constable and was one that found support in the papers. Unemployed people, living in poverty and resentful of the deal they are getting from society are obviously prone to riot and to loot. 'Why put video shops in a black ghetto? We can't afford that'. [65] White looters in Liverpool are 'explained' by reference to assumptions about working-class criminality. A 9-year-old boy directing journalists to trouble spots in Liverpool, said his father 'had gone to Park Road on the grab'. [66] A *Daily Star*[67] cartoon showed a brawny labourer trying to bail out his skinny punk of a son and saying: 'Be reasonable, officer - how can I be responsible for 'im riotin' in Manchester when I was busy lootin' in Liverpool?' But Ilene Mellish, a local resident of Liverpool 8, writing later in the Grassroots section of the *Guardian* [68] saw different looters. 'Well dressed, car owning whites' who pushed shopping trolleys towards private housing, and who were middle-aged, white and in groups.

The inner areas of cities were not disintegrating into general chaos. The disturbances were highly localised and sporadic. Reports marginalised the 'trouble makers and thieves' in several ways but always the same intention of dividing the 'decent' (i.e. law abiding) residents from the rest. Blacks were separated from whites as we have seen through the ghetto construction. Immigration policies were blamed for destroying the white working-class community. The *Daily Mail*, for example, published an article by Ronald Butt [69] who wrote that 'ordinary, decent' people will become angry at being 'stigmatised as a racialist" white society'. They have to 'live with a problem not of their own making as a result of which vast areas of their cities have been changed beyond recognition'. These changes 'on any reckoning have been a major challenge ... to their own sense of identity'. The breakdown in law and order, the decline of the inner cities, the loss of community controls are by implication, the fault of West Indian immigrants.

Few reports were as overtly racist as the *Daily Mail*. For the majority it was sufficient to distance the older generation from the youths on the streets, the 'decent' blacks from the activities of the white looters, and local people from outsiders who were presumed to be coming into the areas either as agitators or looters. The *Daily Telegraph*[70] found an unemployed black man to say: 'It was white kids doing this. They were coming in from other parts of Liverpool ... and getting us blacks the blame for it'. Shocked residents in Liverpool and Moss Side were reported as wanting to quit. Local black women often 'wept' as they commented on the disturbances. 'They are destroying Moss Side. It will never be the same again ... The local boys ... seem to have gone mad'. [71] The *Guardian*[72] took up the theme of local vigilantes helping protect the community against looting outsiders: 'people, particularly blacks' were effectively turning people away. Again, this provides an illustration of contradictory sense. The first proposition states that there is no longer any sense of community in the inner city, that it has been broken down by a combination of large-scale immigration and insensitive, random, piecemeal redevelopment. The second states that local people were organised and supportive of each other, banding together to repel 'outsiders' and trying to protect properties from damage. The contradiction illustrates the conflict between generalised understanding and situated knowledge. Real people in a real context actively defended their homes and streets.

The motives of the people who were on the street - 'the mobs in the great majority of cases remained obscure. Most often, politicians, policemen and journalists provided their own interpretations of the motives behind the actions. The issue of damage to property was a case in point. Was it selective or did it represent the actions of a crazed irrational mob? The majority of reports on the April riots in Brixton saw no justification or reason behind the damage. Exceptions included the *Daily Mirror*[73] which argued that the black community 'despise local businessmen whom they think exploit them' and the *Guardian* reporter [74] in Brixton who wrote that long rows of shops owned or run by ethnic minorities were untouched while the shops of well-known chain stores were damaged. In Liverpool, two *Times* reporters [75] were horrified by the 'collective madness' of the mob and bemoaned the destruction of the 'famous Racquets Club - 104 years of history and many valuable paintings being consumed in minutes'. Several papers carried pictures of the burnt out Rialto cinema in Liverpool 8, which was described as 'a well loved landmark'. The implication again, that the black and white youths have no respect or care for the symbols of the older community. Ilene Mellish [76] gives the local reality. The Rialto had for several years been used as a furniture store, owned by a Conservative Councillor who, for quite specific reasons, was disliked by some local people.

The example illustrates a major point: the actions of the people on the streets were never 'mindless' or 'irrational'. The riots in each place were triggered by specific acts by the police which no longer seemed tolerable and the buildings which were attacked were clearly identifiable symbols for community frustrations and injustices (see Kettle and Hodges, 1982; Clare, 1984). To understand those injustices requires a situated knowledge of the local realities. As the newspaper reports have demonstrated, only a very few journalists began to acquire such an understanding of the lives of the people in any of the three places. The reports are full of crude generalisations, misinterpretations and appropriations of other people's meanings. Ilene Mellish wrote about the rage of young black people in Liverpool 8 and their need to cry out against a certain reality:

> 'of street behaviour arrests, police-defined crime and court room deals; of those offered arson in empty buildings or play in private clubs; who sense themselves the object of public violence, or of private protection. Which is not the reality portrayed by the newspapers, newscasters or political leaders (whether in government or opposition).

For a short time in Liverpool, working-class black and white people were united against local expressions of the injustices of class and colour.

News from Nowhere

In this chapter, I have discussed the social production of news and demonstrated the ways in which media practices determine the selection and presentation of events. The critical concept that allows analysis of the mass media in terms of its role in the maintenance of existing social conditions is that of hegemony. The press relies heavily on the views of representatives of the dominant class: politicians, senior policemen, elite people with known status. It is able to exercise choice in terms of how much and what sort of coverage these views are given. However, through the use of 'social maps' which frame and make sense of events, certain interpretations and commonsense understandings become sedimented into generalised knowledge. It is perfectly possible for people to accept and indeed consent to particular interpretations of how things are while at the same time contesting those interpretations through their personal, situated knowledge of their immediate reality.

The disturbances in 1981 took place in a few streets in a few cities. The framework used by the press to locate and partly to account for those events was *the inner city*. It is clear that the conditions of life in the areas were necessary but not sufficient causes of the disturbances. Inner city policies did not contribute directly to the disturbances. 'Nobody rioted in Toxteth because they weren't being made an enterprise zone and Speke was. Nobody went on to the street of Brixton to demand more government investment in the partnership scheme' (Kettle and Hodges, 1982, p131). It has not been my intention here to argue the role played by the conditions of life in these areas in the disturbances. Rather, I have tried, through close attention to the texts of the newspapers, to see what we are given to understand about inner cities.

The myth of the inner city feeds on four distinct ideological domains. These I identified as being concerned with the physical environment; white working-class culture; black culture and finally, a culture of the street. Each idea has developed in specific historical circumstances and selected features have been taken into the media representations of the 'reality' of life in inner areas of large cities. So, for example, the inner city is described in an imagery which echoes the interpretation of nineteenth-century industrial cities, and carries negative meanings. At the same time, it fuses with certain negatively perceived aspects of post-1945 planning practice, most notably redevelopment and public housing schemes. Similarly, the inner city street signifies not only the 'undisciplined' and 'licentious' activities of the white working class, but also the invasion and destruction of that 'traditional' community by black people who are noisy, violent and criminally inclined. The pathology of the inner city is clearly signalled.

Each domain of the myth thus reflects the dominance of a particular world view, naturalising the environments, values, experiences and demands of white, bourgeois culture. That representative of 'The Establishment', *The Times* newspaper [77] offers its readers a chilling reminder of what can happen when 'the mob' breaks loose

> 'Toxteth ... presented an awful picture of anarchy. We saw looters of all ages, and both sexes, black and white ... around 11 p.m. the savagery of the pitched battle ... went beyond anything that most experienced observers had seen before. The mob screamed, the buildings roared in flames ... the area's very efficient grapevine brought news of impending moves ... the road was littered inches deep in places with shoe boxes and their contents representing one small shopkeeper's life investment, the remainder being spirited away to the gaunt blocks of flats on the nearby housing estates. With them went food and drink ... Behind the burning street the sound of shouting and laughter came from the block of flats.

A wide range of journalists have provided the text for this chapter and they had to produce copy much more quickly than other writers. Deadlines give little time for thought or the gathering of local knowledge. Being charitable, it might be said that the inner city is simply a pastiche of cliches, but the persistence of certain forms, the negative and degrading qualities which were heaped into interpretations of these inner urban areas makes that charitable assumption somewhat difficult to sustain. The empty, hollow form of the myth denies any reality to the places and people being written about. It perpetuates a generalised understanding which 'locates' inner cities as distinct, separate, alien and potentially destructive of 'our civilised way of life'. The myth removes the places and the people who live in them to a grey, shabby, derelict, poverty-ridden fairytale-land which can be conveniently ignored because it has no reality.

NOTES

The following notes provide full details of the newspaper articles cited, including the names of the journalists who wrote them. Headlines are given in upper case and where possible I have classified the report.

1. 'Toxteth' is not the name by which this area of Liverpool is known locally. Sections of the local community know it as Liverpool 8, Granby or the South End. The media labelling caused some friction between residents and press, see **INSIDE THE GHETTO**, by Neil Lyndon, *The Sunday Times*, 4 July 1982, p17

2 **THE LULLABY SOUND OF HOUSES FALLING DOWN**, by Beryl Bainbridge, *The Sunday Times*, 19 July 1981, p36

3 **THE RACE BOMB**, by Jad Adams, Shektar Bhatia and Tony Wedderburn, *Daily Star*, 5-8 May 1981

4 One exception in the national press was a photograph taken by Denis Thorpe of the side-front view of the police in Moss Side standing behind riot shields. The caption read 'Shops burn in Princess Road as the police stand firm against rioters in Moss Side' (*Guardian*, 10 July 1981, p2). The possibilities of an oppositional reading of this shot were shown later in an article by Steven Wright entitled *YOUR UNFRIENDLY NEIGHBOURHOOD BOBBY* (*Guardian*, 16 July 1981, p17). Another shot in the Thorpe sequence was captioned: '... the insect-like image of policemen in full riot gear'.

5 **A NIGHT ON BOTH SIDES OF THE LINE**, by Michael Morris, *Guardian*, 7 July 1981, p3

6 **BLOODY BATTLE**, by staff reporter, *Daily Star*, 7 July 1981, p3

7 A number of events brought the debate back into issues of policing practices in areas with ethnic communities, and techniques for handling street violence. Two stand out in this period to the end of July. It was disclosed on 16 July that the CS gas canisters fired on the night of 5/6 July had caused severe personal injuries. Designed to be fired only against buildings, the guns had been used directly against people. Kenneth Oxford, Chief Constable of Liverpool, approved the use of police vehicles being driven at rioters so as to disperse them. A handicapped man, David Moore, was run down and killed by a police van on the night of 28 July. The officers were acquitted in December.

8 **A WEEK IN THE LIFE OF THE TEMPORARY MINISTER FOR MERSEYSIDE**, by Philip Norman, *The Sunday Times*, 26 July 1981, p13

9 **SOUND THE ALARM**, *The Times*, 7 July 1981 (Editorial)

10 **LOOTERS MOVE IN AS THE FLAMES SPREAD**, by Martin Huckerby, *The Times*, 13 April 1981, p8 (News)

11 **THE 'ALTERNATIVE' LIFE IN RAILTON ROAD**, by Lindsey Mackie, *Guardian*, 13 April 1981, p2 (Feature)

12 **LIVING ON THE FRONT LINE**, by Brian Connell, *Daily Mirror*, 13 April 1981, centre page (Feature)

13 **WEAPONS OF HATE IN THE CITY OF FEAR**, by staff reporters, *Daily Mail*, 6 July 1981, pp2-3 (News)

14 **ANGRY CITY**: 'none of my kids have been to school since the riots started', by Ian Brandes, *Daily Star*, 15 July 1981 (Feature)

15 **ANGRY CITY**: 'I always have an awful fear that I might be attacked', by David Newman, *Daily Star*, 15 July 1981 (Feature)

16 **HE CAME, HE SAW ... BUT DID HE CONQUER?** by David Norris, *Daily Mail*, 5 August 1981 (News)

17 **BRIXTON'S MORNING AFTER**, by Mike Phillips, *Guardian*, 13 April 1981 (Feature); **SCREWDRIVER OR BULLDOZER**, *Daily Mail*, 6 August 1981, p6 (Editorial); **DEVELOPMENT AND RENEWAL PLANS COLLAPSE AS THE CASH DRIES UP**, by Robin Young, *The Times*, 15 April 1981 (Feature)

18 **NO GO AREAS RULED OUT BY POLICE CHIEF**, a staff reporter, *Daily Telegraph*, 6 July 1981, front page (News)

19 **TROUBLE SHOOTER ROPES IN THE INVESTORS**, by John Young, *The Times*3 August 1981 (News)

20 **HATRED OF THE POLICE HAS BEEN FESTERING FOR YEARS**, by Graham Paterson, *Daily Telegraph*, 13 April 1981, p4 (News)

21 Lindsey Mackie, note 11

22 **THE FEAR THAT STALKS THE PEOPLE IN RAILTON ROAD**, by Brenda Parry, *Daily Telegraph*, 15 April 1981, p6 (Feature)

23 **LIVING BEHIND THE FRONTLINE OF VIOLENCE**, by Robert Chesshyre and George Brock, *Observer*, 12 April 1981, p6 (Feature)

24 John Young, note 19

25 **INSTANT RESPONSES**, *Daily Telegraph*, 17 July 1981, p14 (Editorial)

26 **MR HESELTINE LOOKS AND LISTENS**, *Daily Mail*, 21 July 1981, p6 (Editorial)

27 Beryl Bainbridge, note 2

28 **WHERE HELL IS OFTEN A CITY**, *The Times*, 22 July 1981 (Editorial)

29 **MOB VIOLENCE: A TALE OF TWO CITIES**, by Charles Lawrence, *Sunday Telegraph*, 12 July 1981, p3 (Feature)

30 **'MY MUM ASKED ME TO GET A CLOCK'**, by staff reporter, *The Times*, 10 July 1981, p2 (News)

31 **WHY IT DIDN'T WORK IN AMERICA**, by J.B. Weatherby, *Guardian*, 11 July 1981, p9 (Feature)

32 **OUR SHORT HOT SUMMER OF DISCONTENT**, by Laurence Marks, William Keegan, Michael Nally and Kirsty White, *Guardian*, 12 July 1981, pp13-16 (Feature)

33 **NEW CHIEFS FOR CRISIS CITIES**, by Geoffrey Goodman, *Daily Mirror*, 9 July 1981, front page (News)

34 **CLAMP DOWN ON POLICE ROUGHNECKS**, *Sunday People*, 9 August 1981, p10 (Editorial)

35 **GET THEM OFF OUR STREETS**, *Daily Star*, 7 July 1981, front page (Editorial)

36 Philip Norman, note 8

37 **THEY WARNED HER BUT SHE JUST WOULDN'T LISTEN**, by Peter Jenkins, *Guardian*, 8 July 1981, p13 (Feature)

38 **ATTEMPT TO ALTER RACIAL HOUSING IMBALANCE**, by John Young, Robin Young and Diana Geddes, *The Times*, 13 April 1981 (Feature)

39 Graham Paterson, note 20

40 Editorial, *Daily Star*, note 35

41 Ian Brandes, note 14

42 **ANGRY CITY**: 'What is the point of working for nice things when someone comes and steals them', by David Hudson, *Daily Star*, 14 July 1981, pp 12-13 (Feature)

43 **'WHY NICK MARGE WHEN THERE'S BUTTER TO BE HAD?'**, by Anne Robinson, *Daily Mirror*, 10 July 1981, pp16-17

44 Charles Laurence, note 29

45 **WHY THE RIOTS FLARED: CAN MONEY QUENCH THE FIRE?**, by staff reporters, *The Sunday Times*, 12 July 1981, pp16-17 (Feature)

46 **WHY SO MANY CHILDREN TAKE TO THE STREETS**, by Peter Watson, *The Times*, 11 July 1981, p12 (Feature)

47 Graham Paterson, note 20

48 **ECHOES OF AMERICA'S LONG HOT SUMMER**, by Louis Heren, *The Times*, 13 April 1981, p12 (Feature)

49 **PROFILE OF A GHETTO**, by staff reporters, *The Sunday Times*, 12 April 1981, p2 (Feature)

50 Laurence Marks *et al*, note 32

51 **BRIXTON SOUL SEARCHING AS TENSION EASES**, by Ivan Rowan, *Sunday Telegraph*, 19 April 1981 (Feature)

52 Lindsey Mackie, note 11

53 **THE RACE BOMB:** 'a revenge plot ended in riot and bloodshed', by Jad Adams, Shekhar Bhatia and Tony Wedderburn, *Daily Star*, 5 May 1981, p17 (Feature)

54 Brian Connell, note 12

55 Brenda Parry, note 22

56 Graham Paterson, note 20

57 **THE NO GO GHETTO**, by Robert Gibson, *Daily Star*, 13 April 1981, centre page (Feature)

58 *The Sunday Times*, note 49

59 Robert Chesshyre and George Brock, note 23

60 *Daily Mail*, note 13

61 Graham Paterson, note 20

62 **THE SHAPE OF THINGS TO COME**, by Roger Todd, *Daily Mirror*, 13 April 1981, front and back page spread (News); **TOXTETH IS CONNECTED TO GAS**, by Jean Stead, *Guardian*, 15 July 1981. *Sunday People*, 9 August 1981 (Editorial)

63 **THE FORCE OF LAW AND ORDER SEEN IN A NEW LIGHT**, by James Lewis, *Guardian*, 24 July 1981, p2 (News)

64 **AFTER THE BATTLE OF LIVERPOOL 8**by James McClure, *Observer*, 12 July 1981, p15 (Feature)

65 **BLACKS BACK POWELL VIEW OF FUTURE**, by Barry O'Brien, *Daily Telegraph*, 10 July 1981, front and back page (News)

66 **YOUNG THIEVES IN THE NIGHT**, by Steve Crowther and Reginald White, *Daily Mirror*, 8 July 1981, pp2-3 (News)

67 Bill Caldwell cartoon, *Daily Star*, 11 July 1981

68 **RAGE IN A CAGE**, by Ilene Mellish, *Guardian*, 31 July 1981, p8 (Feature)

69 **THE EVIL MISCHIEF MAKERS WHO ARE SO QUICK TO LABEL US ALL AS 'WHITE RACISTS'**, by Ronald Butt, *Daily Mail*, 10 July 1981, pp6-7 (Feature)

70 **STREETS WITHOUT LAW: THE SEED PLANTED IN BRISTOL FLOWERS APPALLINGLY IN TOXTETH**, by staff reporters, *Daily Telegraph*, 6 July 1981, pp2-3 (News)

71 **LOOTERS ON THE RAMPAGE**, by Brian Wood, *Daily Mirror*, 9 July 1981, front page (News)

72 **TOXTETH 'VIGILANTES' DEFY THE LOOTERS**, by Michael Morris and Malcolm Pithers, *Guardian*, 7 July 1981, back page (News)

73 Editorial *Daily Mirror*, 13 April 1981, p2

74 **'WHEN YOU GET A LOT OF PEOPLE WHO ARE TREATED AS BADLY AS THIS, WHAT CAN YOU EXPECT'**, by Malcolm Dean, *Guardian*, 13 April 1981, p13 (Feature)

75 **GREED AND FEROCIOUS VIOLENCE MARK A COLLECTIVE MADNESS**, by Arthur Osman and Nick Timmins, *The Times*, 7 July 1981, p4 (News)

76 Ilene Mellish, note 68

77 Arthur Osman and Nick Timmins, note 75

THIS is the grim face of Toxteth, Liverpool 8 — the rundown area which became front-page news after a weekend of savage rioting.

These pictures, specially taken for the Daily Mirror in March, show the squalor and desolation and what was once a middle-class suburb.

Unemployment in the area, now virtually a black ghetto, is critically high.

Muggings and housebreakings are commonplace.

Red-light girls thrive in the shambles of tatty terraced streets and modern tenement slums.

But it is the despair of unemployment which probably lies at the heart of Toxteth's festering troubles.

A city councils survey last year put the number of jobless in the area at 37 per cent.

Other estimates paint an even more dismal picture .

A recent Liverpool University report on the Liverpool and district put white unemployment at 43 per cent and black at 47 per cent.

In its 1980 report the Merseyside Community Relations Committee claimed that half the black people in the city were out of work.

Latest unemployment figures for the city show 81,000 people chasing just over 1,000 jobs.

At the careers office, with thousands of school-leavers looking for work, there are just twelve vacancies.

Against this background, the ugly and unacceptable face of Toxteth has little hope,

Fig. 9.4

CHAPTER 10: NEWS AND THE DISSEMINATION OF FEAR

Susan J. Smith

Introduction

There is already a large literature discussing the relationship between crime and the mass media. Mostly, it seeks to establish or refute hypothesised links between peoples' exposure to deviance on film, television or in newspapers and their likelihood of turning to crime as a consequence. Yet, many recent studies of urban crime indicate that *fear* is far more widespread and debilitating than victimisation itself, impinging not only on the lives of the victims but also on the well-being of a wider general public. Recognising the importance of this condition, the essay that follows focuses on the institutionalised and informal dissemination of fear, i.e. on the processes by which the intangible effects of crime are carried far beyond the direct experiences of perpetrators and victims.

This study has two main aims which, being interrelated, are pursued in parallel rather than sequentially as the text proceeds. Conceptually, they are linked by the development of Robert Park's often-neglected contribution to humanistic geography (a contribution outlined in some detail by Jackson and Smith, 1981, 1984). First, on the general theoretical level,the function of the press and its contentious relationship with culture and social change are explored. In this respect, Park's writings on the newspaper and his novel conceptualisation of the public prove illuminating. Secondly, my own research on crime in north-central Birmingham, England, is used as the empirical context through which these theoretical questions are approached. Specifically, the problem at this level is to explain why behavioural reactions to crime in the study area were not aligned socially with the incidence of victimisation. In part, this explanation rests on a study of interpersonal communication and, to this end, Park's pioneering enthusiasm for experiential fieldwork in an urban setting offers important methodological guidance.

Crime in the Inner City

The part of north-central Birmingham popularly known as Handsworth, but spanning parts of the wards of All Saints, Aston, Handsworth and Soho, has experienced a long history of race-related civil unrest. During the 1960s and 1970s, the area also acquired a reputation for high crime rates and strained ethnic relations. The presumed link between these two issues is a pervasive feature of daily life (Bishton and Homer, 1978; Plummer, 1978), a recurrent theme in the mass media (Critcher *et al*, 1975; Hall *et al*, 1978), and a central concern of much of the academic literature (Brown, 1977; Cashmore, 1979; Weaver, 1980). In view of this, it came as some surprise to the present author, working in an ethnically mixed community in east 'Handsworth', to find no statistical relationship between racial or ethnic variables and people's experiences as the victims of crime.

In order to fill this gap, a survey was carried out over a twelve-month reference period during 1978-79 on a random sample of residents (reported in detail by Smith, 1982a). The main predictors of victimisation were in fact essentially economic: spare-time activity rates, dwelling rateable value, and class. In contrast, perceptions of and reactions to crime varied most markedly and consistently between racial groups (Smith, 1982b). This apparent incongruity is explained below by way of an analysis of the media by which crime-related information is disseminated. For it is the circulation of news that contains most clues as to why race or ethnicity, rather than any other social attribute, is chosen as the principle by which to organise behavioural responses to crime.

Unfortunately, it is not possible here to offer a full account of *why* ethnicity proves salient as the basis for social action, a matter which can only be explained through a more explicit evaluation of the differential distribution of power in the inner city (Smith, 1984). What follows concerns itself simply with describing the opportunities for, and constraints on, the interpersonal communication of news about crime. Its significance lies in illustrating the process by which structural inequality, (as reflected in the uncertainty of an inner city environment and the marginalisation of coloured ethnic minorities), is translated into the common-sense behaviours and experiences of everyday life.

Coping with Crime

There is now ample evidence that the effects of crime vary between

Table 10.1: Residents' Main sources of Information about Crime

Information source:	West Indian		Asian		Other		Total	
	n	%	n	%	n	%	n	%
Personal experience	3	3.3	6	3.3	8	3.1	17	3.2
Friends' experience	7	7.6	37	20.3	31	12.1	75	14.1
Police	3	3.3	1	0.6	3	1.2	7	1.3
Newspaper	19	20.7	34	18.7	106	41.3	159	29.9
TV/Radio	38	41.3	45	24.7	39	15.2	122	23.0
Hearsay	18	19.6	39	21.4	58	22.6	115	21.7
Total[a]	92	100.0	182	100.0	257	100.0	531	100.0

$x^2 = 51.78$, 10d.f., $p < 0.001$

Note: [a] These totals exceed the sum of the columns, since column entries refer only to people who identified one information source as more important than any other. Totals refer to the total number of all respondents in each ethnic group.

social groups (e.g. Smith, 1976; Kahana *et al*, 1977; Klecka and Bishop, 1978). Tentative evidence for the importance of spatial variations in concern for crime is contained in Boggs's (1971) analysis of rural and urban crime environments, and this is corroborated by Skogan and Maxfield's (1981) discovery that views of the crime problem vary little between cities, but vary markedly among neighbourhoods within cities.

The prospect of crime, irrespective of its potential reality, injects the urban environment with an air of insecurity and uncertainty. The varying success of the reactions of different groups to this uncertainty helps to account for the uneven distribution of crime perceptions and to determine whether these images take the form of fear, concern or merely awareness of crime. According to Garofalo (1981a), 'information seeking' and 'communicative behaviour' are two common responses to environmental uncertainty, implemented when danger is sensed and knowledge is limited. The relevance of these strategies in north-central Birmingham is apparent from Table 10.1 which shows the main sources that survey respondents cited as to their information about crime in the immediate neighbourhood. For over half the population, the local newspaper, television or radio was the primary source of such knowledge, while hearsay or the experience of friends was most important for a further 36 per cent of respondents.

Although the possible influence of television on public opinion has attracted a disproportionate amount of attention in recent years (see Garofalo, 1981b), Table 10.1 indicates that in the study area, slightly more people rely on the local newspaper for their information. This is consistent with the evidence of Piepe *et al* (1978) that in Britain regional newspapers tend to be the preferred medium from which to glean *local* news. However, the provincial press remains a relatively neglected facet of mass communication research. For these reasons, it receives attention below as one mechanism for the dissemination of crime news amongst those 'information seekers' who wish to construct a more coherent map of the dangers threatening their security.

Of late, the mass media have tended to dominate research on public opinions about crime with the consequence that little is known about the interpersonal communication of such information, although this clearly does occur. LeJeune and Alex (1973), for instance, documented the 'ripple effect' caused by victims of mugging who are eager to relate their experiences to friends and acquaintances. In an attempt to specify this process more precisely, an effort was made in the Birmingham study to trace the informal circulation of gossip, rumour, and related 'improvised' news about crime.

Thus, the local press and word of mouth emerge as two relatively neglected media which could be instrumental to the circulation of information within a small urban neighbourhood. These are considered in turn in so far as they influence the dissemination of information about crime.

News as Knowledge

Inspired by his mentor William James, Park (1940a) identified two forms of knowledge. These are *acquaintance with* - 'the sort of knowledge one invariably acquires during the course of one's first hand encounters with the world'; and *knowledge about* - 'fact that has been checked, tagged, regimented, and finally ranged in this or that perspective according to the purposive point of view of the investigator' (Park, 1940a, pp 34, 36). This seems to be a simple distinction between folk and analytical conceptions of reality;

between instinct or intuition and its rational, validated, scientific representation. Yet Park preferred to view these forms of knowledge as two ends of a continuum, and news is allocated a distinctive position between them, for 'news, as a form of knowledge, contributes from its record of events not only to history and to sociology but to folklore and literature; it contributes something not merely to the social sciences but to the humanities' (Park, 1940a, p46). More precisely, the sphere of news is neither the individual's psychology, nor an abstract set of analytical categories. Rather, news is a type of communication that informs the 'mind' of a public; it is to the public what perceptions are to the individual. Neither image is merely informative, for both additionally serve to orientate beliefs.

Park's distinct conception of the news, however, begs two important questions which deserve attention here. They concern the effect of the news media on public opinions, attitudes and behaviours, and the function of the press in modern democratic societies, in particular its relationship to social change. To investigate these contentious issues, the content of Birmingham's daily evening newspaper was monitored for seven months prior to administering the household survey. Full details were collected for all coverage of the police, race, and race-related crime, while coverage of all crime was sampled randomly, on a week-to-week basis so that the equivalent of one day's crime reporting per week was collated. The number, length and type of article was recorded, together with the referenced neighbourhood (where applicable). Content and headline analyses were completed to provide a basis for comparing crime news both with official statistics and with popular images of crime.

News and Public Opinion

One of few points of agreement amongst studies of crime as reported by the mass media is that the news bears little relation to official crime statistics. It reflects neither the proportions in which offences occur, nor their trends over time (e.g. see Davis, 1952; Hauge, 1965; Jones, 1976; Chibnall, 1980). Others have shown how even the most dramatic 'crime waves' are frequently an artefact of journalistic practices. They can arise out of the interaction between bureaucratic news organisations competing for the exposition of particular journalistic themes (Medalia and Larsen, 1958; Fishman, 1978; Hall *et al*,1978) and can also, by virtue of their extreme 'newsworthiness', be contingent upon attempts to boost newspaper circulation (Bell, 1962). The mismatch between crime statistics and the news is no less marked in the present study. Table 10.2 shows the exaggeration of personal violence and robbery at the expense of less newsworthy but much more common crimes such as theft or burglary. From Table 10.3 it is clear, too, that while north-central Birmingham does not rank highly according to known crime rates, it is a preferred setting for crime-related newspaper articles.

Table 10.2: Crime News Compared with Official Crime Statistics over the same Seven Month Period

	Known Crimes		Press Reports	
	n	%	n	%
Crime type:				
Personal violence, robbery and assault with intent to rob	4629	5.4	3584.5	72.7
Theft/burglary	71631	83.9	186.5	3.8
Other	9138	10.7	1160.5	23.5
Total	85398	100.0	4931.5	100.0

Sources: West Midlands Police monthly crime statistics; author's newspaper survey.

Where analysts diverge most bitterly is on the question of whether or not these statistically inaccurate news reports are capable of shaping public opinion. Park (1940b, p107) seemed to think not, maintaining that 'the news announces events rather than interprets them'. However, the *laissez-faire* theory that this appeared to imply [1] elicited a strong reaction from those preferring a 'mass manipulative' model of the relationship between mass media images and public opinion (cf. Cohen and Young, 1973). Mass manipulative theories invest the news media with an active and persuasive ability to shape and mobilise unresisting opinions and they gain support from empirical evidence (e.g. see Davis, 1952; Gordon and Heath, 1981, and Rikardsson, 1981).

Similar evidence can, in fact, be mustered in the present study, which corroborates Walmsley's (1980, 1982) assertion of the importance of news reports as a source of the public's spatial information. In Birmingham, 117 representatives from five inner city communities were asked to rank the city's neighbourhoods according to the severity of their crime problem. As Table 10.3 shows, north-central Birmingham, the preferred location for crime-related news, was consistently perceived to be the worst district. Even within the study area, public opinion greatly inflated the contribution of violence to the overall crime pattern. 'Mugging' and other violent crime, together accounted for less than six per cent of recorded crime, whereas the surveyed public inflated their proportions to 25 per cent and 33 per cent respectively. Moreover, this distortion is not unrelated to people's acquaintance with the provincial press. Those who specified the local newspaper as their main source of information about crime, and those who claimed always to read the evening newspaper studied here, were more likely than other respondents to believe that local crime consists largely of personal violence or vice. They also showed a greater tendency to conceive of crime generally in terms of violent or personal offences.

As the types and locations of crime foremost in the public mind tend to be those accorded most attention by the press, it seems likely that news coverage has some influence in the formation of such images. Nevertheless, it would be over-simplistic and unfaithful to the empirical evidence which follows to interpret this as evidence of a direct and deterministic relationship between crime news and public opinion, and so to deny the public any real autonomy in constructing their perceptions of reality. Indeed, if any such causal link does occur, its direction is far from easily demonstrable (cf. Miller *et al*, 1982). A preferred interpretation is one that seeks the middle ground between *laissez - faire* and mass-manipulative theories, acknowledging the power of the press, but recognising that this is lodged both in the content of the news and in the circumstances under which it is received. I shall argue that it is this middle ground, and not the *laissez - faire* option, that Park preferred, and that this preference rested on a scrupulous theory of the public which is lacking in many current attempts to understand the relationship between the mass media and the public opinion.

Park is often criticised for underplaying the manipulative power of the press. Perhaps, as Turner (1967) suggests, he was unable to distance himself sufficiently from his role as a journalist to comment impartially. He worked for seven years as a reporter in New York, Detroit and Chicago, and often made claims for the detachment and objectivity of the newspaper. Yet, this may reflect less his

Table 10.3: Crime Rates for Birmingham's Inner City Areas compared with Crime in the News and Community Representatives' Estimates of the Severity of the Crime Problem

Location	Intensity of crime[a]		Property crimes[b]		Total crimes[c]		Crime in the news[d]		ECS[e]	
	rate	rank	rate	rank	rate	rank	%	rank	score	rank
City centre	25.1	1	873	1	16.0	2	14.6	4	.29	4
North-central	9.1	3	339	3	13.9	3	34.0	1	.578	1
South-central	12.8	2	406	2	17.4	1	25.2	2	.52	2
East-central	6.9	4	202	5	7.3	5	9.5	5	.366	3
West-central	6.7	5	88	6	8.9	4	1.3	6	.189	5
Inner suburbs	5.1	6	309	4	5.9	6	15.5	3	.178	6

Notes: a Personal crimes per 1000 residents b Property crimes per 1000 households c Total crimes per hectare d Number of articles on crime in the newspaper sample citing each area expressed as a proportion of all articles on crime e Estimated Crime Seriousness (ECS) is based on the rankings produced by 117 representatives of voluntary organisations and decentralised statutory bodies from 5 geographically distinct, ethnically mixed inner city communities. ECS = [E/N (c-1)], where n=number of areas above which each district was ranked, N=total number of respondents, c=number of alternatives that could be assigned a rank. (Thus the index is derived from scores allocated to each area on the basis of the number of neighbourhoods they were ranked above, in the sense of having a more serious crime problem.) ECS varies between 0 and 1, and as ECS tends to 1, interviewees' overall estimates of the severity of the crime problem tend towards a (subjective) maximum.

Sources: West Midlands Police Monthly Crime Statistics; author's newspaper survey; author's interviews.

protectiveness towards the industry than his clear sense of its limitations. He did believe that journalism could have the power to change society (cf. Matthews, 1977, p11) but, equally, from tramping the streets and chatting enthusiastically with his public, he realised just how transient, ephemeral and inconsequential the news could be. The news raises issues, certainly, but this does not guarantee their salience in the public mind. It outlined what appear to be the 'facts', and these facts might be right or wrong, but 'from the newspaper point of view objectivity can go no farther. Facts are, after all, only facts in a universe of discourse and, as I have suggested, every public has its own' (Park, 1940b, p108).

Park's argument, then, is for the agenda-setting role of the press. The newspaper is conceptualised as a form of communication which helps to define the terms by which daily life is practised, without insisting that these terms are accepted uncritically. It does, however, create an awareness of particular issues rather than others, and by delineating and clarifying them, might set some bounds to the nature of social reality. The mass media can suggest what could and should happen by controlling what remains unconceivable and inaccessible, and as a *public* information source its influence might reach beyond individual idiosyncracies to carry implications for groups and areas. As such, news has a cultural role enabling it to 'provide continuity and moral confirmation for established ways of living through its interpretations of local affairs' (Critcher *et al*, 1975, p3; see also Piepe *et al*, 1978). In the context of the present analysis, then, the provincial press may be responsible not so much for transmitting specific fears as for conditioning the ways in which an awareness of crime is orientated or coloured by those it concerns. It remains to identify the agenda set in this respect for the residents of north-central Birmingham, paying particular attention to items which might account for the otherwise inexplicable association of race with crime in this neighbourhood.

News as a Public Agenda

Previous studies indicate that reporting practices might account for many of the stereotypes encountered in the Birmingham example. For instance, Husband *et al* (1974) suggested that the news media have a significant role in defining white people's images of race relations in Britain. Hartmann and Husband (1971) also claimed that these images are most frequently couched in terms of conflict. Moreover, in the West Midlands press Critcher *et al* (1975) showed that when black people appear as individuals they do so primarily as persons suspected or convicted of crime. In so far as editorial policy is concerned, by combining race with crime it is possible to add to the newsworthiness of both topics, and this must have accounted for the bias of many popular images of north-central Birmingham.

To some extent, pressure groups had succeeded in moderating these questionable editorial practices by the end of 1978. In the present study, most articles referring to blacks or Asians contained news of sport, entertainment or other items of human interest. However, there were still important differences in crime reporting according to whether or not the news contained an ethnic element. Coloured offenders were over-represented in reports of the most sensational 'newsworthy'crimes, including sexual offences, robbery and fraud. They were under-represented in articles devoted to less emotive crimes such as theft and burglary.[2] Moreover, Table 10.4 shows that news items linking crime with coloured ethnic minorities centre overwhelmingly on north-central Birmingham. Indeed, in proportional terms the majority of crime reports citing these neighbourhoods contain allusions to coloured offenders. While this is also true of the inner city communities of south Birminghan, the racial bias is not as marked as in the north.

Paradoxically, 'human interest' news, which would tend to portray ethnic minorities in a favourable light is under-represented in those articles concerning the coloured population which refer to the inner city. The benefits of cultural diversity to which they bear witness must seem far removed from the residential milieu of the study area's readers. Suburban images of race thus contrast sharply with the negative picture conjoured up for the inner city where Critcher *et al*'s (1975) conclusions are still appropriate: mass media handling of race-related news perpetuates negative perceptions of coloured minorities and helps define the local structure of social relations in terms of inter-group conflict. As Weaver (1980) states more explicitly, the provincial press portrayed north-central Birmingham as a violent, crime-ridden area throughout the 1960s and 1970s, and tended to locate the problem in the nature of the black people rather than in their disadvantaged position in British society.

The agenda set for the residents of the study area can thus be identified in terms of at least one spatial image and two social stereotypes of the criminal connotations of the coloured population. Spatially, emphasis remains on north-central Birmingham. Here, in one of Britain's 'Race Relations Capitals' (Rex and Tomlinson, 1979,

Table 10.4: The Geography of Crime News

Focus of newspaper articles	Race only		Crime only		Themes linking race and crime		Total	
	n	%	n	%	n	%	n	%
Location cited:								
Inner city:								
North	54	16.4	17	5.7	69	30.9	140	16.4
East	14	4.2	6	2.0	7	3.1	27	3.2
South-east	14	4.2	6	2.0	12	5.4	32	3.8
South	29	8.8	20	6.7	31	13.9	80	9.4
West	8	2.4	7	2.3	13	5.8	28	3.3
City centre	7	2.1	6	2.0	6	2.7	19	2.2
Other Suburban Birmingham	58	17.6	86	28.8	31	13.9	175	20.5
Other West Midlands	82	24.9	68	22.7	33	14.8	183	21.5
Other	64	19.4	83	27.8	21	9.4	168	19.7
Total	330	100.0	299	100.0	223	100.0	852	100.0

$x^2 = 115{,}554$, 16 d.f., $p < 0.001$ Note:These numbers are based on a random sample of crime news over 7 months, all other columns refer to *all* relevant articles which appeared during this period.

p70) is found the 'angry suburb' of Birmingham (*Birmingham Evening Mail*, 5-8 July 1970), a neighbourhood where 'our new multi-racial society sprawls drunkenly with all its conflicts raw, all its squalor exposed' (*Birmingham Post*, 20 Nov. 1977). Additionally, every two or three years since 1967, the *Evening Mail* has run a series of sensational articles on the district which have tended to sustain this image in the public mind.

Socially, the supposedly 'black' crime of mugging, a label generated by allegations of the disproportionate involvement of young blacks in personal robbery, can be traced back as far as Enoch Powell's controversial speeches in 1968. However, the label gained most impetus during the 'moral panic' of 1973 when three newsworthy topics - race, crime and youth - were irrevocably collapsed into a single theme as the consequence of an incident in Handworth itself, which is documented by Hall *et al*(1978, pp106-115). 'Mugging' lingered in the national press for more than two years. It attracted renewed concern in Birmingham following an academic publication which placed a small group of blacks at the centre of the policing problem in part of the same area (Brown, 1977). Shortly afterwards a 'Terror gangs shock' hit the headlines (*Birmingham Evening Mail*, 15 Nov. 1977); the *Morning Post* revealed the 'Stark Truth' about the locale (20 Nov. 1977); and journalists noted how the 'strife-torn' area was again in the limelight as a consequence of a new report 'on the problems caused by 200 rebellious, violent West Indian youngsters' (*Birmingham Evening Mail*, 4 Oct. 1977). By early 1978 even the *Morning Post* had relinquished its neutral stance, asserting under a headline 'The Second City for Robbery' that:

> What everyone knows and no-one likes to say for the best of reasons is that Birmingham's robbery statistics have been raised to disproportionate heights in the last few years by the freakish crime wave among young - and often unemployed - coloured people. (*Birmingham Post*, 28 Jan. 1978).

Towards the end of the decade the sensational connotations of mugging were subdued. More recently, they have been superseded by relationships forged between race and civil unrest in the inner city. However, in the intervening period, (which is that of the present study), the associations between West Indian culture and interpersonal violence were played down, rather than refuted. Images already established in the public mind received continuing support even in the months when excessive dramatisation was successfuly avoided.

A second racial stereotype emerged during this time, drawing attention to Asian criminality. This rarely invoked dangerous or threatening images, but stressed rather elements of stupidity, fraudulence or deceit. A typical example is a front page article telling how an unemployed man's working sons had paid for their father to have a holiday in Bangladesh. It was headlined 'Jobless Dan will jet back to a State handout' (*Birmingham Evening Mail*, 31 Jan. 1979) and written in a style likely to play on people's fears and prejudices. As the Birmingham Community Relations Council (1979, p1) noted:

> Nothing in the story is actually untrue, no accusations are directly made, but the indications are clear. No opportunity, either by turn of phrase or conjunctions of words is missed to lead the reader towards the mistaken conclusion that the fearless Evening Mail has uncovered a real scrounger.

Other articles from the *Evening Mail* described how Asian criminals fail in their attempts at fraud and deception abound: 'Cashing in on car tax cost man job' (5 Feb. 1979); 'Swoop on the benefit fiddlers' (16 Feb. 1979); 'Police dig up a garden of gold' (17 Feb. 1979); 'Goldsmith says "my deals were worth 1M"' (20 Feb. 1979); 'Mail fraud charges' (24 Feb. 1979); 'Wife didn't exist except for tax' (27 Feb. 1979); 'Two face charge' (23 Mar 1979)' 'Dishonest profit from the State (6 Apr. 1979); 'Tighter security moves to beat the scroungers' (7 Apr. 1979); 'Ninth car-hire man jailed for security fiddle' (9 May 1979); 'Trader started blaze to swindle insurance' (22 May 1979). In every case, these articles mentioned an Asian perpetrator. For the most part, the criminals in these stories are presented as bungling and inefficient, attempting to commit offences which could not possibly succeed.

Both this type of news, and those articles documenting intra-familial or sectarian violence within the Asian community, have as much potential for 'marginalising' their subjects as did the mugging panic for the West Indians. The image of coloured ethnic minorities made available through the local press is predominantly one of separation from mainstream society. The association of race with crime, especially in north-central Birmingham, ensures further that New Commonwealth immigrants are cast into the perspective of a racial problem rather than a cultural resource. This, then, is the agenda set by the provincial press for the residents of the study area. Their neighbourhood is defined as high in crime, and the element of risk this introduces is couched in terms of stereotyped images of criminals drawn from the two most obvious minority groups living there.

The Function of the Press

In its role as an agenda-setting form of communication, the provincial press contributes to what Miles and Phisacklea (1978) saw as a national, structural, marginalisation of Britain's coloured ethnic minorities. It also portrays the inner city environment as one which carries the risks and uncertainties of social unrest and a high crime rate (especially in terms of violent, personal offences). What still has not been clarified is the *function* of the newspaper in fulfilling this role. Perhaps the thorniest issue here concerns the relationship of the mass media to social change. The press may passively set an agenda or define the bounds of social reality, but could it be an active agent in the process of social transformation?

Whole volumes have been devoted to this question (e.g. Katz and Szecsko, 1981) and there is a strong argument in the literature that the mass media can be instrumental in creating social change, either by exacerbating inter-group tensions, or by the destruction of cultural diversity. A different perspective is offered by Robinson (1972) who suggested that mass media work against change by reinforcing or accentuating existing conditions. They are fundamentally mechanisms for social integration, which, as Alexander (1981) argued, is necessary in a modernising and differentiating society as a functional substitute for direct contact. The press is only a means of communication, not a self-conscious organiser of norms or director of change, for 'it does not formulate basic goals, which is a political responsibility, or basic values, which is a cultural one' (Alexander, 1981, p35).

For Park, the function of the newspaper was defined by the activities of a public. It was a discriminating public rather than a monolithic press that had the power to effect or inhibit social change. In this sense, the public constituted a very specific form of collective behaviour, which is too often passed over in studies of mass society (Levine, 1972). Park (1904) identified both the crowd and the public as mechanisms for social change and, in this, both stand in contrast to institutionalised social groups such as classes, sects, and political parties:

> The crowd and the public are governed by a collective drive, but one that has not yet crystallised into a norm ... Neither crowds nor publics possess rules, modes of conscious governance, self-consciousness or boundary maintenance. They are limited only by the immanent conditions of spontaneous interaction. (Levine, 1972, p xxx).

The definitive characteristic of a public, in contrast to a crowd, is the critical abilities of its members. Since the news raises issues over which thinking people may divide, it is not surprising that the notion of the public is central to Park's essays on the press. Public opinion forms only through discussion (Park, 1904, p60), and the news is only discussed because it is capable of more than one interpretation (Park, 1940a). The press is powerful, but its power rests in the public opinion that emerges out of debates amongst individuals, each attempting to rationalise their interpretations of the news (Park, 1941). The power of the press is its ability to bring into existence a collective will which might mobilise for action. In this sense the news could, but will not necessarily, prompt social change through the agency of the public.

The Press and the Public

From Park, then, it is possible to derive a theory of the mass media based on their agenda-setting role and their communicative functions: they set the scene and raise issues for public debate. In order to understand fully the impact of the press, (in this instance on perceptions of crime and definitions of criminals), it is necessary to consider not only the restrictions its agenda places on the bounds of social reality, but also the deliberations of a public prompted by their selective interpretations of this news. For, as Robinson (1972) divines from a wide-ranging literature review, the mass media seem fairly ineffective in conveying *specific* pieces of information. The public are often ignorant of particular discrete news items. News is ahistorical and decontextualised, it is for the initiated who make it relevant to a local situation. It circulates only in so far as it is interesting and intelligible and able to excite discussion (cf. Park, 1938).

Public interest in the news is pragmatic rather than indiscriminately appreciative and, as gossip begins, the focus of attention might shift, for 'once discussion has been started the event under discussion soon ceases to become news and, as interpretations of an event differ, discussion turns from the news to the issues it raises' (Park, 1940a, p42). The remainder of this essay considers these issues in the context of race relations and the problem of crime in north-central Birmingham.

Improvised News and the Dissemination of Fear

Park (1940a) described rumour and gossip as types of knowledge which are related to, but less authentic than, news circulated by the mass media. Yet, he forcefully acknowledged that public opinion arose out of selective interpretations and discussions of more formal sources of news. This selectivity depends on the structure of social relations from which it arises and with which it interacts: for news to circulate there must be 'a certain degree of rapport and a certain degree of tension' (Park, 1940a, p49). This process can only be studied using the experiential research methods pioneered by Park himself - methods that are as much a part of the inheritance of urban social geography as the more positivistic traditions with which the Chicago school are often linked (Smith, 1981).

Park and his associates often used case studies to identify basic principles of social and spatial organisation in society. They showed that intensive small-scale studies of events and relationships can illuminate issues which far transcend the parochial, seemingly unique, concerns of each situation. Turner (1976, p xxv) found a clear rationale behind the tendency towards purposive observation rather than representative sampling that this produced:

> There is a very special sense in which Park sees the city as a microcosm in which are exposed and magnified, as under a microscope, the processes taking place in the larger society ... In this special sense, the city is a laboratory in which the investigator can see what he may only infer elsewhere.

Accordingly, the cases discussed below were selected for their explanatory power rather than for their typicality. They were chosen in order to develop theory, such that potentially generalisable relationships did not just turn up, but rather were deliberately pursued among the myriad interactions comprising crime-related gossip or rumour.

According to Turner and Killian (1972), rumour is a definitive characteristic of collective behaviour - the process by which emergent norms develop and a means of problem solving. In my experience, however, rumour generally was not rife in the study area. Moreover, crime-related rumour was extremely particularistic. The only classification that seemed appropriate draws a distinction between 'focused' and 'diffuse' messages. Focused gossip was easily linked with specific events, while unfocused messages contained more abstract news items; events well-absorbed into the conventional wisdom of 'folk knowledge' but periodically re-worked and re-formulated for specific ends. Some instances of both forms of gossip are discussed here in an attempt to integrate their geographical implications with theories grounded in the existing, largely anthropological, literature.

Suttles (1968) identified street life as a vital link in the communications network of the Addams area of Chicago. Face-to-face exchanges were conditioned by the spatial arrangements of the various social groups and their conversations were heavily restricted to the known world of nearby persons and events. The extent to which this proved true in north-central Birmingham varied according to ethnicity, for the most obvious dimensions of residents' social networks were aligned according to birthplace, religious and linguistic affiliations. This alignment both guided and was reinforced by the interpersonal communication of crime news; and at different times, the various ethnic attributes all proved to be effective barriers to the dissemination of rumour. In fact, many intra-ethnic rumours must have completely escaped my notice. A key Bengali informant picked up only snippets of news from the Indian Muslims and Punjabi Sikhs who live close by, and the small community of Pakistani Pathans centred in a nearby General Improvement Area almost totally escaped his notice. While part-time work in a Muslim doctor's surgery gave him access to much of the rumour circulating amongst the Bengalis, his attempts to explain their subtleties to me quickly vindicated the view that the closer the bonds of a relationship, the more intimate and esoteric the gossip, and the more trite and meaningless it appears to outsiders (Gluckman, 1963). Thus, some of the rumours which proved most illuminating were those found at the locus of several social networks. These were usually of the 'specific' rather than the 'diffuse' type.

Focused Rumour: Re-working the News

Specific rumour seemed initially to be merely informative, communicating details about the nature, locations and participants of different types of crime. To some extent, this *was* its role. As such, rumour constituted a source of 'folk wisdom' required by residents for the management of danger in everyday life. Individuals were able to build up maps of varying accuracy of the social and spatial environment for the purely pragmatic purpose of avoiding real or imagined hazards and proceeding unhindered with their daily lives, but the following examples suggest that the significance of rumour extends well beyond its communicative function.

Shortly before I arrived in the study area, an old terraced house had been acquired as an educational and play centre for Asian youths. It was run by a local school teacher and a white community worker, both of whom had lived in the area for some years. A spate of burglaries followed by malicious arson was sufficient to gut the house and disrupt the regular meetings, which variously involved Bengali, Pakistani and Indian women and schoolchildren.

During the course of three weeks, the burglaries caused progressively more damage, and tension increased when no clues about the perpetrators came to light. Speculation as to their identity and motive soon became rife however, and the circumstances of this conjecture are illuminating. A process of social labelling began with allusions to an apparently troublesome group of West Indians living in some nearby multi-occupied terraces. In the past, many Bengalis had complained of harassment, noise, disrespect and intimidation at their hands. Soon, it transpired that a number of these youths had been seen loitering outside the vandalised centre (which stands opposite their dwelling). Suspicion was easily cast upon them by virtue of an obvious escape route to their own nearby home. As no-one was ever charged with the offences, many Bengalis were content to blame the labelled suspects, reasserting and justifying their already apprehensive feelings towards this small group of West Indians.

Given the small proportions of Asians, relative to other ethnic groups, who gain their crime-related information from the local press, Shibutani's (1966) interpretation of rumour as 'improvised' news seems especially applicable here. He suggested that rumour becomes necessary when public demand for news exceeds the supply made available through institutionalised channels. Thus, when no formal account of the culprits was forwarded, the suitable substitute of improvised news was required as a means of dissipating the mounting tension and filling the information vacuum.

The explanation is incomplete, however, for the rumour was not completely exhausted. The interest was quickly aroused of several Indian and Pakistani families in two nearby General Improvement Areas, who had friends or relatives attending the community centre. I did not hear of the rumour again from the first of these areas despite reliable contacts and a close-knit social network in the area, but in the second area it gained further impetus. Here for some time a group of West Indian car mechanics had been a source of discontent amongst other residents - largely because of the congestion caused in the narrow streets by cars being parked and even serviced at the roadside. Already, veiled accusations about stolen excise licences had been mooted, and labelling associated with the burglaries at the community centre provided 'confirmation' of the shady dealings which were assumed to be going on. The rumour was seized upon as a means of clarifying and confirming existing suspicions, defining the extent of social exclusion and spatial avoidance which could justifiably be practised.

Rumour, then, is not merely the creation of informal news. The social centrality of the source incident influenced the spatial extent of related gossip by introducing it to divergent networks. Yet this was not sufficient to ensure its perpetuation, even amongst those receiving little 'formal' news. In the first General Improvement Area the rumour could serve no pragmatic purpose. It was received as purely informative gossip and lost to a host of more intimate and personal disclosures. Elsewhere, however, the rumour 'arrived' at a time when it could help clarify a tense and ambiguous situation, providing the rationale for organising meanings and behaviour. It is in this sense, as 'a recurrent form of communication through which men caught together in an ambiguous situation attempt to construct a meaningful interpretation of it by pooling their intellectual resources', that Shibutani's (1966, p17) interpretation of rumour as improvised news seems most valuable. The key feature of this is not so much distortion, manipulation or evaluation, as the process of social interaction amongst people confronted with inadequately defined situations. Where these involve crime, which itself connotes danger, fear and apprehension, the ambiguity is resolved by excluding, whether spatially or socially, the source of uncertainty. It makes little difference whether the rumour is true or false, for given a lack of formal information and a racist agenda set by the provincial press, people's usual standards of judgment may be suspended and only the rumour offers cues as to how to respond (cf. Turner and Killian, 1972, p31).

There are, however, other principles by which crime-related information seems to spread, as a second example of 'specific' rumour illustrates. This was elicited by tapping a network of white female pensioners. The rumour began when one of the group disturbed a burglar who had gained entry to her home through an insecure window. This was followed not long afterwards by a similar incident in a nearby street where entry was facilitated by a broken French window and a garden fence in disrepair. Discussions centring on these crimes prompted participants to recall similar instances which had afflicted their acquaintances both recently and in the distant part. Although the ethnicity, sex and age of the perpetrators was often known, this was not a central theme of the ensuing gossip. Attention focused rather on the consequences of victims having 'let their standards slip'. For the residual indigenous population of this once-coveted residential area, opportunistic property crime is disproportionately likely to afflict those who cease to maintain their property adequately. In condemning such victims, people develop a mechanism by which to preserve and assert their own social status. In this sense, gossip is only partly about transmitting information; it is largely an evaluative assessment of morality, and an expression and affirmation of norms.

This second example shows how rumour can cut across and re-define normal group boundaries. The given explanation is akin to the structural-functional interpretation of rumour originally formalised by Gluckman (1963, 1968; see also Epstein, 1969). However, Firth's (1956) even earlier research in Tikopea had suggested that certain types of rumour serve as social instruments by which individuals or groups attempt to improve their status; and Bott (1967) had concluded from her study of social relations in a lower-class London neighbourhood that gossip is one of the chief means by which norms are stated and reaffirmed. Crime-related rumour, with its attendant package of moral and ethical piety seems, according to the evidence observed in north-central Birmingham, to be particularly suited to this function.

Diffuse Rumour: News as Received Wisdom

Diffuse or abstract rumour appears to have a different explanation again. Although 'specific' rumours tend to be ephemeral, their quixotic nature invests them with unique adaptability. They may be constantly reworked and re-circulated until they become 'folk ideas', absorbed into the popular history of the neighbourhood. Thus, while Shibutani (1966) saw fit to seek the beginnings and ends of rumours, in this, their most general and abstract form, they are synthesised rather than propagated from the numerous snippets of information contained in a vast reservoir of public news.

Two rumours had been absorbed into this pool of received wisdom well before I arrived in Birmingham. In essence, they concerned a West Indian tenant who had been provoked into murdering his landlord, and a fight between two factions of the Muslim community in a residential grove tucked behind the main thoroughfare. The incidents were variously used, in combination with other fragmented opinions, to elaborate upon the problems of letting and renting properties, the dangers of loitering in back streets, the perils of accommodating members of ethnic minority groups, and the nuisance of poor street lighting, sparse policing and inefficient environmental planning. The incidents themselves had merged into a repertoire of past experiences; they were drawn on pragmatically to resolve ambiguities, and to clarify and legitimise animosity or affect.

Some clues to the interpretation of this type of rumour can be found in the psychoanalytical theories of Festinger *et al* (1948). Their suggestion is that rumours are propagated when individuals entertain and pass on stories which enable them to express anxieties and hostilities that might otherwise remain unacknowledged and suppressed. According to this theory, urban crime, itself a source of tension, could become entangled with a range of other grievances associated with one's neighbourhood of residence. Indeed, a more quantitative study of concern for crime in this area suggests that these other grievances are often translated into anxiety about crime (Smith, 1983).

Psychoanalytical theory tends to examine rumour as a discrete product of social interaction - a message which could be isolated and preserved if only people were more careful in handling it (cf. Allport and Postman, 1947). None the less, the impression of rumour in north-central Birmingham was rather that of a phenomenon which comprises social interaction. It is a process of negotiating shared meanings, rather than a product of social organisation. Thus, on balance, Paine's explanation might be more appropriate than that of the psychoanalysts. Paine (1967, 1968) finds in gossip an informal and indirect sanction which is employed where the risks of open or formal attack are too high. Extending his argument, rumour could be conceptualised as the 'public' equivalent of the crowd behaviour alluded to by Cohen (1980, 1982) in his accounts of the social function of carnivals. Both carnival and gossip are means by which individuals and groups may 'contest territory' in social and physical space. Positions of domination or subordination are negotiated by avoiding overt conflict and entering into a form of 'joking relationship'. This is well illustrated in a conversation that took place between an elderly white resident and her West Indian neighbour, whose delapidated home was a source of her resentment and discontent.

The topic under discussion was a spate of burglaries allegedly committed by a group of West Indian youths. The actual identity of the culprits, of course, was an issue over which opinions divided, but the conversation itself gave both parties a chance to air their grievances, and to allay, if not resolve, their mutual exasperation. The white pensioner gained an opportunity to discuss the 'general' problem of structurally unsound dwellings (though her criticisms were obviously slanted towards her neighbour's unkempt home); the West Indian seized a chance to put forward his views on the unjust labelling of black youths. The rumour itself was quite implausible. Crimes of such magnitude and extent were not recorded either in police files or by the mass media. Yet in discussing a controversial rumour which contained elements of both participants' attitudes, some common ground was cleared for conversation without conflict. In Leinhardt's (1975) view, such 'fantastic' rumours are necessary to resolve certain complexities of public feelings that cannot readily be articulated at a more thoughtful level. Their creation again illustrates Turner and Killian's (1972, p31) point that rumour might work towards social change by cutting across traditional group boundaries: 'strangers who know little about each other except that they share an interest in the ambiguous situation, interact and become part of an emergent collectivity'.

Fantastic or implausible rumour can also be explained in terms of the studied neighbourhood's enduring 'high crime' level. This characterisation, which is particularly evident in mass media reports, makes for an uncertain and unstable environment. This insecurity arises not only from the ostensibly random incidence of crime and its unpredictability, but is also a consequence of the poor inflow of information about crime and, particularly, its perpetrators from official sources. Such ignorance and uncertainty produces an element of tension or suspense which may result in gossip. A close parallel here can be found in the notion of 'wizardry' as conceived by Evans-Pritchard (1937). Merely believing in witchcraft, (or crime in the present context), creates anxieties which are periodically discharged as gossip and accusations. The implication is that once sufficient information is available with which to make a judgment (and regardless of its accuracy), gossip takes the form of a labelling mechanism by which the judgment is executed. Thus, there is only a short, even logical, step from 'diffuse' rumours to totally unfounded gossip if such irrationalism can help to decrease the tensions infusing an uncertain environment. For, as Shibutani (1966) noticed, when unsatisfied demand for news is but moderate, rumour is deliberative and plausible, and limited by existing mechanisms of informal social control. The tension caused by excessive unsatisfied demand, however, prompts extemporaneous rumour which is frequently implausible, but nevertheless eagerly adopted by participants who have surrendered their critical abilities. Such implausibility characterised much crime-related discourse in the study area. I met a number of white residents who claimed not to know any elderly women who had *not* been mugged or burgled 'since the immigrants took over'. Indeed, for much of the time, 'extemporaneous' rumour exerted pressure for social change in the informal sphere, in the same way that the 'moral panics' observed by Hall *et al* (1978) function in an institutional setting.

Thus, while formal news may set the agenda for debate, it is through informal communication channels that the details of events are reconstructed and selectively used by a public. In a reputedly high-risk environment such as north-central Birmingham, deviance is the source of much discussion. In an area where coloured residents are portrayed as a problem, it is convenient, if irrational, to blame them for the worries caused by crime. Yet the news is used pragmatically and discussed critically: people may divide over the issue of a link between race and crime, and rumours sometimes completely ignore the colour of the offender. Nevertheless, for the most part the two themes are associated in the public mind. They are of enough immediate relevance to be worthy of discussion and the bounds of social reality, as set by the mass media, are soon absorbed into the popular wisdom of the neighbourhood.

Conclusion

In this chapter an attempt has been made to derive a theory from the work of Robert Park about the relationship between the provincial press and both culture and social change, in order to help to explain the popular images that link race with crime in north-central Birmingham. Empirical evidence revealed that public opinion is often more closely aligned with the picture of crime drawn by the local newspaper than with official crime statistics. However, in accounting for this, mass manipulative theories were rejected in favour of an explanation assigning the public a more active role in the way that they select and use the news.

The role of the press is theorised as one which provides the agenda within which public scrutiny is exercised. In the present study, the mass media sustained an image of coloured ethnic minorities as separate from mainstream society, particularly when dealing with the inner city. By linking race with crime, the news further defines these groups as part of a problem contributing to the risks of inner city life. The function of this medium, having set some bounds to social reality, is not actively to produce or inhibit change in its own right, but to feed ephemeral snippets of information into the realm of public discourse, so acting as a form of communication or a mechanism for integration. It is the public, not the press, which, as a form of collective behaviour, might act as the agent for social change.

Public opinion arises out of gossip or rumour. Tellers may turn the news to pragmatic or instrumental ends, but they can rarely escape the limitations of an agenda set by the mass media. The evidence in north-central Birmingham is that the provincial press provides a framework, based on established social and spatial stereotypes, which effectively contours any ensuing ripples of gossip. To a certain extent, the news does control what aspects of which issues are made available. The bias that this introduces reflects broader structural tensions in British society, especially those concerning the poverty and uncertainty of the inner city and the marginalisation of ethnic minorities. When these are brought together in the news, fears about crime are linked with apprehension towards social opposites, and structural questions are translated into the commonsense world of daily living. By linking Park's theory of the public with a theory of the press, this chapter has attempted to show how the workings of deeply rooted, and therefore widely experienced, societal structures are played out in detail in social and physical space.

NOTES

1. In other words that, from a variety of conflicting opinions carried by the press, the public abstract only those ideas that conform to their own attitudes.

2. For violence other than robbery, which constitutes the majority of mass media reports, black and white offenders received approximately the same amount of coverage. This, of course, does not preclude mass-media bias, since blacks form a much smaller proportion than do whites of the total population that *could* have appeared in such news reports.

LIST OF CONTRIBUTORS

Susan Brooker-Gross
Associate Professor of Geography,
Virginia Polytechnic Institute and State University

Jacquelin Burgess
Lecturer in Geography,
University College London

John R. Gold
Senior Lecturer in Geography,
Oxford Polytechnic

Peter Gould
Professor of Geography,
Pennsylvania State University

Bob Jarvis
Planner,
Tyne and Wear County Council

Diana M. Liverman
Assistant Professor of Geography,
University of Wisconsin,
Madison

Anne Lyew-Ayee
Lecturer in Geography
University of the West Indies

Douglas R. Sherman
Assistant Professor of Geography,
University of Southern California

Catherine P. Silk
Lecturer in Geography,
Reading College of Technology

John A. Silk
Lecturer in Geography,
Reading College of Technology

Susan J. Smith
Visiting Assistant Professor of Geography,
University of California-Los Angeles

Martin J. Youngs
Research Student,
London School of Economics

Abler, R.F. (1973) 'Monoculture or Miniculture?' in Lanegran, D. and Palm, R. (eds) *Invitation to Geography*: McGraw-Hill, New York, 186-195

Aldgate, T. (1981) 'Ideological Consensus in British Feature Films', in Short, K.R.M. (ed) *Feature Films as History*, Croom Helm, London, 94-112

Alexander, J.C. (1981) 'The Mass News Media in Systemic, Historical and Comparative Perspective', in Katz, E. and Szecsko, T. (eds), *Mass Media and Social Change*, Sage, Beverly Hills, 17-51

Allen, J.L. (1897) *The Choir Invisible*, MacMillan, New York

Allport, G.W. and Postman, L. (1947) *The Psychology of Rumour*, Holt, Rinehart and Winston, New York

Althusser, L. (1971) 'Ideology and Ideological State Apparatuses', in Althusser, L. *Lenin and Philosophy and Other Essays*, New Left Books, London (2nd edition), 121-173

Althusser, L. and Balibar, E. (1970) *Reading Capital*, New Left Books, London

Amin, S. (1977) *Unequal Development*, Harvester, Lewes

Andrews, P. (1980) 'Disaster Novels', *New York Times Book Review*, 27 January, 15

Atkin, R. (1974) *Mathematical Structure in Human Affairs*, Heinemann Educational Books, London

Automobile Association (1980) *The AA Book of British Villages*, Drive Publications, London

Bachrach, P. and Baratz, M. (1970) *Power and Poverty: Theory and Practice*, Oxford University Press, Oxford

Bammer, A. (1981) 'Utopian Futures and Cultural Myopia', *Alternative Futures*, 4 (2-3), 1-16

Banham, R. (1955) 'Machine Aesthetic', *Architectural Review*, 117, 225-228

Banham, R. (1971) *Los Angeles: the Architecture of Four Ecologies*, Allen Lane, London

Banham, R. (1979) 'Hotel Déjà-Quoi?', *New Society*, 59, 5 April, 26-7

Barber, E. (1982) 'Hard News', *Ten. 8*, (7-8), 6-11

Barnouw, E. (1974) *Documentary: a History of the Non-Fiction Film*, Oxford University Press, New York

Barrell, J. (1972) *The Idea of Landscape and the Sense of Place, 1730-1840*, Cambridge University Press, Cambridge

Barrell, J. (1980) *The Dark Side of the Landscape*, Cambridge University Press, Cambridge

Barrell, J. (1982) 'Geographies of Hardy's Wessex', *Journal of Historical Geography*, 8, 347-361

Barsacq, L. (1976) *Caligari's Cabinet and Other Grand Illusions: a History of Film Design*, New American Library, New York

Barsam, R.M. (1974) *Non-Fiction Film: a Critical History*, George Allen and Unwin, London

Barthes, R. (1972) *Mythologies*, Cape, London

Barthes, R. (1977) *Image-Music-Text*, Fontana, London

Barthes, R. (1982) *Camera Lucida*, Cape, London

Bedford, C. (1982) *Weep for the City*, Lion, London

Bell, D. (1962) *The End of Ideology*, Free Press, New York

Bell, D. (1977) 'Ideology', in Bullock, A. and Stallybrass, O. (eds) *The Fontana Dictionary of Modern Thought*, Fontana, London, 298-9

Bennett, T. (1979) *Formalism and Marxism*, Methuen, London

Bennett, T. (1982) 'Theories of the Media, Theories of Society', in Gurevitch, M., Bennett, T., Curran, J. and Woollacott, J. (eds) *Culture, Society and the Media*, Methuen, London, 30-55

Benyon, J. (ed.) (1984) *Scarman and After*, Pergamon Press, Oxford

Berman, R. (1981) *Advertising and Social Change*, Sage, Beverly Hills

Birmingham Community Relations Council (1979) 'The Mail's Two Faces', *Bulletin*, 6, 1

Bishton, D. and Homer, B. (eds) (1978) *Talking Blues*, Affor, Birmingham

Blumer, J.G. and Gurevitch, M. (1982) 'The Political Effects of Mass Communication', in Gurevitch, M., Bennett, T., Curran, J. and Woollacott, J. (eds) *Culture, Society and the Media*, Methuen, London, 236-267

Body, R. (1982) *Agriculture: the Triumph and the Shame*, Temple Smith, London

Boggs, S.L. (1971) 'Formal and Informal Crime Control: an Exploratory Study of Urban, Suburban and Rural Orientations', *The Sociological Quarterly*, 12, 319-327

Bommes, M. and Wright, P. (1982) 'Charms of Residence: the Public and the Past', in Johnson, R. *et al* (eds), *Making Histories*, Centre for Cultural Studies in association with Hutchinson, London

Booker, C. (1980) *The Seventies*, Allen Lane, London

Bott, E. (1957) *Family and Social Network*, Tavistock, London

Bowden, M.J. (1976) 'The Great American Desert in the American Mind: the Historiography of a Geographical Notion', in Lowenthal, D. and Bowden, M.J. (eds) *Geographies of the Mind*, Oxford University Press, New York, 119-148

Boyd, W. (1981) 'Living Out of London XV', *London Magazine*, 217, 56-63

Briggs, A. (1960) *Mass Entertainment: the Origins of a Modern Industry*, Oxford University Press, Oxford

British Film Institute (1981) *Granada: the First 25 Years*, BFI Publications, London

Brock, W.R. (1973) *Conflict and Transformation*, Penguin, Harmondsworth

Brooker-Gross S.R. (1983) 'Spatial Aspects of Newsworthiness', *Geografiska Annaler*, 65B, 1-9

Brown, J. (1977) *Shades of Grey: a Report on Police-West Indian Relations in Handsworth*, Cranfield Institute of Technology, Cranfield

Brunsden, C. and Morley, D. (1978) *Everyday Television: 'Nationwide'*, British Film Institute, London

Buck, P.H. (1937) *The Road to Reunion*, Little, Brown and Co., Boston

Burgess, J.A. (1978) *Image and Identity*, Occasional Paper in Geography No 23, University of Hull

Burgess, J.A. (1981) 'The Misunderstood City', *Landscape*, 25, 20-27

Burgess, J.A. (1982a) 'Selling Places: Environmental Images for the Executive', *Regional Studies*, 16, 1-17

Burgess, J.A. (1982b) 'Filming the Fens: a Visual Interpretation of Regional Character', in Gold, J.R. and Burgess, J.A. (eds) *Valued Environments*, George Allen and Unwin, London, 35-54

Burgess, J.A. and Unwin, D. (1984) 'Exploring "The Living Planet" with David Attenborough', *Journal of Geography in Higher Education*, 8, (in press)

Burgess, J.A. and Wood, P.A. (1984) 'The Role of Advertising in Company Decisions to Locate in London Docklands Enterprise Zone'. Report for the London Docklands Development Corporation

Burns, T. (1977) 'The Organisation of Public Opinion', in Curran, J., Gurevitch, M. and Woollacott, J. (eds), *Mass Communication and Society*, Edward Arnold in association with Open University Press, London, 44-69

Burton, I., Kates, R.W. and White, G.F. (1978) *The Environment as Hazard*, Oxford University Press, New York

Butcher, C.P. (1959) *George W. Cable: The Northampton Years*, Columbia University Press, New York

Calder, A. and Sheridan, D. (1984) *Speak for Yourself: a Mass Observation Anthology 1937-49*, Jonathan Cape, London

Callinicos, A. (1983) *The Revolutionary Ideas of Karl Marx*, Bookmarks, London

Camejo, J. (1976) *Racism, Revolution, Reaction 1861-1877*, Monad, New York
Campbell, R. (1982) *Cinema Strikes Back: Radical Filmmaking in the United States, 1930-1942*, UMI Research Press, Ann Arbor, Michigan
Carey, J.W. (1967) 'Harold Adams Innis and Marshal McLuhan', *The Antioch Review*, 27, 5-39
Carey, J.W. (1969a) 'Courtship Patterns in the Popular Song', *American Journal of Sociology*, 74, 720-731
Carey, J.W. (1969b) 'The Ideology of Autonomy in Popular Lyrics', *Psychiatry*, 32, 150-164
Carey. J.W. (1975) 'Canadian Communication Theory: Extensions and Interpretations of Harold Innis', in Robinson, G.T. and Theall, D.F. *Studies in Canadian Communications*, McGill University, Montreal, 27-59
Carey, J.W. (1977) 'Mass Communications Research and Cultural Studies: an American View', in Curran, J., Gurevitch, M. and Woollacott, J. (eds) *Mass Communication and Society*, Edward Arnold in association with the Open University Press, London, 409-426
Carroll, P.N. and Noble, D.W. (1977) *The Free and the Unfree: a New History of the United States*, Penguin, Harmondsworth
Cash, W.J. (1971) *The Mind of the South*, Thames and Hudson, London
Cashmore, E. (1979) *Rastaman*, George Allen and Unwin, London
Cauthen, N.R., Robinson, I.E. and Krauss, H.H. (1971) 'Stereotypes: a Review of the Literature, 1926-1968', *Journal of Social Psychology*, 84, 103-125
Chanan, M. (1981) *The Dream that Kicks: the Prehistory and Early Years of Cinema in Britain*, Routledge and Kegan Paul, London
Chapman, G. and Johnson, J. (1979) *Television Programme Coding Manual*, International Television Flows Project, Cambridge
Chibnall, S. (1978) *Law and Order News*, Tavistock, London
Chibnall, S. (1980) 'Chronicles of the Gallows: the Social History of Crime Reporting' in Christian, H. (ed) *The Sociology of Journalism and the Press*, University of Keele Press, Keele
Chibnall, S. (1981) 'The Production of Knowledge by Crime Reporters', in Cohen, S. and Young, J. (eds) *The Manufacture of News*, Constable, London, 75-97 (2nd edition)
Clare, J. (1984) 'Eyewitness in Brixton', in Benyon, J. (ed) *Scarman and After*, Pergamon Press, Oxford, 46-53
Clark, M.J. and Allen, W.J. (1977) 'Films: Cities via the Screen', *Geographical Magazine*, 49, 341
Clarke, J., Hall, S., Jefferson, T. and Roberts, B. (1976) 'Subcultures, Cultures and Class' in Hall, S. and Jefferson, T. (eds) *Resistance through Rituals: Youth Subculture in Post War Britain*, Hutchinson, London, 9-74
Cohen, A. (1980) 'Drama and Politics in the Development of a London Carnival', *Man*, 15, 65-87
Cohen, A. (1982) 'A Polyethnic London Carnival as a Contested Cultural Performance', *Ethnic and Racial Studies*, 5, 23-41
Cohen, S. (1980) *Folk Devils and Moral Panics*, Robertson, Oxford (2nd edition)
Cohen, S. and Young, J. (1981) *The Manufacture of News: Deviance, Social Problems and the Mass Media*, Constable, London (2nd edition)
Cole, J.P. (1969) 'Places in Pravda', *Ideas in Geography*, 22, Nottingham University
Cole, J.P. and Whysall, P. (1968) 'Places in the News: a Study of Geographical Information', *Bulletin of Quantitative Date for Geographers*, 17
Conrad, A. (1978) 'Disasters and the American Imagination', *Book Forum*, 4, 204-254
Conrads, U. (1970) *Programmes and Manifestos in Twentieth Century Architecture*, Lund Humphries, London
Cook, R. (1981) Review of The Red and The Black, in *New Musical Express*, December

Copland, A. (1979) Letter, *New Musical Express*, 3 March

Cosgrove, D. (1979) 'John Ruskin and the Geographical Imagination', *Geographical Review*, 69, 43-62

Cowell, D., Jones, T. and Young, J. (eds) (1982) *Policing the Riots*, Junction Books, London

Cox, H. (1968) 'The Restoration of a Sense of Place: a Theological Reflection on the Visual Environment, *Ekistics*, 151, 422-427

Critcher, C., Sondhi, R. and Parker, M. (1975), 'Race in the West Midlands Press', unpublished manuscript, Centre for Contemporary Cultural Studies, University of Birmingham

Crosby, T. (1965) *Architecture: City Sense*, Studio Vista, London

Crumb, R. (1965) *Fritz the Cat in Fritz Bugs Out*, Heavy Duty Comics, Manchester

Cunningham, H. (1980) *Leisure in the Industrial Revolution*, Croom Helm, London

Curl, D.W. (1966) 'The Cincinnati Commercial', *Bulletin of the Cincinnati Historical Society*, 24, 221-231

Curran, J. (1977) 'Capitalism and Control of the Press, 1800-1975', in Curran, J., Gurevitch, M. and Woollacott, J. (eds) *Mass Communication and Society*, Edward Arnold in conjunction with the Open University Press, London, 195-230

Curran, J., Gurevitch, M. and Woollacott, J. (eds) (1977) *Mass Communication and Society*, Edward Arnold in conjunction with the Open University Press, London

Dalton, D. (1981) *The Rolling Stones: the First Twenty Years*, Thames and Hudson, London

Darby, H.C. (1948) 'The Regional Geography of Thomas Hardy's Wessex', *Geographical Review*, 38, 426-443

David, B. (1977) 'Review', *Broadcast*, 822, 4 August, 14

Davis, A. (1982) *Women, Race and Class*, The Women's Press, London

Davis, F.R. (1952) 'Crime News in Colorado Newspapers', *American Journal of Sociology*, 57, 325-330

Deakin, N.D. (1982) 'Lord Scarman's Bran Tub: an Episode in the Politics of Urban Disorder', *The London Journal*, 8, 92-94

Denisoff, R.S. and Levine, M.H. (1971) 'The One Dimensional Approach to Popular Music: a research note', *Journal of Popular Culture*, 4, 911-920

Denisoff, R.S. and Peterson, R.A. (eds) (1972) *The Sounds of Social Change*, Rand McNally, Chicago

Di Maggio, O., Peterson, R. and Esco, J. (1972) 'Country Music: Ballad of the Silent Majority', in Denisoff, R.S. and Peterson, R.A. (eds) *The Sounds of Social Change*, Rand McNally, Chicago

Dixon, T. (Jr)(1903) *The Leopard's Spots*, Doubleday, Page & Co., New York

Dixon, T. (Jr) (1905) *The Clansman: an Historical Romance of the Ku Klux Klan*, Doubleday, Page & Co., New York

Dominick, J.R. (1977) 'Geographical Bias in National TV News', *Journal of Communication*, 27, 94-99

Downs, R.M. and Stea, D. (1977) *Maps in Minds*, Harper and Row, New York

Dunkley, C. (1977) 'Never and Always', *Financial Times*, 22 June, 10

Eagleton, T. (1976) *Criticism and Ideology*, New Left Books, London

Eco, E. (1977) *A Theory of Semiotics*, Macmillan, London

Eisner, L. (1976) *Fritz Lang*, Secker and Warburg, London

Eliot, T.S. (1948) *Notes Towards a Definiton of Culture*, Faber, London

Epstein, A.L. (1969) 'Gossip, Norms and Social Network', in Mitchell, J.C. (ed) *Social Networks in Urban Situations*, Manchester University Press, Manchester

Evans-Pritchard, E.E. (1937) *Witchcraft, Oracles and Magic Among the Azande*, Clarendon Press, Oxford

Eversley, D. (1973) *The Planner in Society: the Changing Role of a Profession*, Faber, London

Festinger, L., Cartwright, D., Barber, K., Fleishi, J., Gottsdanker, J., Keysen, A. and Leavitt, G. (1948) 'A Study of Rumour: its Origin and Spread', *Human Relations*, 1, 464-486

Fiedler, L. (1964) *Waiting for the End*, Penguin, Harmondsworth (Penguin edition published 1967)

Fiedler, L. (1968) *The Return of the Vanishing American*, Granada/Paladin, London (1972 edition)

Field, S. and Southgate, P. (1982) *Public Disorder*, Home Office Research Study No 72, HMSO, London

Fielding, R. (1978) *The March of Time, 1935-51*, Oxford University Press, New York

Finnegan, R. (1973) 'Literacy versus Non-Literacy: the Great Divide', in Horton, R. and Finnegan, R. (eds) *Modes of Thought: Essays on Thinking in Western and Non-Western Societies*, Faber and Faber, London, 112-144

Firth, R. (1956) 'Rumor in a Primitive Society', *Journal of Abnormal and Social Psychology*, 53, 122-132

Fishman, M. (1978) 'Crime Waves as Ideology', *Social Problems*, 25, 531-543. Reprinted in Cohen, S. and Young, J. (eds)(1981) *The Manufacture of News*, Constable, London, 98-117

Fiske, J. and Hartley, J. (1978) *Reading Television*, Methuen, London

Forgas, J.P. (1983) 'What is Social about Social Cognition?', *British Journal of Social Psychology*, 22, 129-144

Forman, D. (1981) *Granada: the First 25 Years*, British Film Institute Publications, London

Fowles, J. (1980) 'Foreword', in *The Sunday Times Book of the Countryside*, Macdonald, London

Franklin, J.H. (1974) *From Slavery to Freedom*, Knopf, New York (4th edition)

Frederickson, S.M. (1971) *The Black Image in the White Mind*, Harper and Row, New York

Frith, S. (1978) *The Sociology of Rock*, Constable, London

Frith, S. (1979) 'Songs Ain't What They Used To Be', *New Society*, 21 June, 722-725

Galtung, J. and Ruge, M. (1965) 'The Structure of Foreign News: the presentation of the Congo, Cuba and Cyprus in four foreign newspapers', *Journal of International Peace Research*, 1, 64-90

Gans, H.J. (1975) 'The Disaster Films', *Social Policy*, 2, 50-51

Garofalo, J. (1981a) 'The Fear of Crime and its Consequences', *Journal of Criminal Law and Criminology*, 72, 839-857

Garofalo, J. (1981b) 'Crime and the Mass Media: a Selective Review of Research', *Journal of Research in Crime and Delinquency*, 18, 319-350

Geddes, P. (1915) *Cities in Evolution*, Williams and Norgate, London

Gerbner, G. and Marvanyi, G. (1977) 'The Many Worlds of the World's Press', *Journal of Communication*, 27, 52-66

Giddings, R. (1978) 'A Myth Riding By', *New Society*, 46, 588-9

Gillet, C. (1970) *The Sound of the City*, London

Glasgow Media Group (1976) *Bad News*, Routledge and Kegan Paul, London

Glasgow Media Group (1980) *More Bad News*, Routledge and Kegan PaulLondon

Gleason, R.J. (1969) *The Jefferson Airplane and the San Francisco Sound*, Ballantine Books, New York

Gluckman, M. (1963) 'Gossip and Scandal', *Current Anthropology*, 4,307-316

Gluckman, M. (1968) 'Psychological, Sociological and Anthropological Explanations of Witchcraft and Gossip: a Clarification', *Man*, 3, 20-34

Gold, J.R. (1974) *Communicating Images of the Environment*, Occasional Paper 29, Centre for Urban and Regional Studies, University of Birmingham

Gold, J.R. (1980) *An Introduction to Behavioural Geography*, Oxford University Press, Oxford

Gold, J.R. (1984a) *The City in Film*, Vance Bibliographies, Monticello, Illinois

Gold, J.R. (1984b) 'The City of the Future and the Future of the City', in King, R. (ed) *Geographical Futures*, Sheffield, Geographical Association (in press)

Gold, J.R. (1984c) 'The Death of the Urban Vision?', *Futures*, 16

Gold, J.R. (in press) *The Urban Vision: Modernism and Twentieth Century Images of the Future City*, Croom Helm, London

Gold, J.R. and Barke, M. (1978) *Communications Media and the Future*, Discussion Paper 4, Geography Section, Oxford Polytechnic

Gold, J.R. and Burgess, J.A. (eds) (1982) *Valued Environments*, George Allen and Unwin, London

Goldberg, T. (1969) 'The Automobile: a Social Institution for Adolescents', *Environment and Behavior*, 1, 157-185

Goldstein, R. (1968) *The Poetry of Rock*, Bantam, New York

Goodey, B. (1971) *Perception of the Environment*, Occasional Paper 17, Centre for Urban and Regional Studies, University of Birmingham

Goodey, B. (1974) *Images of Place*, Occasional Paper 30, Centre forUrban and Regional Studies, University of Birmingham

Goodey, B. (1983) *Houses' Promotion = Community: the Role of Media Coverage in the Creation of a Place'*, Working Paper, Department of Urban Design, Oxford Polytechnic

Gordon, M.T. and Heath, L. (1981) 'The News Business, Crime and Fear', in Lewis, D.A. (ed), *Reactions to Crime*, Sage, Beverly Hills, 227-250

Gould, P. (1984) 'Thinks that Machine', *Integrative Psychiatry*, 2, (in press)

Gould, P. and Lyew-Ayee, A. (1981) *The Structure of Jamaican Television: A Pilot Study*, International Television Flows Project, University Park, Pennsylvania

Gould, P., Johnson, J. and Chapman, G. (1983) *Television: The World of Structure/Structure: the World of Television*, Pion, London

Gouldner, A. (1976) *The Dialectic of Ideology and Technology: the Origins, Grammar and Future of Ideology*, MacMillan, London

Gramsci, A. (1971) *Selections from the Prison Notebooks*, (edited and translated by Hoare, G. and Nowell-Smith, G.), Lawrence and Wishart, London

Gregory, D. (1978) *Ideology, Science and Human Geography*, Hutchinson, London

Gregory, D. (1981) 'Human Agency and Human Geography', *Transactions of the Institute of British Geographers*, 6, 1-18

Grey, M. (1973) *Song and Dance Man: the Art of Bob Dylan*, Abacus, London

Grigsby, M. (1981) *Granada: the First 25 Years*, British Film Institute Publications, London

Grundy, B. (1979) 'A Caning for the Master', *Evening Standard*, 26 July, 21

Gumpert, G. (1970) 'The Rise of Mini-Comm', *Journal of Communication*, 20, 280-290

Gurevitch, M., Bennet, T., Curran, J. and Wollacott, J. (eds) (1982) *Culture, Society and the Media*, Methuen, London

Hall, S. (1977) 'Culture, the Media and the "ideological" effect', in Curran, J., Gurevitch, M. and Woollacott, J. (eds) *Mass Communication and Society*, Edward Arnold in association with the Open University Press, London, 315-349

Hall, S. (1980a) 'Cultural Studies and the Centre: some Problematics and Problems', in Hall, S., Hobson, D., Lowe, A. and Willis, P. (eds) *Culture, Media, Language*, Hutchinson, London, 15-47

Hall, S. (1980b) 'Encoding/decoding', in Hall, S., Hobson, D., Lowe, A. and Willis, P. (eds) *Culture, Media, Language*, Hutchinson, London, 128-138

Hall, S. (1981a) 'Cultural Studies: Two Paradigms', *Media Culture and Society*, 2, 57-72. Reprinted in Bennett, T., Martin, G., Mercer, C. and Woollacott, J. (eds) *Culture, Ideology and Social Process*, Batsford, London, 19-42

Hall, S. (1981b) 'The Determination of News Photographs', in Cohen, S. and Young, J. (eds) *The Manufacture of News*, Constable, London, 226-243 (2nd edition)

Hall, S. (1982) 'The Rediscovery of "Ideology": the Return of the Repressed in Media Studies', in Gurevitch, M., Bennett, T., Curran, J., and Woollacott, J. (eds), *Culture, Society and the Media*, Methuen, London, 56-90

Hall, S. and Jefferson, T. (eds) (1976) *Resistance through Rituals: Youth Subcultures in Post War Britain*, Hutchinson, London

Hall, S., Critchner, C., Jefferson, T., Clarke, and Roberts, B. (1978) *Policing the Crisis: Mugging, the State and Law and Order*, Macmillan, London

Hall, S., Lumley, B. and McLennan, G. (1978) 'Politics and Ideology: Gramsci', in Centre for Contemporary Cultural Studies *On Ideology*, Hutchinson, London 45-76

Hamnett, C. (1983) 'The conditions in England's Inner Cities on the Eve of the 1981 Riots', *Area*, 15, 7-13

Hansen, S. (1982) *Press Coverage of the Summer 1981 Riots*, unpublished MA Dissertation, Centre for Mass Communications Research, University of Leicester

Harbou, T. von (1972) *Metropolis*, Lorrimer, London

Harrison, F. (1982) *Strangeland*, Sedgewick and Jackson, London

Harrisson, T. (1961) *Britain Revisited*, Victor Gollancz

Hartley, J. (1982) *Understanding News*, Methuen, London

Hartmann, P. and Husband, C. (1971) 'The Mass Media and Racial Conflict', *Race*, 12, 268-282

Hartmann, P. and Husband, C. (1974) *Racism and the Mass Media*, Davis-Poynter, London

Hauge, R. (1965) 'Crime and the Press', *Scandinavian Studies in Criminology*, 1, 147-164

Havelock, E.A. (1963) *Preface to Plato*, Harvard University Press, Cambridge, Massachusetts

Harvey, D. (1984) 'On the History and Present Condition of Geography: an Historical Materialist Manifesto', *The Professional Geographer*, 36, 1-110

Hearne, J. (1972) *New Analysis*, broadcast 11 April, typescript, 2

Hebdige, D. (1979) *Subculture: the Meaning of Style*, Methuen, London

Hebdige, D. (1982) 'Towards a Cartography of Taste, 1935-1962', in Waites, B., Bennett, T., and Martin, G. (eds) *Popular Culture: Past and Present*, Croom Helm, London

Herriot, J. (1979) *James Herriot's Yorkshire*, Michael Joseph, London

Hester, A. (1978) 'Five Years of Foreign News on US Television Evening Newscasts', *Gazette*, 24, 86-95

Hewitt, K. (ed) (1983) *Interpretations of Calamity*, George Allen and Unwin, Boston

Hobson, D. (1980) 'Housewives and the Mass Media', in Hall, S., Hobson, D., Lowe, A., and Willis, P. (eds) *Culture, Media, Language*, Hutchinson, London, 105-114

Hoggart, R. (1957) *The Uses of Literacy*, Chatto and Windus, London

Holcombe, H.B. and Beauregard, R.A. (1981) *Revitalised Cities*, Association of American Geographers, Washington DC

Horkheimer, M. and Adorno, T. (1972) *Dialectic of Enlightenment*, Verso, London

Horton, D. (1957) 'The Dialogue of Courtship in Popular Songs', *American Journal of Sociology*, 62, 569-578

Houston, J.M. (1978) 'The Concepts of "Place" and "Land" in the Judaeo-Christian Tradition', in Ley, D. and Samuels, M. (eds) *Humanistic Geography*, Maaroufa Press, Chicago, 224-237

Hubbel, J. (1954) *The South in American Literature*, Duke University Press, Durham, North Carolina

Husband, C., Hartmann, P. and Poynter, D. (1974) *Racism and the Mass Media*, Constable, London

Innis, H.A. (1951) *The Bias of Communication*, University of Toronto Press, Toronto

Innis, H.A. (1952) *Changing Concepts of Time*, University of Toronto Press, Toronto

Jackson, J.B. (1957) 'The Abstract World of the Hot-Rodder', *Landscape*, 7, 22-29. Reprinted in Zube, E.H. and Zube, M.J. (eds)(1977) *Changing Rural Landscapes*, University of Massachusetts Press, Amhurst

Jackson, P., and Smith, S.J. (1981) 'Introduction', in Jackson, P. and Smith, S.J. (eds) *Social Interaction and Ethnic Segregation*, Academic Press, London, 1-17

Jackson, P. and Smith, S.J. (1984) *Exploring Social Geography*, George Allen and Unwin, London

Jackson, R.H. (1972) 'Myth and Reality: Environmental Perception of the Mormon Pioneers', *Rocky Mountain Social Science Journal*, 9, 33-38

Jakle, J.A. (1982) Personal Communication

Jamaica Broadcasting Corporation (1973) *Annual Report for 1973*, Kingston, Jamaica

Jamaica Broadcasting Corporation (1977) *Annual Report for 1977*, Kingston, Jamaica

Janowitz, M. (1968) 'The Study of Mass Communications', *International Encyclopaedia of the Social Sciences*, 3, 41-53

Jay, L.J.C. (1975) 'The Black Country of Francis Brett Young', *Transactions of the Institute of British Geographers*, 66, 57-72

Jeans, D. (1979) 'Some Literary Examples of Humanistic Descriptions of Place', *Australian Geographer*, 14, 207-214

Jenkins, A. (1984) 'Looking at Contemporary China', a paper for the International Television Studies Conference, London

Jenkins, A. and Youngs, M. (1983) 'Geographical Education and Film: An Experimental Course', *Journal of Geography in Higher Education*, 7, 33-44

Johnson, W. (1981) Interview in *New Musical Express*, 30 May

Jones, E.T. (1976) 'The Press as Metropolitan Monitor', *The Public Opinion Quarterly*, 40, 239-244

Joshua, H., Wallace, T. and Booth, H. (1983) *To Ride the Storm: the 1980 Bristol 'Riot' and the State*, Heinemann, London

Kahana, E., Liang, J., Felton, E., Fairchild, T. and Harel, Z. (1977) 'Perspectives of Aged on Victimization, "Ageism" and their Problems in Urban Society', *Gerontologist*, 17, 121-130

Kaplan, F.L. (1975) 'Film Disasters'. *The Progressive*, June 38-39

Kaplan, F.L. (1979) 'The Plight of Foreign News in the US Mass Media: an Assessment', *Gazette*, 25, 233-243

Kariel, H.G. (1978) 'Parochialism among Canadian Cities', *Professional Geographer*, 30, 37-41

Kariel, H.G. and Rosenvall, L.A. (1978) 'Circulation of Newspaper News within Canada', *Canadian Geographer*, 22, 85-111

Kariel, H.G. and Rosenvall, L.A. (1981) 'Analysing News Origin Profiles of Canadian Daily Newspapers', *Journalism Quarterly*, 58, 254-259

Karlins, M., Coffman, T.L. and Walters, G. (1969) 'On the Fading of Social Stereotypes in Three Generations of College Students', *Journal of Personality and Social Psychology*, 13, 1-16

Karp, W. (1982) 'Subliminal Politics in the Evening News: the Networks from Left to Right', *Channels of Communication*, 2, 23-27, 56

Kates, R.W. (1971) 'Natural Hazard in Human Ecological Perspective: Hypotheses and Models', *Economic Geography*, 47, 438-451

Katz, E. and Szecsko, T. (eds) (1981) *Mass Media and Social Change*, Sage, Beverly Hills

Keith, M.J.A. and Peach, K. (1983) 'Reply to Hamnett's Paper', *Area*, 15, 316-319

Kellerman, A. (1984) 'Telecommunications and the Geography of Metropolitan Areas', *Progress in Human Geography*, 8, 222-246

Kettle, M and Hodges, L. (1982) *Uprising: the Police, the People and the Riots in Britain's Cities*, Pan, London

Kirby, J.T. (1978) *Media-Made Dixie*, Louisiana State Press, Baton Rouge and London

Klapper, J. (1960) *The Effects of Mass Communication*, Free Press, Illinois
Klecka, W.R. and Bishop, G.F. (1978) *Neighbourhood Profiles of Senior Citizens in Four American Cities*, National Council of Senior Citizens, Washington DC
Korner, A. (1981) *Humming Birds and Alligators*, unpublished lecture, Newcastle upon Tyne Literary Festival
Kulik, K. (1975) *Alexander Korda: The Man who could Work Miracles*,W.H. Allen, London
Lacan, J. (1968) *The Language of the Self: The Function of Language in Psychoanalysis* (translated by Wilden, A.), Johns Hopkins University, Baltimore
Lane, S. (1979) 'Maryport', *The Morning Star*, 25 July, 3
Larson, J.F. (1979) 'International Affairs Coverage on US Network Television', *Journal of Communication*, 29, 136-47
Lawrence, E. (1982) 'Just Plain Common Sense: the "Roots" of Racism', in Centre for Contemporary Cultural Studies *The Empire Strikes Back: Race and Racism in 70s Britain*, Hutchinson, London, 47-94
Leavis, F.R. and Thompson, D. (1933) *Culture and Environment: the Training of Critical Awareness*, Chatto and Windus, London
Lejeune, R. and Alex, N. (1973) 'On Being Mugged: the Event and its Aftermath', *Urban Life and Culture*, 2, 259-287
Lent, J.A. (1977) 'Foreign News in American Media', *Journal of Communication*, 27, 46-51
Levi-Strauss, C. (1963) *Structural Anthropology*, Basic Books, New York
Levi-Strauss, C. (1966) *The Savage Mind*, Weidenfeld and Nicholson,London
Levin, G.R. (1971) *Documentary Explorations: 15 Interviews with Film Makers*, Doubleday, Garden City, New York
Levine, D.N. (1972) 'Note on the Crowd and the Public', in Elsner, H. (Jr) (ed) *Robert E. Park, The Crowd and The Public and Other Essays*, University of Chicago Press, Chicago, xxvii-xxxii
Lienhardt, P.A. (1975) 'The Interpretation of Rumour', in Beattie, J.H. and Lienhardt, R.G. (eds) *Studies in Social Anthropology*, Clarendon Press, Oxford
Logan, R.W. (1970) *The Negro in the United States, Vol. 1: A History to 1945*, Van Nostrand Reinhold, New York
Lomax-Cook, F., Tyler, T.R., Goetz, E.G., Gordon, M.T., Protess, D., Leff, D.R. and Molotch, H.L. (1983) 'Media and Agenda Setting: Effects on the Public Interest, Group Leaders, Policy Makers and Policy', *Public Opinion Quarterly*, 47, 16-35
Lornell, C. and Mealor, W.T. (1983) 'Traditions and Research Opportunities in Folk Geography', *Professional Geographer*, 35, 51-56
Low, R. (1971) *The History of the British Film, 1918-1929*, George Allen and Unwin, London
Lowenthal, D. (1961) 'Geography, Experience and Imagination: Towards a Geographical Epistemology', *Annals of the Association of American Geographers*, 51, 241-260
Lowenthal, D. (1975) 'Past Time, Present Place: Landscape and Memory', *Geographical Review*, 65, 1-36
Lowenthal, D. (1976) 'Heroes and History: a Commentary, in Moore, G.T. and Golledge, R.G. (eds) *Environmental Knowing*, Dowden, Hutchinson and Ross, Stroudsberg, PA, 291-293
Lowenthal, D, (1977) 'The Bicentennial Landscapes: a Mirror held up to the Past', *Geographical Review*, 67, 253-267
Lowenthal, D, (1982) 'Revisiting Valued Environments', in Gold, J.R. and Burgess, J.A. (eds) *Valued Environments*, George Allen and Unwin, London, 74-99
Lowenthal, D. and Prnce, H.C. (1964) 'The English Landscape', *Geographical Review*, 54, 309-346
Lowenthal, D. and Prince, H.C. (1965) 'English Landscape Tastes', *Geographical Review*, 55, 186-222

MacDonald,D. (1957) 'A Theory of Mass Culture', in Rosenberg, B. and White, D.M. (eds) *Mass Culture: the Popular Arts in America*, Free Press, Glencoe

Macherey, P. (1978) *A Theory of Literary Production*, Routledge and Kegan Paul, London

Marcus, G. (1972) 'A New Awakening', in Dennisoff, R.S. and Peterson, R.A. (eds) *The Sounds of Change*, Rand McNally, Chicago

Marcus, G. (1975) *Mystery Train: Images of America in Rock 'n' Roll Music*, Omnibus, Press, London

Marx, K. and Engels, F. (1974) *The German Ideology*, Lawrence and Wishart, London

Marx, L. (1964) *The Machine in the Garden*, Oxford University Press, Oxford

Mathews, F.H (1977) *Quest for an American Sociology: Robert E. Park and the Chicago School*, McGill-Queen's University Press, Montreal and London

McCombs, M.E., Cole, R.R., Stevenson, R.L. and Shaw, D.L. (1981) 'Precision Journalism: an Emerging Theory and Technique of News Reporting', *Gazette*, 24, 21-34

McLuhan, M. (1964) *Understanding Media: the Extensions of Man*, Signet, New York

McQuail, D. (1983) *Mass Communication Theory: an Introduction*, Macmillan, London

McRobie, A. (1980) 'Settling Accounts with Subculture: a Feminist Critique', *Screen Education*, 34, 37-49

Medalia, N.Z. and Larsen, O.N. (1958) 'Diffusion and Belief in a Collective Delusion: the Seattle Windshield Pitting Epidemic', *American Sociological Review*, 23, 180-186

Medea, A. and Thompson, K. (1975) *Against Rape*, Peter Owen, London

Meinig, D. (1983) 'Geography as an Art', *Transactions of the Institute of British Geographers*, 8, 314-328

Meltzer, R. (1970) *The Asethetics of Rock*, Something Else Press, New York

Miles, R. and Phizacklea, A. (eds) (1978) *Racism and Political Action in Britain*, Routledge and Kegan Paul, London

Miller, W.L., Brand, J. and Jordan, M. (1982) 'On the Power or Vulnerability of the British Press: a Dynamic Analysis', *British Journal of Political Science*, 12, 357-373

Mitchell, D. (1981) *Granada: the First 25 Years*, British Film Institute Publications, London

Moholy-Nagy, L. (1939) *The New Vision: from Material to Architecture*, Faber and Faber, London

Molotoch, H.L. and Lester, M.J. (1974) 'News as Purposive Behaviour', *American Sociological Review*, 39, 101-112

Moore, G.T. and Golledge, R.G. (1976) 'Environmental Knowing: Concepts and Theories', in G.T. Moore and R.G. Golledge (eds) *Environmental Knowing*, Dowden, Hutchinson and Ross, Stroudsberg, PA, 3-24

Morley, D. (1980) 'Texts, Readers, Subjects', in Hall, S., Morley, D. Lowe, A. and Willis, P. (eds) *Culture, Media, Language*, Hutchinson, London, 163-173

Mott, F.L. (1941) *American Journalism: a History of Newspapers in the United States through 250 Years 1690-1940*, New York

Mott, F.L. (1957) *A History of American Magazines 1885-1905*, Belknap Press of Harvard University Press, Cambridge, Mass

Mumford, L. (1938) *The Culture of Cities*, Secker and Warburg, London

Murdoch, G. (1974) 'Mass Communication and the Construction of Meaning', in Armistead, N. (ed) *Reconstructing Social Psychology*, Penguin, Harmondsworth, 205-220

Murdoch, G. (1981) 'Political Deviance: the Press Presentation of a Militant Mass Demonstration', in Cohen, S. and Young, J. (eds) *The Manufacture of News*, Constable, London, 206-225 (2nd edition)

Murdoch, G. (1984) 'Reporting the Riots: images and impacts', in Benyon, J. (ed) *Scarman and After*, Pergamon, Oxford, 73-95

Murdoch, G. and Golding, P. (1978) 'Theories of Communication and Theories of Society', *Communications Research*, 5, 339-356

Murphy, D. (1976) *The Silent Watchdog*, Constable, London

Murphy, D. (1978) 'Control without Censorship', in Curran, J. (ed) *The British Press: a Manifesto*, Macmillan, London, 171-191

Nally, M. (1984) 'Eyewitness in Moss Side', in Benyon, J. (ed) *Scarman and After*, Pergamon, Oxford, 54-62

Nathans, E.S. (1968) *Losing the Peace*, Louisiana State University Press, Baton Rouge

National Academy of Sciences (1980) *Disasters and the Mass Media*, National Academy of Sciences, Washington DC

Newby, H. (1977) *The Deferential Worker*, Allen Lane, LondonNewby, H. (1980a) *Green and Pleasant Land?*, Penguin, Harmondsworth

Newby, H. (1980b) 'A One-Eyed Look at the Countryside', *New Society*, 53, 324-325

North, R. (1979) 'Maryport', *The Listener*, 102, 152

Oakley, R. (1984) 'Ethnic variation in the incidence of street activity in inner city areas in London', Working Paper, Department of Social Policy, Bedford College, University of London

Ong, W.J. (1967) *The Presence of the Word*, Simon and Schuster, New York

Ott, F.W. (1979) *The Films of Fritz Lang*, Citadel Press, Secaucus, New Jersey

Paine, R. (1967) 'What is Gossip About? An Alternative Hypothesis', *Man*, 2, 278-285

Paine, R. (1968) 'Gossip and Transaction', *Man*, 3, 305-308

Park, R.E. (1904) *The Crowd and the Public*(trans. Elsner, C.) in Elsner, H. (Jr) (ed) (1972) *Robert E. Park, The Crowd and the Public and Other Essays*, University of Chicago Press, Chicago, 5-81

Park, R.E. (1938) 'Reflections on Communication and Culture', *American Journal of Sociology*, 44, 187-205

Park, R.E. (1940a) 'News as a Form of Social Control and Collective Behavior', in Turner, R. (ed) (1967) *Robert E. Park on Social Control and Collective Behavior*, University of Chicago Press, Chicago, 33-52. Reprinted from *American Journal of Sociology*, 45, 669-686

Park, R.E. (1940b) 'News and Human Interest Story', in Hughes, E.C., Johnson, C.S., Masuoka, J., Redfield, R. and Wirth, L. (eds) (1955) *Society: the Collected Papers of Robert Ezra Park, Vol. 3*, The Free Press, Illinois, 105-114

Parkin, F. (1972) *Class Inequality and Political Order*, Paladin, London

Patterson, J.P. (1965) 'The Novelist and his Region: Scotland through the Eyes of Sir Walter Scott', *Scottish Geographical Magazine*, 81, 146-152

Paulu, B. (1981) *Television and Radio in the UK*, MacMillan, London

Pawley, M. (1970) 'Caroline - Go To Canvas City Immediately...', *Architectural Design*, 11

Petley, J. (1973) *The Films of Fritz Lang: The Cinema of Destiny*, unpublished MA thesis, University of Exeter

Piepe, A., Crouch, S. and Emerson, M. (1978) *Mass Media and Cultural Relationships*, Saxon House, Westmead

Plummer, J. (1978) *Movement of Jah People: the Growth of Rastafarians*, Press Gang, Birmingham

Pocock, D.C.D. (1979) 'The Novelist's Image of the North', *Transactions of the Institute of British Geographers*, 4, 62-76

Pocock, D.C.D. (ed) (1981a) *Humanistic Geography and Literature*, Croom Helm, London

Pocock, D.C.D. (1981b) 'Place and the Novelist', *Transactions of the Institute of British Geographers*, 6, 337-347

Pocock, D.C.D. and Hudson, R. (1978) *Images of the Urban Environment*, MacMillan London

Porteous, J.D (1977) *Environment and Behaviour*, Addison-Wesley, Reading, Mass

Porteous, J.D. (1978) 'Review of "Place and Placelessness"', *Canadian Geographer*, 22, 74-76

Potter, D. (1977) 'The Spectre at the Harvest Feast', *Sunday Times*, 19 June, 35

Priestley, J.B. (1934) *English Journey*, Heinemann, London

Prince, H.C. (1981) 'George Crabbe's Suffolk Scenes', in Pocock, D.C.D. (ed) *Humanistic Geography and Literature*, Croom Helm, London, 190-208

Pronay, N. (1981) 'The First Reality: Film Censorship in Liberal England', in Short, K.R.M. (ed) *Feature Films as History*, Croom Helm, London, 113-137

Quarantelli, E.L. (ed) (1978) *Disasters: Theory and Research*, Sage, Salifornia

Quarantelli, E.L. (1980) *The Study of Disaster Movies: Research Problems, Findings and Implications*, Disaster Research Centre Paper 64, Ohio State University

Quarantelli, E.L. and Dynes, R.R. (1972) 'When Disaster Strikes', *Psychology Today*, 5, 67-70

Raban, J. (1974) *Soft City*, Hamish Hamilton, London

Rambali, P. (1981) 'Clash Credibility Rule', *New Musical Express*, 10 October

Ravetz, A. (1974) 'From Working Class Tenement to Modern Flat; Local Authorities and Multi-Storey Housing Between the Wars', in Sutcliffe, A. (ed) *Multi-Storey Living: the British Working-Class Experience*, Croom Helm, London, 122-150

Reich, C. (1970) *The Greening of America*, Penguin, Harmondsworth

Relph, E. (1976) *Place and Placelessness*, Pion, London

Rex, J. and Tomlinson, S. (1979) *Colonial Immigrants in a British City*, Routledge and Kegan Paul, London

Rikardsson, G. (1981) 'Newspaper Opinion and Public Opinion: the Middle East Issue', in Rosengren, K.E. (ed) *Advances in Content Analysis*, Sage, Beverly Hills, 215-226

Riley, R.B. (1980) 'Speculations on the New American Landscapes', *Landscape*, 24, 1-9

Robinson, J.P. (1972) 'Mass Communication and Information Diffusion', in Kline, F.G. and Tichenor, P.J. (eds) *Current Perspectives in Mass Communications Research*, Sage, Beverly Hills, 71-93

Rock, P. (1981) 'News as Eternal Recurrence', in Cohen, S. and Young, J. (eds) *The Manufacture of News*, Constable, London, 64-70 (2nd edition)

Rooney, J.F., Zelinsky, W. and Louder, D.R. (1982) *This Remarkable Continent*, The Society for the North American Cultural Survey, Texas A & M University Press, Texas

Roshier, B. (1981) 'The Selection of Crime News by the Press', in Cohen, S. and Young, J. (eds) *The Manufacture of News*, Constable, London, 40-51 (2nd edition)

Rossman, H. (1969) 'Youth as Learning', unpublished manuscript, quoted in Carey, J.T. 'Commentary and Debate', *American Journal of Sociology*, 75, 1040

Ruch, C. (1980) 'Awareness Program Component Assessment', in Baker, E.J. (ed) *Hurricanes and Coastal Storms*, Report 33, Florida Sea Grant College, 143-149

Saarinen, T.F. (1976) *Environmental Planning*, Houghton Mifflin, Boston

Saussure, F. de (1960) *Course in General Linguistics*, P. Owen, London

Scanlon, J.T. (1978) 'Media Coverage of Crises: Better than Reported, Worse than Necessary', *Journalism Quarterly*, 55, 68-72

Scarman, Lord (1981) *The Brixton Disorders, 10-12 April 1981*, (Cmnd 8427), HMSO, London

Shatzkin, R. (1975) 'Disaster Epics: Cashing in on Vicarious Experience', *Society*, 77-79

Sheckley, R. (1978) *Futuropolis: Impossible Cities of Science Fiction and Fantasy*, Bergstrom and Boyle, London

Shibutani, T. (1966) *Improvised News: a Sociological Study of Rumor*, Bobs-Merrill, Indianapolis

Silk, C.P. (1977) 'The Southern Literary Revival of the 1880s and 1890s , unpublished manuscript, Institute of United States Studies, University College, London

Silk, J.A. (1984) 'Beyond Geography and Literature', *Society and Space*, 2, 151-178

Simonon, P.and Jones, M. (1978) *The Words and Music of 20 Clash Songs*, Wise Books, London

Skogan, W.G. and Maxfield, M.G. (1981) *Coping with Crime*, Sage, Beverly Hills

Smith, D.L. (1976) 'The Aftermath of Victimisation: Fear and Suspicion', in Viano, E. (ed) *Victims and Society*, Visage, Washington DC

Smith, S.J. (1981) 'Humanistic Method in Contemporary Social Geography', *Area*, 13, 293-298

Smith, S.J. (1982a) 'Victimisation in the Inner City', *British Journal of Criminology*, 22, 386-402

Smith, S.J. (1982b) 'Race and Reactions to Crime', *New Community*, 10, 233-242

Smith, S.J. (1983) 'Public Policy and the Effects of Crime in the Inner City, *Urban Studies*, 20, 229-239

Smith, S.J. (1984) 'Negotiating Ethnicity in an Uncertain Environment', *Ethnic and Racial Studies*, (in press)

Snow, R.P. (1983) *Creating Media Culture*, Sage, Beverly Hills

Solomon, S.J. (1975) 'The Film as Urban Art', in Eliot Hurst, M. (ed) *I Came to the City*, Houghton-Mifflin, Boston, 369-375

Spolton, L. (1970) 'The Spirit of Place: D.H. Lawrence and the East Midlands', *East Midlands Geographer*, 5, 88-96

Stedman-Jones, G. (1982) 'Working Class Culture and Working Class Politics in London 1870-1900: Notes on the Remaking of a Working Class', in Waites, B., Bennett, T. and Martin, G. (eds) *Popular Culture*, Croom Helm, London, 91-121

Stern, R. (1981) *The Anglo American Suburb*, Special edition of *Architectural Design*, 9-10

Stover, L. (1982) 'Spade House dialectic: Theme and Theory in "Things to Come"', *The Wellsian*, 5, 23-32

Sulzinger, R. (1979) 'Will there be any Truckstops in Heaven?'. unpublished paper, Department of Landscape Architecture, University of Illinois

Sussex, E. (1975) *The Rise and Fall of the British Documentary*, University of California Press, Berkeley

Sutcliffe, A. (1984) 'The Metropolis in the Cinema', in Sutcliffe, A. (ed) *Metropolis, 1890-1940*, Mansell, London, 147-171

Suttles, G.D. (1968) *The Social Order of the Slum*, University of Chicago Press, Chicago

Swallow, N. (1966) *Factual Television*, Focus Press, London

Swingewood, A. (1977) *The Myth of Mass Culture*, MacMillan, London

Taylor, J. (1983) 'The Imaginary Landscape', *Ten-8*, 12, 3-13

Tebbel, J. (1974) *The Media in America*, Thomas Crowell, New York

Thomas, D. (1978) Interview in *New Musical Express*, January

Thomas, D. (1984) 'Black Initiatives in Brixton', in Benyon, J. (ed) *Scarman and After*, Pergamon, Oxford, 184-190

Thompson, E.P. (1963) *The Making of the English Working Class*, Gollancz, London

Thompson, H.S. (1966) *Hell's Angels*, Penguin, Harmondsworth (Penguin edition published in 1970)

Thompson, K. (1969) 'Insalubrious California: Perception and Reality', *Annals of the Association of American Geographers*, 59, 50-64

Time (1975) 'The Deluge of Disastermania', *Time*, 5 March, 84

Trewin, I. (1977) 'Never and Always', *The Times*, 16 June, 12
Tuan, Y.F. (1974) *Topophilia*, Prentice-Hall, Englewood Cliffs, NJ
Tuan, Y.F. (1976a) *Space and Place*, Edward Arnold, London
Tuan, Y.F. (1976b) 'Literature, Experience and Environmental Knowing', in Moor, G.T. and Golledge, R.G. (eds) *Environmental Knowing*, Dowden, Hutchinson and Ross, Stroudsberg, PA, 260-272
Tuan, Y.F. (1978) 'Literature and Geography: Implications for Geographical Research', in Ley, D. and Samuels, M. (eds) *Humanistic Geography: Prospects and Problems*, Croom Helm, London, 194-206
Tuan, Y.F. (1980) 'Rootedness versus Sense of Place', *Landscape*, 24, 3-8
Tuchman, G. (1978) *Making News: a Study in the Construction of Reality*, Free Press,New York
Tulloch, J. (1976) 'Genetic Structuralism and the Cinema: a look at Fritz Lang's "Metropolis"', *Australian Journal of Screen Theory*, 1, 3-50
Tumber, H. (1982) *Television and the Riots*, British Film Institute, London
Tunstall, J. (1982) 'The British Press in the Age of Television', in Whitney, D.C., Wartella, E. and Windhall, S. (eds) *Mass Communication Review Yearbook*, 3, Sage, London, 463-479
Turner, R.H (1967) 'Introduction', in Turner, R.H. (ed) *Robert E. Park on Social Control and Collective Behaviour*, University of Chicago Press, Chicago, ix-xlvi
Turner, R.H and Killian, L.M. (1972) *Collective Behavior*, Prentice-Hall, Englewood Cliffs, New Jersey (2nd edition)
Uzzell, D. (1984) 'A Structuralist Alternative to the Psychology of Tourism Marketing', *Annals of Tourism Research*, II (in press)
Village Voice (1974) 'Technosplat', *Village Voice*, 23 December, 136 Volosinov, V.N. (1973) *Marxism and the Philosophy of Language*, Seminar Press, New York
Waites, B., Bennett, T. and Martin, G. (1982) *Popular Culture*, Croom Helm/Open University Press, London
Wallman, S. (1982) *Living in South London: Perspectives on Battersea, 1871-1981*, Gower, London
Walmsley, D.J. (1980) 'Spatial Bias in Australian News Reporting', *Australian Geographer*, 14, 342-349
Walmsley, D.J. (1982) 'Mass Media and Spatial Awareness', *Tijdschrift voor Economische en Sociale Geografie*, 73, 32-42
Waterhouse, G. (1981) *Daily Mirror Style*, Mirror Books, London
Watson, J.W. (1970/71) 'Image Geography: the Myth of America in the American Scene', *The Advancement of Science*, 27, 1-9
Watson, J.W. (1983) 'The Soul of Geography', *Transactions of the Institute of British Geographers*, 8, 385-399
Watson, J.W. and O'Riordan, T. (eds) (1976) *The American Environment: Perceptions and Policies*, Wiley, London
Weaver, G J. (1980) 'Political Groups and Young Blacks in Handsworth', *Discussion Paper Series C, 38*, Faculty of Commerce and Social Science, Birmingham University
Weedon, C., Tolson, A., and Mort, F. (1980a) 'Introduction to Language Studies at the Centre', in Hall, S., Hobson, D., Lowe, A., and Willis, P. (eds) *Culture, Media, Language*, Hutchinson, London, 177-185
Weedon, C., Tolson, A. and Mort, F. (1980b) 'Theories of Language and Subjectivity', in Hall, S., Hobson, D., Lowe, A. and Willis, P. (eds) *Culture, Media, Language*, Hutchinson, London, 195-216
Weller, P. (1981) Interview 'The Jam Today', *Sunday Times Magazine*, 8 December
Wells, H.G. (1933) *The Shape of Things to Come*, Macmillan, London
Westergaard, J. (1977) 'Power, Class and the Media', in Curran, J., Gurevitch, M. and Wollacott, J. (eds) *Mass Communication and Society*, Edward Arnold in association with the Open University Press, London, 95-115

Wheeler, D. (1977) 'Paradise Lost', *The Listener*, 23 June, 825
White, G.F. (ed) (1974) *Natural Hazards: Local, National, Global*, Oxford University Press, New York
Williams, C. (1980) *Realism and the Cinema*, Routledge and Kegan Paul, London
Williams, M. (1982) '"Apple of My Eye": Carl Sauer and Historical Geography', *Journal of Historical Geography*, 9, 1-18
Williams, R. (1958) *Culture and Society*, Chatto and Windus, London
Williams, R. (1973) *The City and the Country*, Oxford University Press, London
Williams, R. (1976) *Keywords*, Fontana, London
Willis, P. (1978) *Profane Culture*, London
Winyard, S. (1982) *Cold Comfort Farm*, Low Pay Unit, London
Wolfe, T. (1968a) *The Electric Kool-Aid Acid Test*, Bantam, New York
Wolfe, T. (1968b) 'The Noonday Underground', in *The Pump House Gang*, Bantam, New York
Wood, R. (1956) *Magazines in the United States*, The Roland Press, New York (2nd edition)
Woodward, C. vann (1971) *Origins of the New South 1877-1913*, Louisiana State University Press, Baton Rouge (2nd edition) Woodward, C. vann (1974) *The Strange Career of Jim Crow*, Oxford University Press, New York
Woollacott, J. (1982) 'Messages and meanings', in Gurevitch, M., Bennett, T., Curran, J. and Woollacott, J. (eds) *Culture, Society and the Media*, Methuen, London, 91-111
Wright, J.K. (1947) 'Terra Incognitae: the Place of the Imagination in Geography', *Annals of the Association of American Geographers*, 37, 1-15
Youngs, M.J. (1980) *The Ante-Bellum South as an Image Region*, Discussion Papers in Geography, 12, Oxford Polytechnic, Oxford
Youngs, M. and Jenkins, A. (1984) 'Shell-shocked: Critical Film Analysis and Teaching Strategies', *Geography*, 69, 46-53
Zweig, F. (1970) *The Cumbernauld Study*, Urban Research Bureau-Wates Ltd., London

INDEX